Introduction to Leadership and Management in Nursing

SECOND EDITION

Introduction to Leadership and Management in Nursing

SECOND EDITION

Mary Louise Holle
Veterans Administration Medical Center
Perry Point, MD

Mary Elizabeth Blatchley
Purdue University
West Lafayette, IN

JONES AND BARTLETT PUBLISHERS, INC.

BOSTON   MONTEREY

Editorial offices:
Jones and Bartlett Publishers, Inc.,
23720 Spectacular Bid, Monterey, CA 93940.

Sales and customer service offices:
Jones and Bartlett Publishers, Inc.,
20 Park Plaza, Boston, MA 02116.

Printed in the United States of America
10 9 8 7 6 5 4 3 2 1

Library of Congress Cataloging-in-Publication Data

Holle, Mary Louise.
  Introduction to leadership and management in nursing.

  Includes bibliographies and index.
  1. Nursing service administration.   2. Leadership.
I. Blatchley, Mary Elizabeth.   II. Title.   [DNLM:
1. Leadership.   2. Nursing, Supervisory.   WY 105 H737i]
RT89.H64   1987   362.1'7   86-20858

ISBN: 0-86720-380-3

Manuscript Editor: Leesa Stanion
Production Editor: Traci A. Sobocinski
Interior Design: Rafael Millán
Cover Design: Vernon Boes
Cover Art: Morris Louis, *Point of Tranquility*. Photo by Lee Stalsworth. Reproduced with permission of the Hirshhorn Museum and Sculpture Garden, Smithsonian Instituticr. Gift of Joseph H. Hirshhorn, 1966.
Illustrations: John Foster; Rafael Millán

There are three kinds of people:

> *Those who make things happen;*
> *Those who watch things happen;*
> *Those who wonder what happened.*

Anonymous

This book is dedicated to those nurses
who want to make things happen.

Foreword

TODAY, proportionately few nurses are leaders in top executive positions of U.S. health care, political, economic, social, and educational institutions. Holle and Blatchley identify a verity which I believe to be of paramount importance to the objectives of nursing leadership education. Leadership can be learned and all nurses, in whatever position they serve, must have some degree of leadership ability. The seeds of interest, confidence, self-assurance, and challenge should be planted while the student is in basic nursing school and fed with the proper nutrients throughout his or her professional life. When the seeds are properly planted, the individual who is interested and motivated will learn more about what is needed for leadership and try to acquire those essentials. At every level of responsibility he or she will need increased knowledge and skill to perform a leadership role. Nurses should be encouraged to develop their potentialities to the fullest. Outstanding leadership is valuable at any level.

Although there are common threads that run through all levels of management, there are functional differences between first-line supervision, middle management, and top management positions. First-line supervisors have more involvement with employees and associates at the client-care level and, therefore, have the immediate responsibility for quality service that is always imposed upon first-line supervisors. The first-line supervisor must also transmit directives and information to employees and others who are not a part of management. Middle management contact with employees at the client-care level is reduced by the first-line supervisor. Top management has even less contact with those directly responsible for client care. A major responsibility of top management is to preserve balance among organizational units, and to give attention to institution-wide interrelationships as well as outside influences which impact the organization. The emphasis for the beginning nurse must necessarily be upon those leadership and management functions most frequently performed at the client-care level.

Leaders tend to have a strong desire to achieve and to move upward both career-wise and socially. They tend to be proficient in their own specialty, but they also acquire knowledge of many fields, especially those that are closely related to their own area of service. They rarely think of groups with specific goals as separate entities. They understand the interdependence of departments and seek a commonality of thinking that will enable each group to contribute to the larger goal attainment. They have an appreciation for the operation of the organization as a whole, and take advantage of the related services which may be of assistance to them in accomplishing their objectives.

A leader has a positive self-image, integrity, tenacity, steadfastness of purpose, and a vision of where he or she wants to go. The person is an idealist and will undoubtedly pursue goals some of which may only be attainable in the future beyond his or her era of leadership. A leader may set an example to inspire excellence in others. I am reminded of Emerson: "What you are speaks so loudly I cannot hear what you say." Leaders, secure in their own abilities, can prepare qualified people to carry on after them.

The leader's responsibilities at every level involve idea development, contact with people, and complex planning for future action. One of the most important and sometimes least relished responsibilities of nurses is that of financial management. Cost effectiveness has arrived full force in the health care field for both the organization and the client. In her or his role as the client's advocate, the nurse will need to be well informed about the Prospective Payment System and the Peer Review Organization to which a client may be referred who wishes to make an appeal. It is imperative that the leader look ahead to future goals and to the ways and means of realizing them. The decisions of today influence the future. I am reminded of Winston Churchill's remark: "It is always wise to look ahead, but difficult to look further than you can see." The future should be viewed as an improvement of the present.

Leaders are especially noted for the ability to make decisions at the right time and to act on their decisions. They communicate effectively and are both persuasive and stimulating, as it is important to them to win enthusiasm and inspire participation. Their role becomes that of a catalyst resulting in the release of group energies to achieve objectives. The leader's power, influence, and effectiveness come from the people he or she leads. Success may depend upon how others in the work milieu perceive his or her role.

Change is inevitable. The effective leader recognizes this and moves with it, even inviting it at times. Numerous dynamic changes in our social, political, and economic system have taken place in the past twenty years. Nursing, too, has evolved but hardly fast enough to take advantage of the many opportunities presenting themselves. This book was written "to provide the nursing student with the basic concepts and theories needed for the efficient management of client care." It may be the key that opens the door to some future leaders who will speed up nursing's reaction to societal changes. The authors discuss the various roles of a leader. They give emphasis to the basic qualities of human behavior and the importance of working through and with others to accomplish goals. This is truly an exciting time in nursing education!

November, 1986

HELEN R. JOHNSON, R.N., Ed.D.
Professor Emeritus
Purdue University School of Nursing

Preface

NURSING IS an occupation concerned with the care of people. Student nurses have traditionally been taught how to provide this care, but little emphasis has been placed on how best to administer nursing services. It has become clear in recent years, however, that all nurses are or will be involved in administration of care. Administration of nursing services "uses the skills of one discipline, management, to achieve the ends of another discipline, nursing."*

The purpose of this text is to provide the nursing student with the basic concepts and theories needed for the efficient management of client care. Expanded from the first edition, this book includes new material and additional examples useful for staff development programs for nurses in hospital settings, longterm care, and other health care agencies.

The effective health care institution (hospital, longterm care facility, community agency) is a multipurpose organization whose objectives are clear and balanced so that functions, objectives and mission are defined and congruent. Nursing service must follow suit and manage patient care within the constraints of the objectives of the total organization. The role of the professional nurse manager is an emerging one. A core of knowledge regarding nursing management is now available and growing daily. Since the era of Florence Nightingale, who is recognized as the first hospital administrator, management (administration) has been part and parcel of nursing, although we have often functioned by trial-and-error and without a theoretical base. Now we know that management techniques can be developed by nurses or borrowed from other fields and discriminatingly applied.

Not all concepts and techniques learned from business and industry function well in the health care setting. For example, the concept of "assembly-line nursing," promulgated by management engineering programs, is incongruent with current nursing philosophy. This is not to say that nurses cannot learn to be more efficient.

---

*Stevens, B., "Administration of Nursing Services: A Platform for Practice," *NLNS Publication, Nursing Administration, Present and Future* (#20-1739), 1978, p. 1.

Many nurse-leaders excuse their deficiencies in the management of client care and personnel by hiding behind the cliche "It can't be done that way. We're dealing with people, not machines."

This kind of obsolete thinking is described by R. K. Merton* as "... in the beginning, a false definition of the situation evoking a new behavior which makes the originally false conception come true." Thus, if we believe we cannot become more efficient because we deal with people and not things, we go a long way toward making that prediction come true. On the other hand, if we adopt an open mind and look for those principles of management that are useful for us, we can improve the satisfaction of clients, our staffs, and other nurses. Furthermore, we can use management principles on all levels of nursing, including beginning levels. There is literally no position filled by a professional nurse where these selected ideas are not helpful. One might say that learning leadership and management skills is equivalent to having survival skills in today's ever-changing health care arena.

As any experienced practitioner can testify, nurses perform many varied activities and have many roles. We address these activities and roles in the ten chapters of this book. Each chapter describes a managerial role as applied to the working setting. The concepts and approaches are developed from the basic to the complex, and each chapter builds upon the previous one.

Chapter 1 introduces the leadership role. The humanistic role is described in Chapter 2. Management tools and methods are related to each other in Chapter 3. Chapter 3 has been totally revised with new materials and additional examples. Chapters 4 and 5 are two sides of the same coin—professionalism—as both manager and nurse. Chapter 6 deals with the staff-developer role. The personnel-manager role is emphasized in Chapter 7. Chapter 8 points the way to success as an agent of change. The advocacy role is explained in Chapter 9. Chapter 10 deals with strategies and "how-to-put-it-all-together." We conclude with salient points woven into a formula to be used by nurses seeking success as leaders and professional managers.

Additions to the original textbook include such topics as Theory Z, Quality Circles, Prospective Payment, Reduction-In-Force (RIFs), Participative Management, Mentoring, and a program for Manage-

---

*Merton, R. K. The Self-Fulfilling Prophecy. In *Social Theory and Social Structure*. (R. K. Merton, Ed.) New York: Macmillan, 1968.

ment Training. Several examples have been included from public health nursing, longterm care facilities, and the Veterans Administration Nursing Services.

We are both equally accountable for the contents of both editions. Our views were sometimes divergent, but we believe that these differences created a better product. They forced debate, further exploration, and refinement of the material. It is our view that nurses need to do more of this.

November, 1986   M. L. H.
                                                  M. E. B.

Contents

1

The
Leadership
Role

Who Are the Managers of Client Care?

EVERY REGISTERED NURSE is in some way a manager of client care. Today, we are increasingly aware of the need to leave behind the stereotype of nurses who are followers only, and to develop increased management and leadership skills. Without these we cannot contribute fully to solutions for the needs and problems of the consumer in the changing health-care delivery system..

Management and **leadership** are frequently considered synonymous terms that can be used interchangeably. That they refer to two distinct attributes is often overlooked because leadership and management skills often reside in the same individual. However, it is possible to have a manager with no leadership ability or to have a leader with no management skills. Management, in the end, is a specification of a particular job. Leadership is a characteristic of an individual in a particular situation.

Management, like nursing, can be practiced without special training—by natural ability, by instinct, by trial-and-error learning—but, as in nursing, these are not very practical approaches in view of the considerable body of knowledge that exists in this area. Thus, though some of us may have more natural ability to manage than others do, all of us can be better managers by studying and practicing management and leadership skills.

In nursing's long history there have been many leaders and managers. Florence Nightingale's ability to make things happen through leadership was a primary component of her success as the founder of modern nursing. Other early leaders, such as Isabel Hampton Robb, Adelaide Nutting, and Annie Goodrich, are recognized mainly as names heard in history of nursing classes. The importance of their work is not often considered, perhaps because the activities of women in the past have usually been less highly valued than those of men. More recent nursing leaders fare better in this respect as women become more assertive about themselves and their value to society.

Leadership ability and management skills are necessary elements in all positions held by registered professional nurses, from the director of the nursing service to the staff nurse who functions as a team leader or primary nurse. All job specifications in nursing are oriented toward the management of people and things. The principles of management and the techniques used to implement these principles are the same for all nurse managers; the differences among the staff nurse, head nurse, supervisor, and director are based upon the job description and its position on the organizational chart.

According to the American Nurses Association (ANA), the **director of nursing** carries ultimate administrative authority and responsibility in a health-care facility for the nursing service provided to individuals and families. As a member of the administrative staff, such a person participates in formulating agency policy, in devising procedures essential to the achievement of objectives, and in evaluating policies.

The primary function of the **supervisor** of nursing is to help personnel give safe, efficient, and therapeutically effective nursing care. In order to accomplish this function, the supervisor works with nursing personnel in planning, giving, and evaluating nursing care based upon the needs and response of the patient and upon the preparation and competence of the staff. The director of nursing and her supervisors may be engaged in two distinct professions: nursing and management.

The **head nurse**, usually viewed as a middle or first-line manager, is in a pivotal position that links nursing management with nursing care. The **staff nurse** usually functions as a provider/manager depending upon the organization of the nursing-service department. She may serve as a medicine or treatment nurse, team leader, or primary nurse. The leadership that all these nurses must demonstrate is an intangible quality, perhaps easier to recognize than to define.

In summary, there are many different—although not basically conflicting—definitions of leadership and management. **Leadership** is the ability to inspire subordinates to work hard to achieve the goals of the organization, and **management** involves the carrying out of the functions of **planning, organizing, directing,** and **controlling** for the organization. Based on the philosophy that leadership skills can be learned and that managers should also be leaders, these two terms have been used interchangeably throughout this book.

Early History of Leadership

Leadership has existed since human beings first began to organize themselves into families and tribes. Historically, concepts of leadership can be traced through the political and governmental systems of the early Egyptians and Hebrews, the ancient Chinese and Indians, the Romans, and particularly the Greeks. All used principles familiar to us.

Machiavelli's *The Prince*, written during the Renaissance, is the world's most famous study of power, politics, and political success. Neophyte managers, as well as the more experienced, will recognize in this work basic concepts of management used today.

Max Weber's writing in the late 1800s and early 1900s (Etzioni, 1964: 50–55) conceptualized three theories very much evident and current today: division of labor and the related idea of specialization; hierarchy of authority with the concept of implied responsibility; and the free substitution of personnel, i.e., "people come and people go, but the organization remains the same."

Frederick Taylor, a contributor to the scientific management movement which began in the late 1800s and lasted through the early 1900s, proposed that human beings worked because they loved working. Facetiously, one might say that Taylor believed that the people who built the pyramids did so for the joy of it. Those in the scientific management movement also viewed people as appendages of machines who could be interchanged at will. Out of this movement also came the industrial approach of "speed work" and the concept of time and motion studies.

Management science later developed ideas such as the separation of planning and doing as discrete functions, the study of the elements of a job by using a stopwatch, the study of worker motions with a view toward the development of improved work performance, and the piecework method to encourage workers to put forth their best effort.

The universalist approach or management-process school is associated with Henri Fayol. Three important principles are involved in this management concept: authority is inseparable from responsibility; unity of command is necessary (roughly translated, a person should receive orders from one superior only); and communication is important across as well as up and down the organization. Some of Fayol's other ideas, which one can observe being implemented by today's managers, are the definition of the functions of administrators (plan, organize both workers and materials, command, coordinate, control), and the concepts that discipline is essential to business operation, that wages should be fair, that order should be present (a place for everything and everything in its place), that tenure of personnel is desirable, that esprit de corps is needed, and that equity or justice should be tempered with kindness.

A famous longterm investigation, intended to study the effects of worker fatigue on productivity, was conducted by Elton Mayo during the 1920s. Mayo's premise that rest periods would result in a rise in output was tested in the Hawthorne plant, a division of Western Electric. Out of this study came awareness of the well-known "Hawthorne Effect:" the knowledge that any experimental change in conditions will cause an increase in productivity, at least temporarily, presumably because of the increased attention that personnel receive. The human-relations school of management and two critical conclusions resulted from this study: employees are happy and productive if they belong to a cohesive and stable work group, and first-line supervisors are important in the creation and preservation of morale.

This same idea was further developed by Mary Parker Follett. She saw the necessity for group action and for sharing of authority by the leader, so that individuals have control over their own job areas.

Styles of Leadership

In the 1940s, a number of pioneering studies of various styles of leadership were initiated in business and industry. More recent studies have been conducted into what constitutes successful leadership, focusing on the leader's behavior. Several explanatory theories have been developed. Some of these are briefly described below.

In "great-man" approaches, the manager is seen as innately competent and successful, a leader born rather than made. This manager is able to plan, organize, and control the activities of subordinates as well as encourage their participation in decision making. This is a rather negative approach, since it implies that leadership cannot be learned.

Trait theories propose that successful leadership correlates with the personality characteristics of the leader. This proposition offers a basis for developing the underlying elements of success. The traits studied vary from a half-dozen to twenty or more. Those proposed as characteristics of effective leadership have included: perceptiveness, participation in social activities, communication skills, and the ability to assess group goals.

The path-goal theory has also been proposed to explain effective leadership. In this view effective leadership style must be modified according to the existing contingency. When the leader deals with routinized, highly structured tasks, the most effective approach to leadership emphasizes supportive relationship behaviors, but is low on task-related directives: the rationale is that routine tasks are already well understood, boring and frustrating, and that the stress they induce may be mitigated by leader-relationship behavior. On the other hand, unstructured tasks require a leadership style that is high on task behavior and low on relationship behavior. The rationale is that in an unstructured situation the nature of a given job is unclear so task direction is needed more than relationship behavior.

In the life-cycle theory of situational management, the most effective leadership style is predictable from the level of maturity of the followers. The originators, Hersey and Blanchard (1982), designed a four-quadrant model (Figure 1–1) that depicts on the vertical axis a continuum of low-to-high emphasis on interpersonal relationships, on the horizontal axis another continuum of low-to-high emphasis on accomplishment of tasks, and beneath the quadrant a third continuum of high-to-low maturity. Using this model, a leader can decide whether to employ an approach that emphasizes structure (high task emphasis) or one that emphasizes interpersonal relationships. To do this, the leader plots the estimated maturity level of the person or

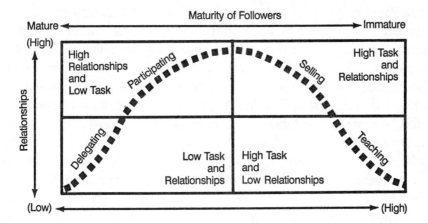

Figure 1–1   (From Paul Hersey and Kenneth H. Blanchard, *Management of Organizational Behavior: Utilizing Human Resources*, 4th Edition, © 1982, p. 152. Reprinted by permission of Prentice-Hall Inc., Englewood Cliffs, N.J.)

group on the maturity continuum, projecting a line upward from that point to the place where it intersects the curvilinear line on the diagram. Thus, a person who appears to be very immature would require much emphasis on task behavior and little emphasis on personal relationships. If he is somewhat less immature, but still does not fall in the "moderate maturity" area on the continuum, he will respond best to a lesser emphasis on task completion and a greater emphasis on a personal relationship with the leader.

The contingency theory of Fiedler (1967) proposes that the amount of ambiguity in the situation coupled with the worker's liking for the leader will affect whether directive or considerate and accepting leadership is most effective. Thus, different kinds of leadership are appropriate at different times. The important idea is that no one style of leadership is applicable to all people in all situations. Success is evaluated according to how well the group responds to the leader. The leader's strength lies in the ability to assess the situation and to coordinate personal motives and group goals so that individuals find meaning and satisfaction in their work.

Some leaders manage the "situation" using a problem-solving approach that involves considering the personnel available and the immediacy of the decision to be made. They set high but attainable goals and are willing to take responsibility for them. These goals are considered only in relationship to the particular situation. They are not seen as character traits of an individual. Thus, leaders decide on an appropriate leadership style by assessing the level of maturity of the individuals or groups involved, then base their actions on that assessment. This is how the four-quadrant model of Hersey and Blanchard is meant to be used (Figure 1–1). The leader chooses how much structure and task supervision is needed and estimates how important personal relationships will be for successful attainment of goals. A nurse's aide who has performed conscientiously and well over the years but who has shown a need for recognition of dependability (as most of us would), will be most productive when the head nurse pays attention to relationship behavior. A nurse who seems to take too casual an approach to the job, on the other hand, may require more structure and supervision from the same head nurse for best performance.

If all nurse managers were alike, there would be no reason to include a discussion of leadership styles in this work, but all nurses are different—individually, educationally, and experientially. Managers are likely to develop leadership styles that reflect their own value systems, personal relationships, expectations, and leadership inclinations. Most authors who write about management styles and leadership recognize several styles of supervision. It is difficult to isolate pure examples, although certain recognizable characteristics are present.

The autocratic style of leadership is one that most nursing staffs have had some experience with at one time or another. The terms "head nurse" and "supervisor" have been almost synonymous with authoritarian leaders who believe that fear is the best stimulus for motivation. These leaders are dictatorial, and their power is absolute. On their nursing units, management is carried on by giving orders: the staff is dependent on them for every decision. Communication is downward, clearcut, and difficult. Within the context of a very tight control system, these leaders frequently use the term "I," are highly critical of others, and in their zeal to "get the job done," may not recognize employees' needs.

The bureaucratic style is easily identifiable in nursing. Bureaucrats are persons who live by the rule book. Their focus of management is the organization, and management by memo is their style. They act in an "official" capacity, relate impersonally to their staff, and cannot make a decision if there are no standards or norms available for guidelines. Their power is derived from the system of written directives, policies, and procedures. Change is frequently an impossibility. These leaders may be afraid of staff and thus write many notes to avoid talking to them directly.

Another easily identifiable leadership style is recognized as the parental approach. This leader is "too good" and never disciplines anyone. Dependency is the primary condition fostered consciously or unconsciously by the leader. In return for deference and obedience, the parent figure attempts to recognize the individual and reward him with the "good things." Controls are loose when all goes well. When problems occur in the work situation, the leader frequently responds with "after all I've done for them. . . ." Communications primarily come from above, but there is some upward motion. The chief problem with this approach is that most adults do not like to be treated as children.

Another commonly seen leadership style is the democratic or participative. This leader is the quarterback of the team. In this group-oriented approach the leader is viewed as a helper who belongs to the group but is the organizer of teamwork. Communication usually goes both ways. Morale is usually high because all members of the group feel that they belong. The main assumption made by those who utilize this style is that, if people are treated as adults, they are more likely to respond as adults. The leader's power, influence, and effectiveness come from the staff that is supervised. Communication is multidirectional with a minimum of written rules and regulations.

The laissez-faire style refers to "do-nothing" leaders. These persons, by virtue of their position, are designated leaders but deliberately abstain from directing the staff. There are no formal structures or controls. The atmosphere in the work situation is permissive. These leaders foster freedom for everyone and do not direct or interfere in any way in what the staff does. They attempt to manage by making no enemies and by being a friend to all. Essentially, therefore, this is a leaderless style.

The multicratic style of leadership incorporates a number of theories and research findings. It combines the best points of three traditional styles: autocratic, democratic, and laissez-faire. The multicratic leader combines flexibility of approach and concern for people in order to arrive at the goal of effective administration.

One can conclude that there are many types of leadership approaches available to the nurse manager. Perhaps the trend today is more toward the democratic than it has been previously. In any case, to be truly effective, the leader must be capable of undertaking various approaches to leadership. See Table 1–1 for a summary of leadership styles.

Using a single style is not usually practical. In the health-care system, with its multiple foci, the nurse's style of leadership must be dynamic. Each situation must be considered on its own merits. There is no leadership style that is correct for all times. Management today employs a variety of methods to determine goals, plan for ways in which the goals can be achieved by human effort, and create the most compatible environment in which to operate.

Leadership styles can be translated into observable behaviors. These behaviors are: telling, persuading, consulting, joining, and delegating. The "telling" pattern is nearly the same as the autocratic style of leadership. The "persuading" pattern utilizes many of the same approaches as the parental style. The "consulting" pattern is group oriented and has many of the elements found in the democratic style. The "joining" pattern has elements of the democratic style as well as the laissez-faire, since this leader becomes a member of the group. The "delegation" pattern is similar to the democratic style. Delegation is usually viewed as a management function as well as a leadership style.

The nurse who is a recognized leader of a group of nursing personnel has certain powers commensurate with the authority and responsibilities of the position. How the leader utilizes this power will affect not only productivity but the decision-making freedom of the staff. As the leader uses less authority and power, the staff gains greater freedom in problem solving. This is the trend today and can be seen where primary nursing is fully developed. Qualified staff act automatically and take full responsibility for 24-hour nursing care of assigned patients. In the traditional approach the leader uses more power and the staff has less freedom to make decisions. The former behavior may be described as "group centered" and the latter as "leader centered."

Table 1–1. Comparison of Leadership Styles

	Autocratic	Bureaucratic	Democratic or Participative	Parental	Laissez-Faire
Concept	Authority centered	Rule centered	Group centered	Individual centered	Deliberately abstaining from direction or interference
Image	Autocrat	Bureaucrat	Team leader	Diplomat	Nonleader
Frame of reference	"I"	"They"	"We"	"You"	"You"
Role of leader	Critic	Regulator	Helper	Persuader	None
Source of authority	Leader	Rules	Group	Individual	Self
Personal approach	Trial and error	Rote and repetition	Participation and involvement	Rewards and penalties	Do your own thing
Objectives	Develop self	Develop system	Develop group	Develop individual	Be a friend to all, make no enemies
Leader needs	Power	Stability	Acceptance	Recognition	Friendship
Behavior desired	Dependent	Consistent	Belonging	Developing	Friendly
Focus	Work demands	Organization	Management of group	Management of individual	None
Demands on employee	Obedience	Loyalty	Cooperation	Ambition	None
Climate	Authoritarian	Official	Democratic	Variable	Permissive
Morale of employee	Antagonistic	Apathetic	Team oriented	Competitive	Poor
Weakness	Independence	Changeability	Crisis proneness	Rivalry	No cooperation
Strength	Decision and action	Standards and norms	Group response	Individual response	Allows individual development

Multicratic — Best of All Styles — Situational Management

A newer approach is "management by confrontation." Managers who subscribe to this philosophy experience a redirecting of skills in the practice of management in nursing. Psychiatric nurses are already familiar with this technique in the therapeutic environment. Using it, leaders do not allow problems to drift along uncorrected. They confront the individual or individuals involved by telling them how the situation appears to them and asking for a rational and reasonable solution. This nontraditional organizational approach allows the nurse manager to maintain control by initiating actions promptly, by actively confronting the individual concerned, and by requiring a solution that is usually best for all concerned.

A leader is influenced not only by personal leadership inclinations but also by other leaders in the organization. The one person who most influences a leader's pattern of behavior is the direct superior in the organization. In other words, how the leader leads is most influenced by how the leader's boss leads.

It follows that the climate created by the top manager affects every appointed leader. Motivation methods, philosophies of leadership, communication patterns, and the type of organization are related to the leadership inclination of the person in top management.

"Leadership is a way of behaving — a set of skills — which can be identified, learned, practiced, and applied. Realistically, it must be recognized, as with any skill, that all people do not have equal potential for leadership, but most can improve their own performance by the application of appropriate behaviors, and by avoidance of inappropriate behaviors." (Quoted from *Journal of Nursing Administration*, January, 1971, cover.) A leader needs clinical and technical knowledge and proficiency, knowledge of human behavior, willingness to develop personnel for higher positions for the good of the organization, sensitivity to the needs of others, and last, but not least, the ability to write and speak.

Success depends on how well the individual uses self and personality to meet the needs of subordinates and thus facilitate the meeting of organizational goals. Leaders need to understand how their actions affect others, and for this they need reliable feedback from subordinates. When conflicts arise, as they will, leaders need to know how to manage them, confronting problems directly when necessary. Over all, leaders need to create an atmosphere in which the primary work groups of subordinates are satisfying and provide opportunities for growth and development. Research has shown that productivity is optimal in circumstances such as these.

Followership, The Complementary Role

A characteristic of leadership not often considered is that leadership does not exist without followership. Leaders may give orders or make suggestions as often as they please, but if followers do not accept the authority of the leader and honor the orders, nothing will happen. The leader's power depends on the willingness of subordinates to follow. Therefore, since people tend to follow those who are seen as most likely to meet their needs (ask any politician), it is crucial to understand the needs and motivations of subordinates. The goals of the group, as identified by the leader, need to be congruent with the goals of individual followers. Nurse leaders as well as other leaders need to appreciate this fact.

No one is a leader in all situations. Sometimes people choose to be followers. Our knowledge of what it is to be a follower helps us to understand the role of a leader (Figure 1–2).

John Naisbitt in *Megatrends* (1982) states that leadership involves finding a parade and getting in front of it. Beginning leaders/managers need to analyze this statement. "Finding a parade" is not the same as developing one. Most nurses, when placed in a leadership position, find that they do not select the staff. Personnel are already there, in the job, with their own beliefs and values. An informal organization is in place. Performance norms are already established. Followers may feel that the way they have been doing things needs no improvement. Indirectly, they may project the feeling, "It was good enough before *you* came" to a new leader introducing a change.

Feelings concerning the relationship between the previous leader and the followers also affect the characteristics of the "parade." A previous leader who was well-liked may make acceptance of a new leader more difficult than if the previous leader was not valued. Leadership requires that strategies be developed to deal with these common human situations, so that the leader can indeed get in front and the parade will follow.

LEADERS	FOLLOWERS
Study and create new ideas	Test new ideas
Make decisions	Challenge where indicated
Assign appropriate responsibilities	Know when to accept responsibility and carry it out
Create an environment of trust resulting in freedom	Use freedom responsibly
Take risks	Risk following
Are reliable	Are trustworthy and respectful
Are loyal to followers	Are loyal to leaders
Are self-confident	Know oneself
Assume leadership position	Follow when appropriate; use the organizational structure

Figure 1–2   Leadership/Followership: Complementary Roles

Followers must agree to be influenced by the leader. If the subordinates are not happy with the job situation, or if the authority is too harsh, they may leave, rebel, or not do the work in the expected manner. If the follower needs the job he or she may comply, but unwillingly.

Learning the Leadership Role

The shortage of prepared administrators of nursing service has been recognized. Multiple sources present statistics that reveal that few administrators in nursing have a master's degree, not very many have a B.S. degree, and the majority have little preparation for leadership positions beyond basic nursing education and staff nursing experience. This insufficient knowledge base contributes to the leadership crisis in nursing. Obviously, nurse leaders filling top leadership posts are operating without benefit of education in the area of management. Managing is a distinct and professional type of work that can be taught and learned. Managers are judged not only by what they do but by what their followers can do. Managers make things happen and work more through organization than through personal effort. They are oriented to results and responsibilities.

Leadership roles are either ascribed or achieved (Douglass and Bevis, 1979). If they are ascribed, we are born to them or learn them by socialization. The role of the daughter in the family, for example, is ascribed. The role of the nurse, on the other hand, is an achieved one that we actively set out to learn.

Sometimes ascribed and achieved roles may be in conflict with each other, because our expectations of a role do not conform to the reality of it, or previous acceptance of an ascribed role is not compatible with characteristics of a role to be achieved. For example, persons may find that their image of themselves as sons or daughters of the family (ascribed role) may not fit with the role of assertive nurse leaders (achieved role). For the son, the conflict may be because the achieved role is usually associated with the female. For the daughter, the conflict may arise because the achieved role is assertive. It is helpful to think out role priorities or role combinations so that expectations may be met.

To learn the leadership role, it is necessary to learn not only the individual parts of the position but also, and most important, the interrelationship of these parts. The whole picture can then be visualized, and for this to happen, practice in a situation requiring all the appropriate behaviors and their interactions is necessary.

All leadership-management development is self-development, a unique personal process. Growth, development, and change can come only from within the individual. Success is determined by ability, willingness to apply oneself, and the quality of personal efforts. Conceptual understanding is an indispensable requirement of leadership and the key to understanding and change.

Management education must prepare the manager to deal with the situation that cannot be foreseen. It must engender development of intellectual abilities and skills so that they may be applied to any situation. Concepts and policies already learned should become relevant to new or unique situations. A knowledge of facts alone is not enough, since facts change or become irrelevant to the situation, and new facts are needed. On the other hand, intellectual abilities and skills, once developed, can be applied to other situations. This calls for a carefully planned and integrated longterm approach to the self-development of the manager.

Management training must concentrate on the individual's development: ability, accomplishments, ambitions, potential, and needs will determine the kind of manager an individual will be. Perceptive assertiveness, flexibility, and creativity have been found to be desirable traits for managers. A person with all three can be the right kind of manager for any business.

Manager development should be work centered: the focus should be on the present job. Improvement in job performance is a major determinant of promotion and increased responsibility. The acquisition of management skills can take place only by doing. New knowledge and insights can be acquired through reading and study.

The nurse leader whose educational background does not include management courses is in a particularly tenuous position. If the employing institution does not have a manager/training program, it becomes each nurse leader's responsibility to design a program of self-development.

What Motivational Factors Influence the Success of a Leader?

There are several approaches to this thorny problem. First of all, the nurse needs to do a self-assessment of strengths and weaknesses in the area of management skills. Second, the nurse's own motivation to manage needs to be measured.

John B. Miner (1973) cites six main contributors to the motivation to manage. First, the manager must have a favorable attitude toward authority. This implies that a manager has a positive relationship with supervisors. The nurse manager thus is able to represent the staff to a higher level of management in the organization and obtain support from this higher level for actions taken. Second, the manager must have a desire to compete. An effective manager must compete for available rewards for self and staff. A strong competitive element is a part of any managerial position. Third, manager behavior is based upon assertive motivation. A manager must be able to take charge, make decisions, take disciplinary action whenever necessary, and protect other members of the group. Fourth, the manager must have the desire to exercise power and be able to tell others what to do, backing words with action. Often this is a behavior female nurses find disturbing, probably because of the traditional female role in society. Fifth, the person must have a desire for a distinctive position. Nurses who are in a management position tend to behave differently from their staff nurses. They must willingly assume a position of higher visibility and be able to stick to their convictions even though they are subject to criticism from the staff, peers, and higher management. Sixth, the manager must have a sense of responsibility. Nurse managers are expected to "get the work done now;" this requires a person who is able to stay on top of routine demands and forms, evaluate staff, make salary recommendations, and so forth. In order to balance the variety of demands, the leader must be able to accept delays and deal with frustrations.

Every nurse perceives leadership problems in a unique way, related to individual background, knowledge, and experiences. Internal factors that affect leadership style are value systems, confidence in the staff, one's own leadership inclinations, and one's feelings of security in uncertain situations. Managers must assess the background, knowledge, and experience of the staff. They need to understand certain things about the groups they are leading: their readiness to assume responsibilities for decision making, their tolerance and acceptance of the unavoidable ambiguity in their leadership, and the degree of independence of the group. Additionally, nurse managers must analyze the environmental pressures from the organization in which they are employed. Nurse leaders, because they provide the services of care to other people, have to adjust their behavior patterns on the basis of urgency, uniqueness, and special requirements of the health-care facility. The nurse may complete the activities required by the job without being really effective as a leader.

Nursing services need leaders who are dynamic, imaginative, decisive, persuasive, and skillful at human relations. Nurse leaders must recognize that their leadership behavior is influenced by their direct organizational supervisors and that this same phenomenon prevails in their relationships with subordinates. Modern administrative nurses will want to consider long-range objectives in their approach to human problems. Some of these goals may be: furthering the individual development of staff members, raising the level of staff motivation, developing teamwork and morale, increasing staff readiness to accept change, and improving the quality of decisions made by the leader and the staff.

One method of accomplishing these goals, not widely used in nursing service, is through the technique known as "team building." Team building is based on collaborative behaviors. Essential components are role clarity (everyone knows precisely what the job is), communication skills and the fostering of feelings of self-worth in each individual without "arrogance or turfism." (Jacobson-Webb, 1985) Health care facilities in general, and nursing services specifically, might benefit from application of these principles to leader-follower relationships.

Some of the myths associated with acquisition of management skills need to be eliminated. Among these is the idea that management training is a separate entity, apart from the day-to-day operations of the various departments, in which only middle managers (top management is often seen as immune to a need for managerial-skills training) and personnel people participate. Within this myth the success of the training is measured by the number of persons who attend or the positiveness of their evaluations.

In reality, for management training to be of true value to the organization and its employees, it needs to be totally integrated into the goals and objectives of the organization so that all levels of management are involved. Its success should be measured by its effects on those goals and objectives.

Management Functions of Nurse Managers

There are several standard lists of management functions available for the nurse who is employed in a charge position. In any list the first function is **planning**. A simple formula for insuring a complete plan is the journalistic checklist: who, why, what, where, when, and how. The second function usually listed in any management scheme is **organizing**: this includes such things as making objective decisions about what work needs to be done and who will do the work.

A corequisite of organization is **coordination**. Nursing service plays a pivotal role in the integration of nursing care with the provision of care from the other hospital services. The nurse leader must view coordination as part of the daily routine.

Another function is **staffing** and **scheduling**. The proper number and kind of employees are the keys to the effectiveness of the care delivered.

A further important factor is **direction**. Though the nurse leader may have outlined the day's plan of action to the staff, there are always problems and opportunities for learning that arise during the normal work day. In a crisis situation, minute-to-minute direction may be necessary. Often a change of direction must be made several times during the work day because of the pressures and complexity of running a busy nursing unit.

A complementary function of direction is **delegation**. Effective delegation implies that the leader shares a segment of responsibility, delegates a specific segment of corresponding authority, and demands accountability.

Another managerial function is **control** or, in nursing terms, evaluation. This function determines how well the job has been done and what progress toward objectives has been accomplished.

Communication is viewed as a function by some management authors and as a subfunction by others. Whatever the leader's viewpoint, communication is critical to work accomplishment.

Two other functions that frequently appear in listings are **innovation** and **representation**. Both seem particularly pertinent to the nursing profession. Nurses need to develop new ideas and approaches to the provision of services. Nurses also need leaders who are not afraid to be visible, have the courage of their own convictions, and are responsible representatives of the profession. Above all, the profession demands nurse leaders who are willing to take risks. Today, leadership in nursing is an opportunity, a challenge, a chance for self-actualization.

Summary

Leadership is

> the ability to inspire and influence others toward achievement
> a learned behavior pattern
> the dynamic force that stimulates and motivates an organization
> the catalyst for nursing management's goal of providing quality care

Exercise

J. V. is a staff nurse on a medical-surgical unit with two years' experience. She has recently been appointed to a leadership position, that of chairman of the Patient Care Standards Committee, of which she has been a member for the past year. Prior to this time she has not had a formal leadership role in the work setting. Imagine yourself in her situation and plan the steps to be taken to ensure effective leadership of the committee.

An answer to this exercise may be found on p. 270.

Bibliography

Brown, Billye. Follow the Leader. *Nursing Outlook* (June 1980): 357–359.

Douglass, L. M., and Bevis, E. M. *Nursing Management and Leadership in Action.* St. Louis: C. V. Mosby, 1979: 7.

Etizioni, Amitai. *Modern Organizations.* Englewood Cliffs: Prentice-Hall, 1964.

Fiedler, Fred E., Chemers, Martin M., and Mahon, Linda. *Improving Leadership Effectiveness.* New York: John Wiley, 1976.

Foreman, W. D. Administrators Analyze the Effectiveness of Their Directors of Nursing Services. *Hospital Management* I (1969).

George, Claude S. *The History of Management Thought.* Englewood Cliffs: Prentice-Hall, 1972.

Hersey, Paul, and Blanchard, Kenneth H. *Management of Organizational Behavior, Utilizing Human Resources,* 4th edition. Englewood Cliffs: 1982.

Jacobson-Webb, Marilyn-Lu. Team Building: Key to Executive Success. *The Journal of Nursing Administration.* (February, 1985): 16–20.

Josefowicz, Natasha. *Paths to Power, A Woman's Guide From First Job to Top Executive.* Reading: Addison-Wesley, 1980.

Machiavelli, Niccolo. *The Prince.* New York: Washington Square Press, 1963 (Originally written in 1513.)

Marriner, Ann. Theories of Leadership. *Nursing Leadership* I (1978).

Miner, John B. The Real Crunch in Managerial Manpower. *Harvard Business Review* (November–December, 1973).

Moloney, Margaret M. *Leadership in Nursing.* St. Louis: C. V. Mosby, 1979.

Nesbitt, John. *Megatrends,* New York: Warner Books, Inc., 1982.

Safier, Gwendolyn. *Contemporary American Leaders in Nursing.* New York: McGraw-Hill, 1977.

Tyndall, Antoinette, Situational Leadership Theory. *Nursing Leadership* 2 (1979).

2

The
Human Relations
Role

THE ABILITY TO LEAD is undoubtedly one of the most valuable of human characteristics. The functions of management (planning, organizing, directing, controlling) are the kinds of activities in which a leader engages. The essence of leadership is the ability to make decisions, delegate, and communicate. These functions are extremely pertinent when one looks at the work necessary for promotion of a good health-care system. Not only must the nurse manager work with material resources, but he or she must be able to utilize, understand, and tap the resource potential of the staff. One commonly accepted definition of management is the ability to work with other people to get the job done. In summary, it is necessary to learn to deal effectively with other people in an honest way. To do so, the nurse manager must examine her own beliefs and attitudes.

Attitudes and Beliefs

Nurse leaders' attitudes toward people play a most important part in their success or failure as leaders. If they believe that people are important, if they believe in what they are doing, and if they believe that nursing-service administrators must care about their employees and meet their needs, then they will possess the basics of success as human engineers.

An attitude is a state of mind with which an individual approaches a situation. In every nurse's educational experience there is exposure to information about attitudes, beliefs and value systems. Most student nurses have developed a philosophy of patient care as a class assignment. Afterward, this paper is usually filed away and never intended to be used again. But, when a nurse is appointed to a leadership position, just such a thoughtful philosophy is needed. Conscientious review of that philosophy is a first step toward identifying beliefs and attitudes. These attitudes affect how a leader looks, what a leader says, and what a leader does. They largely affect how successfully a person will achieve life purposes. Attitudes may be expressed both positively and negatively. One nurse can approach life with the feeling "Today is a new day: I'm really going to get things done." Another can feel "Another lousy day—two more days till I have the weekend off." It is not difficult to guess which of those two attitudes is likely to be most successful.

Nurses who contemplate being in any leadership role should ask themselves the following questions:

1. Am I sincerely interested in others, their purposes and problems?
2. Do I try to understand the other person's point of view?
3. Am I a good listener?
4. Do I try to learn something from others?
5. Am I able to work with others to achieve common goals?

A "yes" answer to these questions indicates a positive attitude toward others.

Beliefs also have an effect on success in the leadership role. Belief is defined as confidence in the truth, in the existence or the reliability of something without absolute proof. Only if one believes in something can one act purposefully. What is the difference between success or failure in leaders actions? Why do some nurses have energy and drive but others are listless and drifting? Why do some nurses lead lives of satisfaction and accomplishment and others continually face frustration? The answer may be found in personal beliefs about the self, nursing, and work.

Questions a prospective leader may address include:

1. Does your belief activate?
2. Does it motivate you toward your hopes and dreams and goals?

Success is a journey, not a destination. One can learn to believe in success for oneself and others.

Attitudes and Beliefs Expressed in Philosophy

An accepted definition of philosophy is "a reasoned belief." In any organization those who survive and achieve success must have a sound set of beliefs and attitudes upon which to base policies and actions. The same applies to the nurse who wants to be a successful leader.

The individual's philosophy must dovetail with the philosophy of the nursing-service department. In turn, the philosophy of the nursing-service department must be compatible with the institution's overall philosophies and objectives. These philosophies must carefully and succinctly explain the meaning of nursing, nursing care, comprehensive nursing, nursing services, and administration. Additionally, in the nursing-service philosophy, such concepts as the worth of the individual and the holistic view of man and of the patient/client as a person must be related to the overall objectives and goals of nursing services. Most philosophies express a view of the role of education in relation to the client, the family, employees, and the community at large.

Relationships to the other hospital departments, medical staff, and other disciplines are usually defined in a nursing-service philosophy. Also, at times, a democratic work climate, model employee relationships, recruitment of personnel, survey studies, and research are described. Sometimes included are statements concerning the significance of cooperation, coordination of client-care services, personal growth and development, the utilization of qualified personnel, and the significance of interpersonal relationships. No one philosophy epitomizes all these concepts. Each group identifies those beliefs that apply best to it and to its department. The real test of the worth of any philosophy is its applicability to the everyday activities and situations to be handled.

The director of nursing is responsible for assuming leadership in defining a philosophy of nursing care. As the key nursing person, the director is the one to whom the nursing staff, administration, and medical staff look for leadership to create the character and tone of the nursing service. But assuming leadership when defining a philosophy does not imply that the director formulates and writes a set of beliefs and imposes them on the departments. Various means can be used to arrive at a set of beliefs, concepts, and attitudes that reflect both staff and nursing management's views. Staff members, both individually and in groups, can be encouraged to define their personal philosophies. An example of a personal philosophy may be seen below.

An Example of a Personal Philosophy

I believe in the dignity and worth of man regardless of race, color, religion, age or economic status.

I believe that each person is an individual with physical and mental endowments similar to and yet different from all other individuals'.

I believe that most individuals are basically good; all have strengths; all have weaknesses.

I believe in the democratic way of life and the interdependence of independent individuals.

I believe in a Supreme Being and respect the other person's spiritual point of view and religious affiliation.

I believe in the intrinsic value of all individuals regardless of socioeconomic or educational differences.

I believe in the importance of individuals to their loved ones, to their life's work, and to their community.

As a hospital worker, I will endeavor to profess and practice my personal beliefs every day—at the hospital, at home, in community activities, wherever I may be.

Everyone has a philosophy, even if it has not been identified as such. The director can create opportunities for discussion of this idea. If the unit staff is small, all members can participate. In a larger setting representatives from each unit can be chosen to participate in the development of a philosophy acceptable to all the staff.

Once the beliefs, concepts, and attitudes to be used are accepted by each unit, the director initiates the process of synthesizing these beliefs into a philosophical statement for the nursing department as a whole. Staff should receive a copy to comment upon before the final form is adopted.

Once the members of the nursing staff agree on the goals they are attempting to meet in client care, then the philosophy of the department of nursing can be presented to the administration for acceptance. Overall goals are useful to guide the development of a philosophy, but they must also be made operational if they are to have an effect on nursing care. The obvious overall goal of nursing service is "to give good nursing care to each client," but this statement is too broad. Several questions must be raised. The key concept to be discussed is: what is meant by good nursing care? This point must be thoroughly examined, so that the results of the discussion can be seen in the document.

In setting down a philosophy, objectives or goals there are certain points to keep in mind (See Box 2–1):

Box 2–1 *BETH ISRAEL HOSPITAL NURSING SERVICES*

PHILOSOPHY

Nursing is the unique process of caring by which a patient is supported throughout his ever-changing level of wellness. It involves the application of an art, specific to satisfying the health-related needs of others. It incorporates scientific knowledge and principles into the trained ability and judgment necessary to assess patient needs accurately, select nursing actions wisely, assure effective implementation of a plan of care, and evaluate patient and family responses appropriately. Through this process, the patient senses a profound commitment to his best interest; his rights are preserved and the essence of humaneness and dignity perpetuated.

We are concerned with creating and preserving an environment for patients and staff that will ensure excellence of care and will support continuing research and education in nursing practice.

We believe that patients have a right to expect that their care will be personalized and will be planned for and evaluated by a professional registered nurse. Patients have a right to the best care available and care which promotes continuity and incorporates them and their family in decision making.

We believe that nurses have a right to provide care in a manner that maximizes their knowledge and skill and optimizes their own professional practice. These rights include the right to enter into the decision-making process for patient care and services and the right to assume accountability for their own practice.

We believe the hospital, as a health-care facility dedicated to the provision of quality care to the community, has a right to expect that care will be provided in an efficient, comprehensive, and cost-effective manner.

Courtesy of Beth Israel Hospital Nursing Services, Boston, MA.

1. Have reasonable targets, including both short and longterm goals.
2. Use meaningful words that are easily understood and agreed upon.
3. Be consistent with the philosophy of the institution. Set up a schedule for review, make revisions as necessary, and be realistic.

Motivation

In many ways people in the United States are biologically, psychologically, politically, and culturally similar. However, no matter how much alike they are, two people looking at the same thing at the same time will rarely see exactly the same image. Differences in value systems, attitudes, knowledge, and beliefs account for this variability in perception. Perception of the meaning of success also varies among people. For some, success means wealth. For others it is power, or recognition, or security.

Personal and organizational philosophies reflect value systems—what individuals believe to be important. We must know why we act and think as we do and then try to understand others. The key to better human relations is the ability to get along with others in spite of differences in value systems.

Human behavior is seldom random in nature. There is a reason for the way people act. Behavior is usually directed toward specific goals or incentives, which is another way to say that it is motivated. Personal motivation, like growth, is inherent in people, and leadership can serve as the "unleashing" factor so that motivation can be identified. The more leaders can help others to discover their own personal philosophies, the more they can help others behave rationally, flexibly, and creatively.

Unless people are blocked, they tend to change their point of view and behavior in reaction to others' behavior. Thus, feedback is a valuable tool in effecting behavioral changes. The nurse leader should be careful not to judge what someone can do simply on the basis of that person's current actions. The effect of past experiences and the potential for future growth must be recognized.

The effective leader must also recognize that individuals behave in ways that make sense to them. Individual perception influences behavior. Thus, the **self-concept** influences an individual's actions and picture of reality. We need to feel that we are competent people, able to deal with problems and worthy of our own respect. If we do not see ourselves this way, we tend to be made helpless by challenge rather than stimulated by it.

The age group to which a person belongs also will affect his or her behavior. Sociologists have proposed that past generations were more inner directed than are people today. We seem to absorb more of our values from our peer group and fewer from our parents. Our actions reflect this change. We are more cooperative with, and dependent on the group but less likely to act on principle alone. Thus it is not surprising that success in such service-oriented industries as health and education (which make up a larger proportion of our total economy than they used to) is largely dependent on interpersonal skills and "other-directedness."

Many theorists have made insightful contributions to knowledge of human motivation. None of these has all the answers, but all of them improve our understanding. Maslow (1954), in his scheme of basic human needs, recognized that a person strives to become what he is capable of becoming and that all people share the same basic needs. In summary, the first need is for survival: to have food, drink, shelter, raise a family, be protected from harm. Second is the need to be wanted: to have the approval, love, and appreciation of others. Third is the need to grow: to get increased satisfaction out of living. Embedded in this last need is the concept of self-esteem. Branden (1971) calls this our reputation with ourselves. Dealing with it is an important part of the nurse manager's role. Self-esteem has been seen as composed of a sense of personal competence and a sense of personal worth. To maintain or increase it, the manager needs to look for opportunities for both staff and self to effectively solve problems and be recognized for doing it.

Frederick Herzberg's two factor motivation theory has been available to assist managers for work redesign since the 1950s. Herzberg labels these factors "maintenance" and "motivation." Maintenance factors relate to employee benefit packages, pay and so forth. According to Herzberg, maintenance factors alone will not lead to happy workers. Managers must be aware of the motivational aspects of the work, the intrinsic possibilities of the job itself and how employees feel about what they are doing. This is basic to understanding the motivation concept (see Figure 2–1).

Herzberg's motivation study concentrated on job outcome. Later studies have taken a further look at what it is in the job itself that makes the work more meaningful. Hackman and Oldham (1981) defined five "core job characteristics" which make work meaningful to people: 1) task identity, 2) skill variety, 3) task significance, 4) autonomy, and 5) feedback from the job itself. A tool, the Job Diagnostic Survey (JDS), has been developed to measure these four dimensions, the critical psychological states, and subsequent personal and work outcomes. The JDS has been modified specifically for health care jobs. Guthrie, Mauer, Zawacki and Couger call their adaptation the Health Professional Motivation Inventory (HPMI). This tool can be used to assist managers to match people to their jobs more effectively.

Previous studies of nursing motivation have focused primarily on staff nurses and models of nursing. The HPMI has also been used to survey nursing managers to explore how well suited they are to their positions. Overall the variables measured by the survey demonstrated

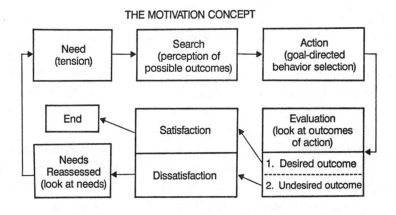

Figure 2–1 (From Michael B. Guthrie, George Mauer, Robert A. Zawacki and J. Daniel Couger. Productivity: How Much Does This Job Mean? *Nursing Management.* February, 1985.)

a remarkably good fit between the high "growth need strength" of nursing managers and the high "motivating potential scores" for the jobs which they occupy. Further research is planned to report similar variables and results for staff nurses, LPNs, and nursing assistants in many different settings.

Leadership is primarily concerned with development of people. The nurse leader must have insight into human needs within the work situation.

Creating a Climate for Excellence

Managers must learn that they cannot directly change the motivation of employees. Internal factors are the most important sources of motivation. Instead what the leader can encourage is the establishment of an environment in which the employee chooses to perform at a high level (Lancaster, 1985). To do this, the leader must understand not only human motivation but also the characteristics of an environment that inspires excellence.

The first requirement is that the leader accurately assess the needs of employees. McClelland (1961) has proposed a theory of human motivation that is useful. In the theory, everyone is seen as having needs, to some extent, for affiliation, influence and achievement. Variability among people arises because for each of us, one of these three motivators tends to be dominant. People with high affiliation needs will work for the establishment of close, caring relationships with others. Those with high influence needs will desire to have power over others. Achievement oriented people, on the other hand, will feel satisfied when they can see the results of their efforts. In the light generated by this theory it can be seen that a climate for excellence depends, first, on understanding the staff well enough to know which of these needs is most important for each of them, so that ways to assist each person to achieve satisfaction can be planned.

Associated with the necessity to find out what motivates employees is the necessity to find out what causes people to go beyond mere satisfaction and actively feel good about themselves and their jobs (Herzberg, Mausner and Synderman 1959). Managers must juggle people, jobs and working conditions to help employees to this level.

Lancaster (1985) has identified some explicit actions that can help achieve this aim. First, everyone needs to know in a specific way, what the goals of the organization are and what their own goals are. Employees must feel that their own goals and those of the employing institution are compatible. The implication is that the manager must make sure that employees are aware of specific organizational goals, and must encourage employees to set their own goals if they have not yet done so.

Second, expectations concerning the job must be clear. Employees must know exactly what their roles are, when deadlines must be met, what resources are available, and so forth. A system of feedback and reinforcement is the next needed factor. People need to know how they are doing. Feedback is most useful when given promptly. Reinforcement also functions well when it is given promptly. The guiding principle for rewarding staff is to reinforce only when it is deserved, but to never miss an opportunity to do so. Threats are usually only effective for a short time and are best used only sparingly if at all.

Individual responsibility and accountability for actions are a part of a climate for excellence. The manager's job is to identify the appropriate level of responsibility and accountability for each employee, so that neither too much nor too little is demanded.

The final elements of the climate for excellence are open communication and trust. People must be able to feel that they will not be continually criticized, and that they will be heard when they feel they need to be. If all these components are present, the probability increases that employees will be self-motivated and will feel good about the excellent job they are doing.

Job Satisfaction and Productivity

Optimally, work is a source of satisfaction gained from knowing that full value has been given for the paycheck received. Also, work usually means that pleasant associations have been gained from working with others to achieve a mutual goal and that money is available to buy life's goods, services, and pleasures.

Any leader can greatly influence the attitude of staff members toward happiness in their work. Managers have influence on many factors that promote job satisfaction: the work itself, responsibility, achievement, recognition, and advancement.

Schrieber and Sloan (1969) have studied why people work in hospitals and how satisfied they are with their jobs. Their research has revealed that administrative-management employees are the most satisfied occupational group with regard to opportunities for achievement, recognition, and advancement. Service workers are the least satisfied of any occupational group in their sense of achievement and opportunities for recognition. Service and clerical workers are least satisfied with their opportunities for advancement. Service workers, craftsmen, and operators are least satisfied of any occupational group with their opportunities for job-related status. Professional-technical employees are most satisfied of any occupational group with regard to salary. Craftsmen and operators are by far the least satisfied in this respect.

In another study, Everly and Falcione (1976) found that interpersonal relationships with co-workers, immediate supervisors, and other supervisory personnel are of great importance to job satisfaction of nursing personnel. The results and conclusions drawn from these studies can be used by nursing-service managers to minimize job dissatisfactions among staff. Personal benefits, inservice education programs, and management and supervision programs can be designed with a view to motivating employees positively. The most important finding is that the individual manager tends to be the significant motivator, more significant than the system in which the employee works. Supervisors and head nurses are major sources of recognition for employee achievement. Skill and effort are necessary to provide opportunities for individual growth and development.

Job satisfaction has been divided into components such as: interpersonal relations, achievement, responsibility, advancement, the work itself, recognition, supervision, working conditions, salary, and status. All of these relate in some way to employee productivity. Additionally, effective communication and employee participation are crucial to better management of productivity.

Many nursing-service administrative personnel in the past have been reluctant to attack the task of improving staff efficiency and productivity. Nurses themselves have not made efficiency a high priority, because they have felt it was impossible to do so where the prime responsibility is caring for individual human beings whose needs are not easily routinized. Most of us have heard nurses say "We work with *people*, not things," implying that the efficiency techniques of industry cannot apply. But productivity and efficiency can be improved in "people" situations. Often nurse managers are unaware of tools available to them or of the basic techniques that provide a foundation for effective use of personnel and equipment. Staff productivity is not determined solely by how hard and how well employees work. Improvement occurs when nurse managers have knowledge concerning individuals and their needs and are aware of the social and physical conditions that affect the work environment and the job to be done. They also need a great understanding of motivation—their own and others.

Nursing schools' philosophers often embrace the holistic concept of man. Nursing-care systems have been designed to incorporate this concept into the care of the client. Nurse managers should apply those concepts to the nursing staff as well. For example, it may be possible to work for the adoption of a fringe benefit whereby staff are given two or three personal days off that they may take when a special need arises—"mental-health days" is a synonymous term. Such a policy reduces abuse of sick times and lets staff know that management is aware that employees have personal and family needs that are real and must be considered.

Another example concerns the use of rotating shifts. If these are necessary, it may be possible to reduce the loss in sleep and productivity that results from this practice by using cyclical staffing, as suggested by Felton (1976), wherein the schedule pattern is set up for eight to twelve weeks in advance. Rotation of night and evening duty is thus minimized unless particular personnel express a preference for those hours. Or it may be that some personnel might benefit more from a "nap" break than a coffee break, even if they have had adequate sleep. Is there a quiet lounge area that could be made available to personnel who fall into this category?

In short, a leader who can individualize approaches to staff as well as to clients will probably promote a high level of job satisfaction.

Circadian Rhythms and Shift Work

Timothy Monk, Ph.D., research psychologist at the Institute of Chronobiology, New York Hospital-Cornell Medical Center, cites a growing body of evidence that a great number of shiftworkers have difficulty adjusting to their hours. This affects their quality of life, relationships with family and friends, and job performance.

Many hospital managers have begun to develop shift pattern systems that attempt to make the adjustment for nurses easier. Schedules that violate known circadian principles must be carefully scrutinized. Three important aspects of the shift-worker's life are often adversely affected: daily regular variation in level of temperature and circulating hormones, the quality and quantity of sleep, and the disruption of family/personal life patterns.

There is some evidence that the night shift nurses take significantly more sick leave than those on afternoon shifts; that the demands of off-the-job activities tend to take priority over the need for sleep; and that the disturbance in circadian body temperature rhythm "probably" caused the "substandard" performance (as measured by their supervisors using an objective grading system) found for nurses on rotating shifts (Jamal, 1982).

It is well recognized that there are no perfect shift schedules. Jamal's study of Canadian nurses identifies a critical aspect of determining the consequences for patient care and for the nurse. Shift workers have to contend with the internal timing problem as well as sleep disturbances due to external events such as unavoidable light, heat, noise, telephone calls, and so forth.

Weekly rotating shift systems are undesirable. Most systems call for a day-night-evening rotation. The Utah Experiment (Czeisler, 1981) established a nine-week rotation schedule using a forward direction of day-evening-night. This schedule implementation seems to minimize employee circadian adjustment problems and maximize employee satisfaction. Forward rotation moves with the body's natural cycles; backward rotation violates circadian principles.

Evidence from both laboratory and field studies suggest that the nurse managers need to identify and understand human problems of the disruption of the sleep-wake cycle among nursing personnel. Once this step has been taken, nurse managers can influence staff satisfaction and job performance by utilization of these principles in the staffing-scheduling function.

Self-Assessment

It is important that the nurse promote self-understanding as well as understanding of others. One should make a self-assessment by asking such questions as:

1. How well do I get along with people?
2. Am I doing the kind of work I want to do?
3. Am I making a good living and getting some fun out of life?

The nurse manager can then ask these same questions when assessing coworkers. In actuality, we understand others by first of all understanding ourselves. There are certain truisms that are useful as background ideas. First, each person is biologically unique. Second, each person is unique in life experiences. Thus, we have some characteristics in common and some characteristics that differ, and any of these can change over time. As individual purposes change, so the world of the individual changes. As infants we have simple needs that others can understand readily. But as time passes and we grow, our world becomes more complex, and our goals change. These changes of purpose make it more difficult for others to understand us. Understanding this constant change in individual purposes is a major key to human relations and the ability to get along in spite of differences.

Attitudes of both leader and followers largely determine how successful the team will be in achieving its purposes. A positive attitude toward self and others is a plus for the nurse leader. The following may give insight into whether or not a positive attitude toward oneself is present:

1. Do I try to learn?
2. Do I try to do a better job?

3. Do I demonstrate enthusiasm?
4. Am I willing to grow?
5. Am I willing to welcome changes?
6. Do I cultivate a sense of humor?

Other questions will indicate whether the nurse leader has a positive attitude toward staff. Some of these are:

1. Am I sincerely interested in them?
2. Do I try to understand their point of view?
3. Am I a good listener?
4. Am I able to work with the staff to achieve common goals?

Although talent is important and knowledge essential, success for the nurse leader depends mostly on attitude and state of mind.

The staff members, for their part, will also judge their leader's attitude. The following criteria are often used: dependability, pride in work, respect for rights of others, consideration for others, knowledge of the job, and enthusiasm (even better when it's enthusiasm with a smile).

The nurse manager's approach to the work to be accomplished is crucial to the staff's attitude. To most people (but not all), work is a source of satisfaction. Leaders can greatly influence the happiness of staff members in their work by showing enthusiasm themselves.

Managers also have input into many decisions that influence job satisfaction. By providing personnel with opportunities to utilize their skills and to participate in decision making, an effective manager can keep satisfaction with the job at the high level. In short, as previously noted, to do a good job we need to feel good about ourselves.

How to Do It All

Certain actions and attitudes are very useful in the work situation but do not appear in the ordinary job description. Some of these are:

1. Use good communication skills for optimal working relationships.
2. Encourage personnel to contribute new ideas.
3. Be sure to give credit where it is due.

4. Show no partiality: don't permit personal likes and dislikes to influence your work.
5. Give advance notice of changes that will affect personnel.
6. Be punctual.
7. Be cheerful: it is a positive motivation for all who must be around you.
8. Be courteous and polite.
9. Admit mistakes when you make them.
10. Be sure that when you make a promise you keep it.
11. Cultivate an attitude of patience and helpfulness. It is a critical factor.

Some things take a lot of time to be accomplished in the right way. A genuine interest in personnel as people will help to speed the job along. The successful nurse leader resists falling into a pessimistic frame of mind and practices positive thinking, in spite of the fact that it is very easy to become negative when what is usually heard is the bad in a situation, rarely the good.

Dealing decisively with complaints is a crucial aspect of a nurse manager's job. In listening to complaints, an effective nurse leader aims to improve relationships, thereby boosting morale and efficiency. When criticism originates from clients and staff, it may be ignored because the leader does not know how to approach the situation or does not want to admit mistakes.

Complaints of some kind are an everyday part of the work situation. No one is perfect; no work situation is perfect. Yet most people feel they are trying to do a good job. It is necessary to accept these ideas and to search out problems, sensing when they are developing and resolving to take care of them before they become major issues. If there are new procedures or equipment to be introduced, permit employees to participate in the planning for their use.

One must be geared to respond to complaints and to look behind what is actually being said. The truly effective leader listens carefully, is sensitive to employees, and attempts to understand them in the context of their needs.

A leader's first action should be to determine what kind of worker is complaining. It has been found, contrary to the opinion of many, that the best workers do the most criticizing. Good workers feel a greater involvement with the job than do poor workers, and thus their complaints usually have to do with things that prevent them from doing the job well, such as inadequate staffing, equipment, or supplies. Poor workers, on the other hand, usually have complaints dealing with their personal discomfort. They tend to be concerned about days off, more time for lunch, coffee breaks, or a need for more personal recognition. With the good worker, therefore, the leader needs to take complaints seriously and attempt to correct them. Poor workers can often, but not always, be made happier in the job by complimenting them and making them feel needed and appreciated. These feelings may then encourage them to do a better job.

If a complaint must be dismissed or a request denied, an explanation should always be given. A supportive approach will usually work, but sometimes it is necessary for the manager to insist that the complaint cannot be acted upon. It must be remembered that in this case the employee will not be motivated to do more than a minimum job.

Another kind of employee, one that is difficult to deal with, is the one who is chronically discontented. Usually the quality and the quantity of this malcontent's performance deteriorates with time and generates a negative effect on the morale and productivity of the rest of the staff. Of course, there may sometimes be a valid basis for complaint. The nurse manager must deal with the situation promptly in order to avert further problems and promote resolution.

For example, suppose a head nurse has an evening nurse who is a chronic complainer. Rarely is anything on the day or night shifts done to the satisfaction of the evening nurse. Frequently this nurse leaves indignant notes for personnel on the next shift. The head nurse must act before a full-scale war between the shifts develops, first deciding as objectively as possible which of the evening nurse's complaints are legitimate.

It is very easy to dismiss all complaints as unfounded when they are frequent. But some of them probably do have merit. When the true problems have been identified, there are several actions open to nurse managers. They can deal with the real problems and let complainers know that this has been done. This is probably the most effective move. They can plan for intershift meetings at times convenient to the majority of the staff, where constructive solutions to identified problems can be sought. In the case of the dissatisfied evening nurse, some experience on the other shifts might be useful so that this nurse may gain a better perspective on other people's problems.

If action is not taken a bad situation will probably get worse. Most persons employed in nursing services are not very good at playing roles they do not feel. Frustrations and unhappiness are picked up by clients. People problems are perhaps the most difficult of those with which the nurse manager deals.

Encouraging Input to Solving Problems

Nurse leaders should encourage imagination and creativity among staff members and in their own personal approaches to the job. Suggestion boxes, employee idea programs (wherein employees' ideas for increased productivity are recognized by management) and incentive systems (wherein employee contributions are recognized and paid for by management) have been used by industry for many years. The innovative nurse leader may be able to utilize these concepts to promote a creative climate in the nursing unit. It must be recognized that a supportive environment favors the fullest possible utilization of the abilities of the staff. The caring leader looks at all staff needs carefully, recognizing that experienced personnel and new workers must be managed differently.

Time Management

Time and money, often synonymous, are scarce resources for both individuals and organizations. In the work setting (and out of it), it is usually advantageous to the individual to be able to manage time well. Nurses in particular may tend to confuse being a good manager with being a martyr who puts in many extra hours in getting the job done. Instead, the good manager is the one who can make proper choices, set the proper priorities, and usually finish within the allotted time.

Of course, in any good job concerned with people, there will always be unexpected complications that upset even the best plans. In that kind of situation, effective managers will not be discouraged, but will continue to make the best use of the time they have.

One procedure for making good use of time is as follows:

1. Rank the tasks to be done in order of importance.
2. Determine which of them can be delegated.
3. Make a list or chart of planned steps, estimating the time each will take.
4. Follow up on the list to be sure that the tasks have been completed and that the time has been spent efficiently.

Management of time requires self-discipline. Leaders must not allow the time spent on coffee breaks or casual conversation to get out of hand. Time can also be saved by using slack periods to work on projects not yet due, so that last-minute crises may be avoided.

The use of an appointment book or planning calendar allows the leader to plot out all required activities in advance so that nothing is forgotten or is scheduled at the same time as another commitment.

If these ideas are being conscientiously applied and the manager is still overworked and unable to complete required tasks in the allotted time, perhaps there is need for an assistant. Managers can often make this clear to their own superiors by documenting all activities and showing how an assistant could be used to improve job performance.

Facilitating an Assistant's Development

Astute nurse leaders recognize that it is as necessary for their assistants or understudies to be efficient as it is that they themselves be good leaders. Part of the overall role of professional manager of care is the responsibility for providing a model of behavior for others. The term **role** can be defined as a set of behaviors attributed to or expected of an individual who occupies a particular position within the structure of an organization. Nurses who see behavior modeling as their role can make significant contributions to the effectiveness of the organization. They set an example for the staff and, in particular, for their assistants.

There are several important actions that nurse leaders should take in order to develop their assistants. They should keep them thoroughly posted on plans for the nursing unit. They should require their assistants to get into the habit of giving frequent feedback reports, demonstrating by example how this is done. They should allow assistants to analyze situations for themselves and teach them to save time by thinking problems through carefully before presenting them for discussion.

Particularly when assistants are new, responsibilities should be handed over to them gradually. One new responsibility at a time is usually enough, with the recognition that accomplishment of goals will be slow. Certain parts of the work should be the sole responsibility of the assistant, although the leaders must continue to check the work that is being done. When an assistant feels ready for more responsibility, the leader should be informed. Any order issued by the assistant should be considered as important as one issued by the superior. A climate in which the assistant feels supported and free to make a mistake will promote growth and readiness. When a mistake is made, it should be possible for the assistant to admit it directly so that it can be discussed and a solution to the problem developed in a constructive manner.

Many of these same ideas apply to the secretarial assistant. A secretary not only can be an enormous help carrying out routine work, but presents to the public and the staff an image of the nurse as leader. Because of this position, a secretary should understand the activities and objectives of the department.

Special Problems

New Employees

The new employee may be a very special problem for the nurse leader. Often new graduates are not readily accepted or integrated into the nursing service. Older, more experienced staff frequently operate under the wait-and-see rule; that is, they do not accept the new person readily but wait to see what the neophyte can accomplish first. Kramer (1974) has defined the concept of **reality shock**, which is the reaction of the new graduate to the discovery that school-bred values conflict with work-world values. Reality shock occurs because most students learn a "whole-task" approach to patient care, in which every possible need is met for one or two patients. Graduate nurses, however, must usually deal with a "part-task" organization of the work load, in which single needs of many patients must be considered. In this situation, the new graduate will be assigned to take the temperatures of all patients on the unit but may not have the satisfaction of having truly met any patient's total needs.

Reality shock follows a fairly predictable pattern consisting of several phases:

1. The "honeymoon"—Everything is wonderful. The new graduate loves the new job, the new options, and having money, freedom, and so on.
2. Shock or rejection—Some goals begin to be blocked by personal inadequacies or by deterrents within the system itself.
3. Recovery—When a sense of humor returns and it is possible to realize that it is pointless to get upset over things that cannot be changed.
4. Resolution—The growth-producing period of self-actualization when one realizes that one can make a difference in quality of care after all.

Kramer has also shown that preparation for the introduction of a new staff member must be carefully made by the nurse leader. Many new graduate nurses are lost to nursing when faced with the reality of the work environment. A prepared, planned individual program for the new graduate as well as for unit staff members is imperative to insure that the needs of the idealistic newcomer are met and to prevent the feelings that are in the situation described in Box 2–2.

The Recycled Nurse

Another worker who requires this same thoughtfully planned program is the "recycled" nurse. The person who has not practiced nursing in a work setting for a number of years often has many of the same difficulties and anxieties as the new graduate. A refresher course, if available in the community, should help the returning nurse to catch up with changes in technical skills needed to be job ready. If no refresher courses are available, the nursing department's orientation must include the review of and introduction to new technical skills as well as the other information normally included in the general orientation.

Box 2–2 *ODYSSEY OF AN EMPLOYEE*

ANONYMOUS

I came fresh from school, full of ideas. There were some things to do that were either not of interest or stymied other people. I said I would do them, and I did, and everyone seemed pleased.

When the initially assigned tasks were done, I undertook some related tasks that seemed appropriate to me and to others. Related agreeable tasks took quite some time. Then I got around to some disagreeable tasks. Insights I had gained indicated changes that were needed. Some tasks involved battles that others had fought before, had lost.

Everything I tried was not successful. Some of my weaknesses were known by now. I could be put off with "Remember when you tried such and such and it didn't work," or "You don't understand," or "It's not your concern." I was:

—laughed at. It's most discouraging not to be taken seriously.
—ignored. "Put it in writing" is a good stall.
—criticized—whittled down to nothing.
—answered with instructions to wait.

The message I had read in the books began coming through loud and clear. Priority was placed on maintenance of the peace: "Do as I say, not as I do."

Minor successes pose a threat and are also written off as for personal gain. I am consistently asked to separate personal interests from work interests, but I find this almost impossible. Most of my life is invested in my work, and my work must be integrated into my life's goals.

The organization seems to perpetuate what I'll call the "puppeteer" concept. When it is your turn to perform in the orchestration, the strings are pulled, and you are supposed to move. But it is a lifeless, dehumanized system. The options are:

1. Conform, give up, speak when spoken to, fill the requirements and fill the hours.
2. Sublimate. Make it on the work scene, but put your real energy into something else.
3. Persist, but be satisfied with an occasional breakthrough. Play it cool.
4. Resist the pressure to conform, through a variety of approaches— attempt to contribute, to show that you care, to change the system, and to encourage discussion and consideration of a variety of solutions.

The first two are dishonest, the third is like walking a tightrope, and the fourth is destroying me.

I know that my experience and understanding are limited, but I must have hope that they can be tested and expanded through my work and my life. At this point, after three years of employment, I'm not sure that hope exists.

In addition, the "recycled" nurse, often low in confidence, especially appreciates positive reinforcement for correct performance. It may be necessary to provide reassurance that lost skills will return, that the complexity of the unit will sort itself out in time, and that recovery from this special form of reality shock will occur.

The Burned-out Nurse

The burned-out nurse is another type who is not infrequently seen, especially on high-stress locations such as intensive care units. Burnout is a phenomenon not limited to nursing. It occurs when one has worked too hard for too long or has endured too much frustration in the work setting in too short a time. Its symptoms and their degree vary with each individual. The normally satisfied and competent worker may exhibit exhaustion, apathy, disillusionment, frustration, disorganization, resignation to the situation, or a general negative attitude.

The nurse leader needs to learn to recognize these signs both in self and in staff. Three personality types appear to be most prone to burnout. One is the individual who has a felt need to be successful and satisfies this need through work. If the work situation deteriorates, the individual's response to it is to work harder. The second type is the overcommitted person who takes on too many jobs with enthusiasm and may be overwhelmed. The third type of individual has a pronounced need to control. Such a person, seeing the job as one that no one else is qualified to do, rarely delegates any tasks and seldom requests help.

Sometimes the problem is not related to personality type, but simply to genuinely being overworked. Whatever the cause, the nurse leader needs to look for practical ways to even the workload of the staff and to promote a team approach to the accomplishment of unit objectives.

The Handicapped Employee

With recent legislative changes another category of worker is appearing in health-care facilities—the handicapped person. This pool of potential employees should not be overlooked because some of its members cannot run down the hall as fast as others. Care must be exercised in placing handicapped individuals in jobs where they can perform well. Of course, this same consideration should be made with the hiring and placement of anyone.

The Male Worker

The male worker in a nursing service is still a fairly rare specimen in a predominantly female society. As more men are entering the field, attitudes are changing, but nursing is still generally viewed as a female occupation. The nurse leader needs to utilize the special skills and interest a man brings to his job just as would be done for other workers. He should not be used as a glorified orderly or as a genito-urinary technician only.

The Older Employee

The older employee who is not as productive as in the past creates a special problem for management. It is important to remember that older workers will probably want to protect and preserve the position and status they have gained in their working years and may find the need to accept change and learn new skills threatening. However, it has been shown that, although older people may require a little more practice and encouragement, they do perform as well as younger people once a skill has been mastered.

The knowledge and experience of the older worker should not be wasted. It may be possible to place this person in a position that does not require a great deal of walking, if walking is a problem. Encouraging the acquisition of new glasses or a hearing aid may help keep the older worker active longer. Undue fatigue can be prevented by rearranging the work schedule so that long stretches of work days are avoided.

The Dead-End Employee

Dead-end employees have reached the highest level possible in a given position and for all practical purposes have run out of opportunities for advancement (McConnell, 1984). The top of the pay-scale has been reached. Worse yet, such employees often realize that they have gone as far as they can and that they are not perceived as candidates for any of the management jobs above them in the hierarchy. The manager may find these employees to be a particular challenge. It has been recommended that the best solution lies in helping such employees to find satisfaction in the job itself. This can be done by giving them as much decision making responsibility as possible, by using them to train new employees, by asking them for suggestions, by giving them special assignments, and in general by providing as much recognition of their contributions to the organization as it is possible to do.

The Ill or Disabled Worker

The employee who is ill or disabled and not working up to par also requires special consideration by the nurse manager. Balancing the needs of these individuals with the needs of the job may require innovative approaches not spelled out in the policy manual. Making use of their experiences for the benefit of others is usually the key to success.

Psychological Paycheck

In any nursing-service department there are a variety of backgrounds (and feelings about them) represented in its workers. "I'm just an aide;" "I'm only a staff nurse." The astute nurse leader knows that some members of the staff have these kinds of feelings. There are several reasons for this nonconfident attitude: lack of education, low status within the organization, devaluing of unit activities as "scutwork," and so forth. Feelings of importance, so necessary to job satisfaction, are often overlooked in day-to-day operation. A "psychological paycheck," as simple as saying thank you for a job well done, is an event that a nurse leader must make happen for every employee as often as honestly possible.

Discipline

Disciplinary action is also a part of a nurse manager's job. Usually it is not a well-liked part, but it is sometimes necessary because of the need to maintain morale by seeing that the work environment is a professional one. Additionally, because it is expensive to orient new personnel and costs must always be considered, it is better for all concerned if those who are not conforming can be helped to see the need for agency regulations. The manager needs to be sure that communication concerning necessary rules and regulations is good. New employees should each routinely receive a copy of relevant policies. Frequently misunderstood or violated rules should be emphasized and explained in formal orientation classes and discussed again periodically at staff meetings.

Most institutions have adopted a formal system for disciplinary action:

1. There may be an oral warning. This does not appear on the employee's record and should be accompanied by listening (What is the individual's side of the story?) and counseling.
2. If this is not sufficient to cause correction of the problem, the oral warning may be followed by a more formal procedure, whereby a written warning is given. The manager needs to be sure that all the facts are complete and documented and that the severity of the problem and any mitigating circumstances are considered. The written warning will be placed in the employee's personnel file. Suspension or termination may result if corrective steps are not taken by the employee at this time. In any case, the manager must be fair to both the employee and the institution.

Attitudes Toward Clients

The nurse leader sets the tone for the atmosphere on the unit and also plays the major role in influencing the attitude of the staff toward clients. Occasionally, personnel must be reminded that clients are really people. The totally effective nurse is one who can readily change places mentally with the client.

One anonymous quotation that reflects this philosophy is: "A patient is a person in a strange environment on an involuntary basis, going through one of the most unpleasant experiences of his life with persons who are not of his choosing."

An Effective Approach

The effective nurse leader behaves ethically with staff, superiors, and clients. Personal peculiarities are not discussed. Justice is dispensed within the organizational system. An attempt is made to be fair in all matters and decisions. Individuals are not criticized in front of others, nor are staff or clients subjected to moralistic cutdown and punitive actions because of their lifestyles.

Too many nurses operate as if their beliefs, attitudes, and values are set in concrete. Being a part of an everchanging society should inspire nurse leaders to review their commitments periodically. They must identify what is worth preserving and what is not, while adhering to the basic beliefs about nursing service and about organizational life.

Over twenty years ago, Erwin H. Schell in "Design for a Career" (in Goodwin and Moore, 1967) wrote that managing

> Is more than a method of thought—it demands a philosophy
> Is more than a task—it is a manner of living
> Is more than a kind of doing—it is a kind of being
> Is more than an affair of mind, body and estate—it is an affair of the spirit
> Is more than a form of leadership—it is a form of trusteeship.

To sum up, nurse leaders are judged by what they are and by what they do. Their attitude toward people may be the key to success or failure as a leader.

Summary

Effective human relations is

> Genuine interest in people, combined with sensitivity to their needs.
> Generous in praise, but cautious in criticism.

Concerned with the development of people.

The ability to motivate others to provide quality nursing care.

Exercise

It is 2:50 PM. K. W. is in charge of a surgical unit for the 3:00-to-11:00 shift and is about to hear report. In the past she has frequently been late getting off duty; she needs to improve her management of time. The following is a description of the first few hours of the shift. Determine how her time could be managed more effectively.

Number of Action	Time	Action
1	2:50–3:05 PM	Listen to report.
2	3:05–3:10	Aide interrupts report—a patient needs medication for pain. Give medication.
3	3:10–3:20	Continue report.
4	3:20–3:25	New patient brought to unit by admitting clerk. Assign aide to take patient to room and orient him to his surroundings.
5	3:25–3:40	Finish report.
6	3:40–3:45	Count narcotics with day charge nurse.
7	3:45–4:05	Assign patient care to two aides. Orient new student to unit and assign her to give 4:00 PM meds.
8	4:05–4:20	Doctor on unit orders IV stat. No setups in supply cabinet. Go to Central Supply for needed equipment.
9	4:20–4:30	Set up IV. No IV pole under bed. Find one under bed in room next door. Start IV.
10	4:30–4:40	Begin rounds. Called by clerk to desk to take phone orders from Emergency Room. A patient who has been injured in an automobile accident will be admitted. He has multiple lacerations and is "shocky." Ask ward clerk to process orders for patient from E.R.

11	4:40–4:50	Go to see patient who was admitted during report—introduce self.
12	4:50–4:55	Patient arrives from E.R. Assess immediate situation, assign student nurse to take vital signs.
13	4:55–5:30	Continue making rounds.
14	5:30–5:45	Patient calls—electric bed has become stuck in high Fowler's position. Manipulate all controls—no success in lowering bed. Call maintenance—they say bed cannot be repaired until morning. Move patient to another room overnight.
16	5:45–6:00	Finish making rounds.
17	6:00	Go to supper.

An answer to this exercise may be found on p. 271.

Bibliography

Branden, Nathaniel. *The Psychology of Self-Esteem*. New York: Bantam Books, 1971: 109–124.

Czeisler, C. A. et al. Human sleep: Its duration and organization depend on its circadian phase. *Science* 210 (1980) (4475): 1264–1267.

Everly, George S., III, and Falcione, Raymond L. Perceived Dimensions of Job Satisfaction for Staff Registered Nurses. *Nursing Research* 25 (1976): 346–348.

Felton, Geraldene. Body Rhythm Effects on Rotating Work Shifts. *Nursing Digest* 1 (1976): 29–32.

Goodwin, H. T., and Moore, L. B. (Eds.). *Management Thought and Action in the Works of Erwin H. Schell*. Cambridge: MIT Press, 1967.

Gorman, M. Leah, Conscious Repatterning of Human Behavior, *American Journal of Nursing* (October, 1975): 1752–1754.

Guthrie, Michael, Mauer, George, Zawacki, Robert, and Couger, Jim Daniel. Productivity: How Much Does This Job Mean? *Nursing Management* (February, 1985): 16–20.

Hackman, Richard, and Oldham, Greg. *Work Redesign*. Reading: Addison-Wesley, 1981.

Herzberg, Frederick, Mausner, Bernard, and Synderman, Barbara. *The Motivation To Work*. New York: John Wiley, 1959.

Hoskins, Carol. Chronobiology and Health. *Nursing Outlook* (October, 1981).

Institute for Social Research, University of Michigan. Boring Jobs Are Hardest on Health. *IRS Newsletter* 3 (1975).

Jamal, M. Shift work related to job attitudes, social participation and withdrawal behavior: A study of nurses and industrial workers. *Personnel Psychology* 6 (1982): 535.

Kramer, Marlene. *Reality Shock*. St. Louis: C. V. Mosby, 1974.

Lancaster, Jeanette. Creating a Climate for Excellence. *Journal of Nursing Administration* (January, 1985): 16–19.

Maslow, Abraham. *Motivation and Personality*. New York: Harper & Row, 1954.

McClelland, David C. *The Achieving Society*. New York: D. Van Nostrand Company, 1961.

McConnell, Charles R. *Managing the Health Care Professional*. Rockville: Aspen, 1984.

McKay, Rita. Is Charles a Motivated Worker? *Modern Health Care* (April 1976).

Overstreet, Barnard W. *Understanding Fear*. Toronto: Collier-MacMillan, Canada, 1969.

Peter, Lawrence J., and Hall, Raymond. *The Peter Principle*. New York: William Morrow, 1969.

Rose, Michael. Shift Work, How Does It Affect You? *American Journal of Nursing* (April 1984) 442–447.

Schrieber, David E., and Sloan, Stanley. Occupational Analysis of Job Satisfaction in a Public Hospital. *Hospital Management* 8 (1969): 26–32.

Sloane, Robert M. Your Management Role in Handling People Problems at Work. *Hospital Topics* 5 (1974).

Steinmetz, Lawrence L., and Middlemist, R. Dennis. Maintaining the Job Performance of the Aging Employee. *Journal of Nursing Administration* 2 (1971).

Tracy, Lane. Postscript to the Peter Principle. *Journal of Nursing Administration* 3 (1973).

3

The
Organization
Role

WHEN STAFF NURSES are asked to transfer to a managerial position the only thing they may initially find in common between the new role and the old one is that both require problem solving. They may soon perceive a conflict between the goals of management and the goals of bedside care. The key to a successful transition is to keep in mind that the role of management is to coordinate and facilitate the process of client care in the heath-care environment.

The Nurse Manager and the System

Administrative success consists of several elements. First, nurse leaders need to know the rules of the game. They need to know how to organize the work of the staff they directly supervise. Once the organization is established, supervisors can then delegate authority and responsibility. They need to understand the nature of communications within the institution. Because part of the supervisory role requires them to administer and support hospital policies, they need to understand and be able to interpret policies to answer questions properly. Additionally, they need the ability to show subordinates how to accomplish their goals in the required manner and within the required time span.

Characteristics of Untrained Managers

If nurses in management positions are asked what they do, they are most likely to describe activities in which they plan, organize, coordinate, and evaluate. If they are observed in actual practice, especially if they have not been educated for management, it might be surprising to note that often their words and actions are incongruent. The "how-to" of management sometimes eludes them; what managers subscribe to in theory and what occurs in actual practice often are very far apart. For instance, managers are supposed to be reflective, systematic planners. Study after study has shown that managers actually are constantly active, even frenetic; that their activities are generally characterized by brevity, variety, and discontinuity; and that they are strongly oriented to action, disliking reflective activities. Most managers would be more effective if they were better at planning, communicating, and evaluating.

To the observer it may appear that the manager has no regular duties to perform. The fact is that managerial work involves performing a number of regular duties. For inexperienced managers some of these may be ritualistic, following in the footsteps of their predecessor. How often have nurses said "We've always done it this way?"

Because communication is critical to effective operation, most organizations have a variety of techniques for disseminating information. Untrained managers tend to strongly favor the oral media: namely, telephone calls and face-to-face meetings. Also, many managers' systems for scheduling time, processing information, making decisions, and so on remain locked deep inside their brains. These managers have not learned to organize effectively.

Organization Defined

The key to success is organization. An organization may be informally defined as a combination of two or more people who together do a job. All health-care institutions should have available a written framework, a formal organizational structure, which in visual form denotes such things as division of work, unity of command, authority, communication, and hierarchy. Most organization charts still reflect the traditional system, which is based on the military model; that is, there is a chief executive officer at the top with a scalar arrangement beneath showing managers and departments (see Figure 3–1).

In recent years other systems have begun to appear. One organizational chart, which is a series of concentric circles, shows the patient in the center, the personnel closest contact to him in the first circle, and those providing support within the institution in successive circles (see Figure 3–2). Another new structure employs the systems approach, in which the organization has departments

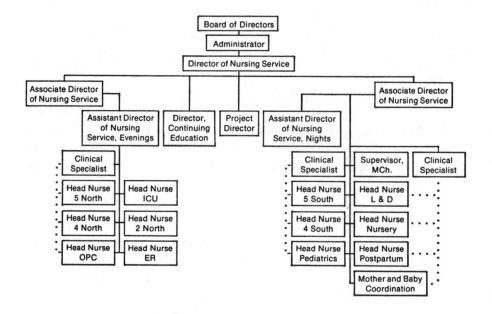

Figure 3–1 Organization Chart—Sample

formed on the basis of similar functions. In this structure, divisions may be patient-care services, physical services, and environment services.

Organizing Defined

The managerial function known as **organizing** can be defined as relating people and things to each other in such a way that they form a unit capable of being directed toward organizational goals. Poor organization lies at the root of many of the problems nurse managers face daily.

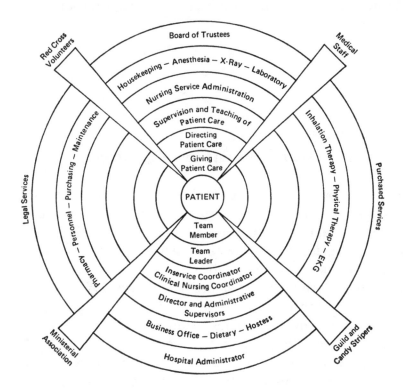

Figure 3–2   Patient-Centered Organization Chart—Sample.

Requirements of an Effective Organizer

The effective manager must have technical skills and the know-how to carry out procedures, the proper equipment, and the ability to get the job done. As described in the previous chapter, human-relations skills are needed, including the ability to judge people and to understand behavior. Also needed are the ability to work with people in the organization. The manager must be able to see the relationship of the unit to the other units in the organization and how to manage time. Priorities must be established so that the most important work is done in the available time. The amount of time may be increased by improving the organization of the work, so that more is accomplished in a given period. Planning is essential. If the plan is ineffectively made, then the organization for carrying out the plan will also be ineffective.

Management by Objectives

One system for preventing an ineffective plan is **management by objectives**. The basis for this organizational approach is the identification, definition, and interpretation of the institution's **goals** and **objectives**. Leaders must know both where they are and where they are going in order to get there. The next step must be communication of goals and objectives to all personnel at all levels of the institution so that efforts and activities are directed uniformly and effectively. Management by objectives promotes teamwork. There is less misdirection, less wasted effort, and less personal frustration. Friction and conflict are kept at a minimum. This system provides for leadership and motivation and also is a basis for review or evaluation.

The primary function of managers, regardless of their position in the organization, is to get things done through people. The establishment of goals and objectives is critical for accomplishing this task.

Although the terms are sometimes used interchangeably, objectives and goals are not synonymous terms. Objectives are stepping-stones toward the accomplishment of the broader goals. An objective should normally be a statement that describes results expected from a single activity. For example, a broad goal would be to improve safety practices within the health-care setting. Objectives that could serve as stepping-stones toward this goal would be such aims as "to identify safe practices for employee and client," "to write policies and procedures to ensure general knowledge of safe practices by all concerned," and "to improve lighting by installing ceiling fixtures in all patient rooms." The overall hospital objectives are the core from which departmental objectives must evolve. Departmental objectives are formulated through the cooperative effort of the departmental director and selected members of the staff.

Writing Objectives

Writing objectives can be a threatening experience for both manager and staff, because it fixes responsibility for contributing to the successful operation of the department and the institution.

Preparing concisely stated objectives and goals accompanied by description is putting sound management principles into practice. The planning activity filters down throughout the entire organization. Planning starts with the review of the organization's goals by top management. Department heads then decide how their department's operations must be modified to accommodate needed changes. The individual staff members must be able to see the relationship of their tasks to the department's contribution to overall organizational goals. In the entire program of management by objectives, nothing is more critical than the point at which the superior and the subordinate come together to sit down and agree upon goals and objectives. Individuals must develop their ideas and bring them to the conference with the superior. The objectives should be measurable.

After discussion and acceptance of the subordinate's objectives by the superior, these objectives must be mutually agreed upon and put into a timetable for accomplishment. From a manager's standpoint, having individual workers establish their own objectives permits the prediction of behavior. This system is a dynamic process, involving a never-ending cycle of evaluation and revision. Managers can evaluate the work performance of subordinates and can analyze their own experiences with the goal-setting procedure. Both can then improve their own performances (see Figure 3–3). Ideally, any manager so inclined can incorporate the system within one nursing unit or one area of the institution.

Writing goals and objectives is an art, and practice is required. One of the problems that frequently occurs in goal setting is that too many objectives are developed to allow for accomplishment within the designated time period. Another difficulty is that often objectives are not realistic, they are unattainable. Objectives must be real and must be established in light of all the factors that can be foreseen when they are adopted, such as time schedules, personnel available, physical facilities, costs, equipment, supplies, and the organization's

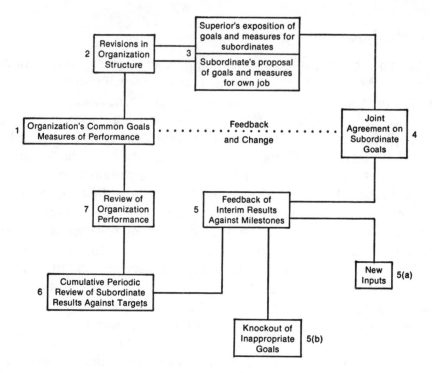

Figure 3–3   Cycle of Management by Objectives

system for providing care. It should be recognized, moreover, that forecasting is never complete. Nevertheless, after giving the matter serious thought, nurse managers must get on with the goal-setting job even though there may be other important factors affecting outcome that they have not been able to consider.

Attainable goals act as a stimulus; unattainable ones are soon ignored. Usually an objective involves more than one department, so that it is important that these are not at cross-purposes with each other. Objectives established and mutually agreed upon can be an effective bridge to cooperation between individuals on different services. Objectives must not be considered as permanently set. They must change or be considered for change on a regularly established basis (see Box 3–1).

Box 3–1 *MANAGEMENT BY OBJECTIVES*

I. Goals for next 12 months:
  1. To improve nursing care:
     Objectives:
     A. Workable plan for the implementation and maintenance of client-care plans.
     B. Establishment of guidelines for more comprehensive discharge planning, including coordination with Medical-Social Services, Home Care, Physical Therapy, Meals on Wheels, Respiratory Therapy, and Speech and Hearing.
     C. Implementation of an improved method of intravenous therapy.
     D. Initiation of a teaching program for post-coronary patients.
     E. Continuation of ward conferences with emphasis on planning and assessment of client care.
  2. To better utilize personnel, time, equipment, and supplies:
     Objectives:
     A. Initiation of unit-dose delivery system in cooperation with Pharmacy.
     B. Better system for issuing passes and controlling visitors.
     C. Continuation of joint-shift conferences on a regular basis.
  3. To obtain a more complete method of evaluating staff/nursing, care /service:
     Objectives:
     A. Joint client-care audits with Medical Staff Records Committee.
     B. Utilization of the skills inventory checklist to keep an updated assessment of skills of the professional staff.
  4. To establish a well-coordinated ambulance service.
  5. To improve public relations:
     Objectives:
     A. Stress on professional ethics and behavior.
     B. Individual demonstration of what "professional ethics" means in the hospital.
II. Goals for the next three to five years:
  1. To develop an Out-patient Service Area.
  2. To evaluate need for expansion of Home Care Services.
  3. To improve isolation facilities and procedures.
  4. To develop modified family-centered maternity unit.

Management by Exception

A concept related to management by objectives is called **management by exception**. Management by exception means planning to assure that only those decisions that no one else can handle are made by the manager. All others should be made by members of the manager's staff. The manager's attention must be devoted to areas where activities are deviating from their planned levels. Expected results must be clearly stated, so that everyone is aware of what the job is and what the acceptable performance levels for it are.

Policies and Procedures

All organizations have **policies** and **procedures**. Such policies and procedures may not be in writing, and they may not even be called by those names. Instead, they may be called routines or simply referred to as "the way we always do it." Whatever the name, they are important guides to decision making and to efficient management. A policy is generally defined as a guide for decision making: a procedure describes how to do something in step-by-step terms. To be most effective, policies and procedures should be formally established and put into writing. One method for doing this is to develop an **administrative manual**. This facilitates consistent interpretation of policy and standardization of action throughout the institution.

Written policies and procedures usually improve efficiency and safety in the institution and either directly or indirectly result in better patient care. They are important tools for administrative staff members who must make policy-based decisions and for other employees who must implement these decisions. Box 3–2 is an example of a policy statement.

The development of administrative manuals is a time-consuming project. A practical approach would be to designate one staff person to be responsible for the overall coordination of the project and to use key staff to help decide what should be included in the manual.

Box 3–2 *EXAMPLE OF A POLICY STATEMENT*

POLICY

The hospital supports the attendance of conventions, institutes, and educational and professional meetings on the part of its employees.

PURPOSE

To encourage employees to keep abreast of developments in their particular field of responsibility.

SPECIAL INSTRUCTIONS

1. Prior to attending any of these job-related programs, employees must obtain approval from the appropriate department head and the Executive Director.
2. Employees attending these functions will receive their regular salary as well as reimbursement for registration fees, lodging, meals, and necessary travel expenses.
3. Without prior approval as indicated above, the hospital will assume no responsibility for salary or expenses incurred. Requests for personnel to attend an educational function on their own time will be evaluated in regard to the staffing needs of their department or unit.

Many nurse managers complain that manuals are written but are not used. When staff help to write policy, they tend to participate in its implementation. There is less likely to be fault finding and resentment if the people who are going to be using the manual help to create it.

To keep any manual current, a system must be set up for periodically reviewing it. There may be review by committee, by personnel in each department, by department heads, or by an administrative assistant. An annual review of the manual is suggested by accrediting and licensing bodies.

Budgets

The **budget** is another managerial tool that often appears ominous to a new nurse manager. A budget is as reliable as the people who compile it. Budgets are not static or unchanging. They function only as guidelines for action. Some flexibility is necessary to allow for comprehensive nursing care on all shifts. Before a budget can be developed, it is necessary to determine the proposed goals and objectives for all concerned levels of management in the budgetary period. After these have been determined, the process of **forecasting** begins. Forecasting involves translating the objectives into personnel, supply, and equipment needs and assigning a dollar value to these. For the head nurse, the procedure is to study past unit performance as a basis for development of nondepartmental objectives. A **plan** is then made to implement the objectives in terms of specific activities, and the activities are translated into measurable units such as hours of work and dollars.

Whether or not the nurse manager participates in budget planning depends upon the institution in which the work is being done. There are various philosophies in administration regarding budget preparation. It may be that the accounting department makes up the entire budget. If so, this is often a source of friction between the accounting department and other departments. Sometimes the administrator appoints a budget coordinator who does the initial work on the basis of the previous year's experience with the department and then works with the appropriate nurse manager in finishing each section. In other instances, the nurse manager compiles the budget and submits it to a higher authority for approval.

Budgets ordinarily are categorized into three parts: **operating-expense budget, capital expenditures**, and **cash flow**. The nurse manager is directly involved in the operating expenses, as most authorities recognize that nursing service makes up the largest segment of the "people" budget. In Box 3–3, a number of terms commonly used in budgeting are defined.

Box 3–3 *BUDGET TERMINOLOGY*

1. A **budget** is a systematic program, in numerical terms, of projections of revenue and expenses for a specific period of time that reflects anticipated expense allocations, sources of revenue, and results of carefully conceived plans to attain the goals of the institution. The **departmental budget** is a systematic presentation in numerical terms of what the department hopes to accomplish and the means by which its objectives can be reached.
2. **Cash flow** is the rate at which monies are received and disbursed.
3. **Cost accounting** is an extension of general accounting costs broken down and reported on a unit basis, the unit being a department function or other item to which cost can be assigned.
4. **An income forecast** is a budgetary plan that predicts how the meeting of objectives may increase or decrease the amount of income for the year, and where money is coming from to pay for the costs of approved programs related to specific objectives.
5. **Operating expenses** are day-to-day costs of maintaining and running a hospital or other health-care agency (controlled by hospital administration and department heads).
6. **Controlling** is a continuing process of comparing actual performance with planned performance, investigating significant deviations, and taking corrective action. It is not accomplished by the mere act of planning. It involves recording and reporting results, appraising actual results in relation to planned results, and taking necessary action to achieve planned results. In order to have good controls, data and feedback must be available for evaluation and analysis by all levels of management. Responsibility must be delegated and individuals held responsible.
7. **Budget development** must be accomplished with the participation of department directors, managers, and supervisors, since the plans of management at all levels must be coordinated into a clear and concise financial program. The fundamental objectives of budgeting are:
   A. **Planning** involves the establishment of goals and objectives, foreseeing problems that will arise in operational activities, and deciding in advance how to meet these problems.
   B. **Forecasting** involves translating the activities into personnel, supply, and equipment needs, which are then translated into dollar values. Steps in forecasting:
      (1) Setting up objectives for the department
      (2) Studying past performance

---

(3) Studying the list of assumptions and objectives by the administrator as a basis for forecasting the needs of the department

(4) Planning how the objectives of the department are to be met in terms of activities

(5) Translating activities into measurable units

8. **Client-care hours** are the hours of care provided per client per day by various levels of personnel—a numerical allocation by worker-hours guiding design of staffing patterns per 24-hour period.

9. **Client/family needs classification** is a system of identifying client and family nursing needs to arrive at a category level that determines the assignment of client caseloads, staffing patterns, and projected budget allocations.

10. **Position allocations** refers to the allocation of approximate numbers and types of positions on the basis of guidelines, including client-care-hour determination, usual client population, client-care programs, and anticipated projects for the clinical area.

11. **Capital Expenses** refers to those items such as equipment, renovation materials, furnishings, or softwear costing over a preset dollar amount, such as $100.00. These are budgeted in anticipation of purchase, with a description of item, cost, and justification.

12. **Expendable supplies** are those supplies that are consumed through their use.

Nursing-Service Needs

The nursing budget for department or unit is based on the kind and number of staff and the system of nursing (primary, team, functional) that is being utilized. Many factors determine nursing-service needs as reflected in the budget:

1. the type of client (medical, surgical, maternity, pediatric, communicable disease, chronically ill)
2. the length of stay and the acuteness of the illness
3. the size of the institution and its bed occupancy
4. the physical layout of the institution, and the size and plan of the ward (open wards, small units, or private rooms)
5. personnel policies with regard to staffing, and salaries paid to various types of nursing personnel, including pay for overtime

6. the length of the work week and work periods, flexibility of hours, vacation, holidays, and sick leave
7. provisions for inservice educational programs including instructional staff as well as relief staff
8. provision for development of staff through university preparation and refresher courses

In addition, standards of nursing care will affect the number of hours of bedside nursing: the frequency of giving baths, changing beds, or repositioning clients. The need for teaching clients or assisting them in being independent are more examples. Other factors that affect the provision of nursing service are:

1. the methods of performing nursing procedures, simple or complex
2. the proportion of nursing care provided by professional nurses as compared to that provided by auxiliary personnel
3. the amount and quality of supervision available and provided
4. the efficiency of job descriptions and job classifications and the method of client assignment

Additional considerations in budgeting are:

1. the amount and level of labor-saving equipment and devices
2. the amount of centralized supply services provided and the amount of clerical assistance available
3. requirements of the medical staff
4. reports required by administration

All of these matters have bearing on how the nursing-service organization functions, the amount of staff required, and the amount of budget needed in order to provide the necessary nursing care.

Budgeting Process

Most nursing departments have budgeted their operations on a historical basis: next year's budget is last year's plus new services or factors. Often, very little concrete goal setting has been formally factored into the budget. The result of this practice has been the widespread misunderstanding, underestimation, and overspending of nursing budgets across the United States. Two key elements must be included in all budgets to prevent this from happening: 1) a formal statement of what goals are to be achieved; and 2) documentation of the personnel required to achieve these goals.

Recent events such as federal prospective payment requirements have limited the funds available to hospitals. Third-party payors (Blue Cross, Medicaid, Medicare, commercial insurance carriers, and private paying patients) are becoming very skeptical of hospital costs and have put ceilings, restraints, and denials on hospital operations. In these cases, a priority system for ranking goals is most important. In this way, cutbacks can be made without losing the entire character of the service. Across-the-board cuts merely aggravate any inequities that already exist.

It has estimated that over 95 percent of the nursing departments in this country budget incorrectly. They make two basic mistakes: 1) not documenting the time lost through benefits, orientation, and training; and 2) lack of care in factoring time lost effects into a complete staffing plan.

Determining On-Duty Full-Time Equivalents.   The first step is to determine the *Full-Time Equivalent* (FTE) for each employee. A full-time-equivalent is the number of hours of work for which a full-time employee is scheduled weekly.

> Thus, 1.0 FTE = 5 eight-hour days of staffing = 40 hours of staffing
> One position covered 7 days a week = 7/5 FTE = 1.4 FTE
> On an hourly basis, 7 eight-hour days of coverage = 56/40 = 1.4 FTE

For example, a head-nurse position requiring seven days a week needs 1.4 FTE in worked time to cover all seven days.

Covering Vacation, Holiday, and Illness.   To this point the fact that full times do not work full time has been ignored. In reality, full time employees are paid to take time off for vacation, holiday, and illness. Even though sick leave is a privilege, not a right, a realistic expected use of the benefits package must be considered. To start the whole process, it is necessary to know just how much time to allow.

For example, a new employee usually gets two weeks of vacation per year. By staying on the job in the hospital a number of years, extra vacation, possibly even up to 5 or more weeks, can be earned.

Employees in big inner-city hospitals with unions often earn even more. To find accurate values for vacations taken without getting involved in a lot of detail, one can:

1. Get last year's payroll run and find the "Total Paid Hours of Vacation." Divide this total by the normal working day of eight hours to determine the equivalent number of days of vacation taken.
2. Find the year's total paid FTE for the nursing department by dividing the total hours paid by 2080 hours (the numbers of hours in 52 forty-hour weeks). (Do not include administration, supervision, or inservice in either of the first two steps.)
3. Divide the answer in Step 1 by the answer from Step 2, giving the average number of days of vacation taken per FTE.

Covering for Orientation and Training.   Orientation and training are very large components of lost time in today's health-agency environment. Inservice is not of concern here, since it is concerned with upgrading the skills of existing staff. Two basic facts are related to the current situation: 1) Formerly, qualified individuals almost straight out of school could be put to work on a floor with a few days of administrative orientation; and 2) The amount of lost time due to this orientation was relatively small and was almost never formally documented.

Today's environment is a bit different. The new RN graduate often has less bedside nursing experience and may have to undergo a rigorous six-to-eight-week training program, only to leave because of disillusionment with the real world. Training-program costs may be double, since the trainee may be lost permanently, and a good portion of the orientation manager's time is lost as well. This manager is often part of the working staff on a floor, and therefore the orientation function may not be documented as part of the job, although it should be. For accurate cost accounting and to establish the value of the nurse's teaching function, costs associated with this training time should be charged to inservice education.

The typical training period for a new RN is about six to eight weeks in most hospitals. The LPN usually undergoes a four-to-five-week program, and the nurse assistants are usually trained in two weeks. Is all this time really productive? Yes and no. During the first phase of the program, it is terribly unproductive in that a fair day's work is not received from either member of the trainer-trainee pair. At the end of the period both may be up to normal productivity.

How can orientation and training be figured into the budget? Orientation costs usually must be spread over all working personnel. This in no way minimizes responsibility for documentation of orientation activities carried out by individual staff members. One can use a step-by-step approach:

1. Make a list of all new hires for the last year (by skill).
2. List their orientation and training period in days.
3. Add it all up for all new hires.
4. Divide this sum by the total FTE in nursing, excluding administration, supervision, and inservice education.

Determining Budget FTE.   The first step in any budgeting process is to figure out exactly what the goals are. The second is to figure just what it will cost to achieve these goals. Once there is a specified staffing plan, and the time that will be lost with real people has been accounted for, one can determine the number of staff to be paid.

The objective in the budgeting process is to obtain enough funding to do what must be done. In addition, extra allowance should be made for special projects and extra activities that will improve care.

To begin, consider a full-time employee who is paid to work five days a week and 52 weeks a year, or $52 \times 5 = 260$ days. As we have noted, some of this paid time will not actually be worked. Holiday, vacation, illness, orientation, and continuing-education time fall into this category. The total lost time must be subtracted from the scheduled work time to obtain a projection for the cost of one staff member in the budgetary period. This process must be carried out for each individual on the staff and totaled for the entire unit.

Activity Analysis.   Nurse leaders who have not previously done so should analyze the activities performed by their staffs. In some cases administration has employed an outside firm to do an activity study. The result of this study may or may not be the recommendation to reduce staff.

In studying activities one's first task is to construct a job description. Job descriptions (or position descriptions) typically are one- or two-page summaries of the basic tasks performed on a job. They are a direct reflection of the job design.

The factual basis for a job description can vary all the way from the employer's mental image of a job to an elaborate investigation and analysis of the job using such methods as interview and detailed checklist. Such a systematic investigation is the first step in a job description called a **job analysis**.

Many times the terms **job description** and **job specification** are used interchangeably. This is not entirely correct. Job descriptions relate to the duties of the job as a whole; job specifications, a part of the job description, are the skills, training, and experience necessary to perform the particular duties of this position. Therefore, job description includes job specifications. The overall relationship is one in which job specifications and job analysis are a part of the job description, which in turn is a part of activity analysis.

In constructing the job description certain basic information should be obtained: the job title, scope, particular duties, need for special equipment, physical requirements, formal training, experience required, special conditions, normal work hours, wage, range, and possibly alternative routes for promotion.

Job descriptions have several important uses. One, as previously noted, is the development of job specifications, a summary of the qualifications needed by workers on the job. The job description is useful to manpower planning and recruitment. Job descriptions can also be used to orient new employees to basic responsibilities and duties. The job description is the basic document used in developing performance standards. Finally, a job description is used to provide basic information for **job evaluation**.

Job evaluation is the process of determining the relative worth of the various jobs within the organization. Job evaluation assumes that it is logical to pay the most for jobs that contribute the most to attaining organizational goals and that people will feel they have been fairly treated if wages are based on the relative worth of their jobs.

Evaluation of some kind is a universal phenomenon in organizations that pay wages. Most formal job-evaluation plans make use of the job data recorded in job descriptions. Several methods have been devised to determine how one goes about judging the worth of a job. These include **ranking** or **grading**, **job classification**, the **factor-comparison method**, the **point-assignment** system, or a combination of all four.

The ranking or grading method is the simplest system that can be used. It consists simply of arranging every job in the organization in order of difficulty, from the easiest to the most difficult.

The job-classification method is a modification of the ranking system. Jobs are placed at predetermined levels on the basis of the current wages in effect. The method consists of assigning rates of pay for each level according to its importance to the institution.

The factor-comparison method ranks job against job within the organization and considers the major factors for which the institution compensates its employees and to what extent each factor is a part of each job.

The point-assignment method is the system most widely used in job evaluation. This system is based on the premise that it is possible to assign points to all of the factors in any job. The total of these points will give a significant indication of the value of that particular job. All of these methods are based upon job descriptions.

Staffing

Job satisfaction depends on many factors. In part it is based upon goodness of fit between job requirements and personal capacity; in other words, in the effectiveness of the person's pursuit of happiness in the individual work setting. In most cases, appropriate staffing is the key to that happiness.

Any nurse leader will tell you that staffing is a recurring problem. In health-care institutions the constant need for human resources uses up the largest part of the budget, and of that segment nursing is the largest component. In the past this cost has been kept down by low salaries. Now, as salaries have improved to some extent, need for staff must be justified.

Most staffing plans consider one or more variables; the number of positions in the department or the unit, the number of personnel, the type of personnel, the placement, the availability, and other specific details basic to staffing, planning, and control.

There are three kinds of staffing plans. The first is **employment control**, in which all positions are described word by word and service by service. It shows vacancies and the status of employees (whether full or part time) and also tentatively filled positions. The second type of plan, used for **budget projection**, is usually found in the central nursing office. It is a longterm plan, duplicating all things in the first plan and adding projected dates for future needs. A third plan is used for control of hourly coverage and is usually found in a division office and/or a nursing unit. This is the familiar **unit-time schedule**. Some may show class times, benefits, and absences — authorized and also unauthorized. Coverage is designed to meet clinical nursing objectives.

Historically, there have been a variety of staffing patterns. Modern nursing started with rooming-in by the nurse, 24 hours a day. By the 1930s nurses were down to twelve-hour tours of duty. During the Depression the first eight-hours three-shift duty appeared. After World War II eight hours became the norm. In the 1950s, most nurses still worked six days a week, and still, occasionally, ten hours a day. Now a 40-hour, five-day week is usual, but it too may yield to the forces of change. Currently, a different staffing pattern being tried is a ten- or twelve-hour day with a four-day week.

Cost Analysis

A **cost-analysis** approach, which came out of emerging modern technology, has been used in the past by many institutions. The current watch-word for nursing service administrators is **cost containment**. The high cost of health care plus the advent of prospective payment have made it mandatory that managers attempt to keep all charges down. There is no hard-and-fast formula for predicting staffing needs. The problem for the staffing planner becomes one of determining what is average. How many people will be needed in a given unit most of the time? People who are ill do not always fit the average projection for service needed, service given. Thus formulas are only guidelines and cannot take into consideration emergencies or the unusual. It is not usually financially feasible to staff for every possible situation.

Many factors other than money affect the staffing pattern. Of prime importance is the availability of sufficient professional and nonprofessional staff. When nurses are in short supply, nursing units have had to be closed for lack of qualified personnel. Even worse are the units that should have been closed but were not, so that an inadequate number of people had to try to do the impossible.

Other factors to be considered are the type of patients (medical or surgical), the type of institution (acute care or longterm care), the type of patient accommodations (semi-private or private), the quality of supervision, the quality of nursing care, administrator's expectations of what will be done in each unit (for example, does the nursing staff have any responsibility for food service?), the demands of the medical staff, staff responsibility for ordering and maintaining supplies, and institutional personnel policies.

Flexibility of nursing staff is also important. Can personnel be easily shifted to meet the changing demands of the various units? If not, alternative approaches to meeting short-term needs must be developed. For example, an **outside staffing service** may be tried. These services offer the advantage of availability to handle peak census conditions or to provide short-term temporary assistance whenever a part of the regular staff is ill.

Another alternative whereby temporary staffing needs can be met is the **shared-personnel service** which can operate when a group of agencies work together to organize a pool of nursing personnel for use by any one of them in time of need.

The importance of adequate staffing is soon apparent. Without it, the best nurses in the world cannot provide good patient care. The nurse in charge must spend much time finding people to do the work. No one has energy left for more than physical care of the patient and carrying out the specifically written orders. Thus, quality care and good staffing go hand in hand. When staffing is done properly, there is a blend of good professional nursing judgment, an efficient clerical system, and an understanding by employers and employees of the rights and responsibilities of each. Staffing trends for the future include the use of computers and of a central staffing office run by nonnursing clerical personnel.

Methods of Assignment

The method of assignment used within the nursing service has a direct relationship to staffing and budget. The oldest in existence is the **case method**, wherein complete care of one or more clients is assigned to one member of the nursing staff. Responsibility for care is clear, and a supportive nurse-client relationship can be established, but a large nursing staff must be maintained. Another method, the **functional**, is the assignment of a selected function to a particular staff member. For example, one nurse gives all the medications. No one person is responsible for total care of individual clients. The advantage of this method is that a great deal of work gets done in a short time. The disadvantage is that client care becomes fragmented and accountability for it becomes difficult to establish. A combination case-functional system may be used in institutions having nursing students. Case method is used in the morning or evening when the students are on the unit. The system of organization reverts to functional at mealtime or when certain staff members are not pre-pared to provide for all the needs of the client.

Since the 1950s another method, **team nursing**, has been heavily utilized. In team nursing everyone works together as a team to provide client care. The professional nurse is in charge of a team composed of staff nurses, licensed practical nurses, and aides. A democratic approach is used to involve all team members in plan-ning and executing care for a group of clients. The head nurse shares responsibility with the team leader. This makes one nurse, with her team, responsible for a group of clients.

Three components of team nursing have particular value. One is the **written care plan**, which serves to keep all members of the team abreast of changes in the client's condition. Another is the **team conference**, where all members have input into problem solving. Third, the attempt of the team leader to match individual client needs with individual nursing skills of team members can produce the best nursing care at the lowest cost. The major disadvantage is that in practice the system is often only partially implemented. Many nurses do not see the value of the potential strengths of the system (nursing-care plans, team conferences, and matching), and thus these are eliminated and care becomes more fragmented than ever.

The most recent assignment method is that of **primary nursing**. Here, as in the case method, the nurse is responsible for total care of a certain number of clients. The difference between them lies in the fact that in primary care the responsibility extends over the entire 24-hour period, when others are carrying out the primary care the primary nurse has planned. The major advantage of this system for clients is the increased continuity of the care they receive. When clients say "my nurse," they have a specific person in mind. A second advantage is that ideally the nurse can practice with much more autonomy and decision-making power, leading to increased job satisfaction. In primary nursing, it is possible to utilize the often-neglected skills learned in nursing school to truly individualize patient care. High-level systematic planning often results. Evidence is accumulating that primary care using a greater proportion of RNs as care givers costs no more than other methods (VanServellen and Mowry, 1985) but in these cost-conscious days full acceptance has not yet been achieved.

Impact of DRGs on Nursing

In the last few years, legislative changes have made major financial impact on all parts of the health care delivery systems, including nursing. More change is expected as effects are felt. These changes derive from the response of the federal government to the high cost of health care. In 1983 legislation was passed enacting a system of prospective reimbursement of hospitals for the care of Medicare patients. The meaning of this for hospital financial officers is that reimbursement for Medicare and Medicaid patients, which had been based on the number of days the patient spent in the hospital now is based on a set predetermined amount which is paid to the hospital upon discharge. Health insurance providers will probably adopt the system also. Payment received is not related to length of stay in the hospital, but is instead determined by the disease category in which the patient falls. The underlying notion is that patients with similar diagnoses will utilize similar amounts of hospital resources and therefore can be classified together in payment categories. To operationalize this concept, 23 Major Diagnostic Categories (MDCs) were established and then further subdivided into several hundred Diagnostic Related Groupings (DRGs). The number of DRGs identified has already increased since inception.

The DRGs are themselves subdivided according to the patients age and the presence or absence of complications. The amount paid to the hospital for each DRG is based on past average cost data for a given hospital and region, adjusted for inflation. If the Medicare patient's length of stay is longer than expected, the hospital must absorb the cost of the extra days. Cost containment, already important, becomes a critical issue.

Definitions of terms related to prospective payment are found in Box 3–4. For nursing costs of care have historically been included in the cost of the room, along with costs for laundry, housekeeping, and the dietary department. Under prospective payment, this is still true. But nursing administrators realize that direct nursing care costs must be identified and cost of care established. DRGs, although sensitive to age and possible complications, do not so far take into account differences in severity or individual psychosocial or cultural differences among patients. Professional nurses need the freedom to individualize care for patients as people, within DRGs. To do this, nurses must be able to show that individualized nursing care makes a difference to the patient's health status, and can help them to recover and leave the hospital within the prescribed length of stay.

Although prospective payment has caused much concern within the nursing community because of the potential it brings for layoffs in nursing positions, it can also be seen as an opportunity which can improve care and also establish nurses' value as professionals.

Much research is in process to identify the costs of individualized nursing care. Most of these studies are aimed at establishing costs through levels of patient acuity (Curtin, 1983). That is, sicker patients are allotted more nursing time. Eventually, acuity levels and patient needs and problems as reflected in nursing diagnoses must be tied to DRGs so that accurate costing can occur. Computerized programs are being generated to carry out these activities.

Box 3–4 *DEFINITIONS OF PROSPECTIVE PAYMENTS TERMS*

1. LOS	Length of stay
2. Trim Points	Low and high days LOS allowable for each DRG
3. Inliers	Patients whose cost of care falls within the trim points
4. Outliers	Patients whose cost of care falls outside the trim points
5. Case reference index	Factor that identifies the complexity (on the average) of cases treated by an institution

---

There are many other implications of prospective payment. Nurses will be asked to consider all possible methods of cost containment in the use of supplies. Non-nursing activities will be delegated to less costly personnel. Head Nurses will become more important and more accountable, since they control allocation of nursing resources.

Home nursing care sources for patients who are no longer able to recuperate fully in the hospital have become more important and some hospitals are organizing to fill this need. As less sick patients are discharged, and only those who are acutely ill remain, nurses will need to sharpen their assessment skills and emphasize discharge planning and patient teaching.

Reports and Records

Nurse managers spend many hours preparing reports and records. The one that can be most valuable to them is an **annual report** on their unit's area of responsibility. Annual reports are useful to nurse managers in several ways. With them, the managers can point out to the administration and in the nursing department the objectives that have been met during the year. They are a means of patting oneself on the back without appearing to be a braggart and, additionally, a means of giving information about nursing philosophy and needs to the Board of Trustees.

Some of the contents of an annual report might be:

1. messages from the departmental director and other nurse managers
2. the highlights of the current year
3. the goals for future years
4. any meaningful special reports and statistics on services given

Theory Z: Challenges For Health Services Management

William Ouchi, in his book describing the "Americanized" version of the Japanese management system, presents an integrated model of organizational development which leads to a more holistic approach to relationships between the employee and the organization. Ouchi provides new insights into how to develop the organization in a form that will increase quality and productivity.

The secret to Japanese success is not technology, but a way of organizing and managing people. Given the "Theory Z" organization and the health care organization, numerous contrasts are readily apparent, and while hospitals certainly differ from other industries, the problems are parallel. Hospitals are hierarchical, are organized around discrete disciplines, and have problems with coordination, cooperation, and humane care when more than one department is involved (which is most of the time). Supervision and management for discipline-based units is provided by persons in that discipline (usually through Joint Commission Accreditation of Hospitals mandate), and result in "local objectives" which at times conflict with overall hospital philosophy. Employee commitment to organizational goals is generally secondary to personal goals. Employee turnover is a constant problem as is the frustration of "dead-end" jobs with little opportunity for career growth. Health service organizations have relatively short-term perspectives, reacting primarily to reimbursement guidelines rather than to longterm philosophy. *Theory Z* is designed to address precisely these negative aspects of health service organization.

The challenge of *Theory Z* to health organizations is that its incorporation would require a radically different form of organization, governance, and operation. The change would necessitate 10–15 years of slow, orderly development. According to Clark (1981), there are several approaches to be considered.

1. Hospitals should systematically determine in a collaborative manner the longterm values, goals and objectives, organizational procedures, and relationships with clients, and with community into a formal philosophical statement which guides the behavior of the organization. The philosophical statement should replace formal, bureaucratic rules and regulations as the organization approaches "Theory Z."
2. Institutions must be willing to take more longterm perspectives, and thus, be willing to invest heavily in staff development on both the individual employee level and in relation to the development of "Theory Z" behaviors. The goal should include a commitment to life-long employment and nonspecialized career paths.
3. Participative management must become a reality, not a method of cooperation, and eventually encompass the entire organization.
4. Organizational structure revolving around specialty areas should be dismantled in favor of integrated workgroups revolving around generic client problem areas in a matrix organizational design.
5. Given the different organizational structure, supervision can now circulate across departments within a hospital. Employees on all levels, particularly management, can be rotated to maintain enthusiasm, effectiveness, coordination and collaboration.

These suggestions are certainly more easily stated than implemented. We are sure they are controversial to many. However, in the long run we think they may be workable and lead us more closely to that collaborative, comprehensive form of health care we have been seeking.

Organizations of the Future

Organization has four very basic purposes. It reduces frustration, saves time, makes order out of chaos, and, in the case of the health industry, can sometimes save lives. All of us can improve our organizational skills. Some nurses feel that they cannot organize. They need to think more positively, applying what they have already learned about organizing their own personal lives so that obligations are met. Organizing in the health-care setting operates in the same manner as it does in daily life.

Today's methods build on yesterday's, as tomorrow's will build on today's. Experts predict that, in the future, agency organizations will be better able to adapt quickly to changing situations than they do now. Adaptability means flexibility, the sense that change is occurring and new responses are required. The absence of this sense can make a progressive management obsolescent through complacency in a very short time. Another trend is an increased recognition on the part of human satisfactions experienced by employees. If management provides a work climate of confidence and respect, then everyone's life can be enriched by the job satisfaction generated.

Service institutions such as hospitals and schools are becoming an increasingly important part of the contemporary economy. They have many similarities with business enterprises; the main difference is that the product of the service organization is performance, and the goal is to provide a service rather than a tangible item that yields a profit.

Drucker (1974) predicts that the service organization of the future will function more effectively because there will be an increased emphasis on specific, clearly defined objectives and on standards for service that measure performance. These will require that priorities be set to allow the attainment of objectives at acceptable standards and that an ongoing feedback mechanism operates to provide continuous evaluation.

Trends to reduce bureaucracy, increase diversity, instill a greater sense of community among health-care workers, and increase appreciation of managerial ability are emerging. Nursing leadership will affect all of these. The trend to primary nursing is an example of reduced bureaucracy as well as greater diversification, in that holistic health care of the client can also often be accomplished under this system. Additionally, greater collegiality can replace the stereotypical "doctor-nurse" game in primary nursing. The increased interest in development of managerial abilities is shown by the many publications, courses, and continuing-education programs being offered in this area. Many present-day hospital nurses are feeling a need for more autonomy and a desire for increased input into decision making concerning quality of care. A partial answer to this need could be the establishment of a **nursing-staff organization**, similar in structure to the medical-staff organization and with the same relationship to hospital administration.

Kimbro and Gifford (1980) have suggested that such an organization could consist of all the nurses practicing in the institution, regardless of the department through which they are paid. Its officers would have direct access to the board of trustees and to administration, as do the officers of the medical-staff organization. The general function of the organization would be to provide advice and make recommendations to administration in matters where nurses are experts—that is, in the area of nursing care. This function could include responsibility for peer review, quality assurance, the setting of standards for staff qualifications, and resolution of any problems concerning substandard nursing care. The organization's function would also include the granting of clinical privileges to appropriately prepared nurses. The need for this function arises from the fact that nurse practitioners and others with expanded skills have been required to have "visiting privileges" granted by the medical-staff organization. This is not appropriate; nurses are licensed under specific acts of the various state legislatures and are legally responsible for their own practice. A mechanism is needed whereby nurses can approve the practical and clinical practice of nurses, including those in the expanded role. A staff organization can fill this role.

This organization, of course, would not replace the department of nursing service or interfere with the functions of nursing administrators. Accountability would be different for those two organizational entities: nursing service would continue to carry full responsibility for provision of continuous nursing care. Each entity would need to clearly understand the function of the other.

The ability of nurses to control their own practice could also be expanded by the department of nursing service through a more democratic structure. For example, could staff nurses nominate qualified candidates for head nurse when that position is open on the unit, as Spencer (1979) has proposed? Peers are often well qualified to evaluate strengths and weaknesses of those with whom they work. Better patient care and increased job satisfaction can result when staff has input into the appointment process.

Summary

Organization is

the key to bringing order out of chaos
the framework with which the nursing staff, the materials, and the
    machines are interrelated so as to provide quality nursing care
a means of facilitating cost containment
oriented to the needs of the future

Exercise

Mrs. P. R. is a head nurse on a Pediatric unit. Match the examples on
the right with the organizational functions of a nurse-manager listed
on the left.

1. _____ Interpret hospital policies.

2. _____ See the relationship of the unit to other units.

3. _____ Delegate responsibility and authority.

4. _____ Analyze costs.

5. _____ Show personnel how to accomplish organizational goals.

a. Plan meeting to discuss ways of saving money on supplies used by unit.

b. Make the patient assignment for the day.

c. Describe this year's objectives for the Pediatric unit to new staff member and relate to hospital objectives.

d. Write memo describing infection-control policies applied to use of the playroom.

e. Send RN who is not needed for patient care today to Pediatric Intensive Care Unit, which is short-staffed.

An answer to this exercise may be found on p. 271.

Bibliography

American Hospital Association. *The Management of Hospital Employee Productivity*. Chicago: American Hospital Association, 1973.

Clark, Dan. Theory Z: Challenges For Health Services Management. *Prospectus for Change*. Center for Interdisciplinary Education in Allied Health, Lexington (September–October, 1981).

Clifford, Joyce C. The Potential of Primary Nursing. *Health Care for the 1980s*, New York: National League for Nursing, 1979.

Curtin, Leah. Determining Costs of Nursing Services per DRG, *Nursing Management* (April, 1983): 16–20.

Department of Nursing. *Massachusetts General Hospital Manual of Nursing Procedures*. Boston: Little, Brown, 1975.

Drucker, Peter F. *Management Tasks/Responsibilities/Practices*. New York: Harper & Row, 1974.

Fraser, Lorraine P. *Contemporary Staffing Techniques in Nursing*. Appleton-Century-Crofts, Norwalk: 1984.

Kimbro, C. D., and Gifford, A. J. The Nursing Staff Organization: A Needed Development. *Nursing Outlook* (October, 1980): 610–616.

Magula, Mary. Understanding Organizations, A Guide for the Nurse Executive, *Nursing Resources* Wakefield (1982).

Nield, Margaret. Developing a Projected Nurse Staffing Program. *Supervisor Nurse* (July, 1975).

Olsson, David E. *Management by Objectives*. Palo Alto: Pacific Books, 1968.

Price, Elmira M. Staffing: The Most Basic Nursing Service Problem. *Supervisor Nurse* (July, 1975).

Smith, Howard, Reinow, Franklin and Reid, Richard. Japanese Management, Implications for Nursing Administration. *Journal of Nursing Administration* (September, 1984): 33–39.

Spencer, C. E. Nurses Need Feedback—But From Whom? *RN* (July, 1979): 63–64.

Spitzer, Roxanne. Making Primary Nursing Work. *Supervisor Nurse* (January, 1979).

Van Servellen, Given and Mowry, Mychelle. DRGs and Primary Nursing: Are They Compatible? *Journal of Nursing Administration* (April, 1985): 32–37.

Zandes, Karen. Second Generation Primary Nursing, A New Agenda. *Journal of Nursing Administration* (March, 1985): 18–24.

The
Professional
Managerial
Role

IN CHAPTER ONE a distinction was made between leadership and management. This chapter focuses on the functions of the manager.

There are nurses who would say that all management activities are just necessary evils that take time from bedside nursing. These nurses do not recognize that management, like nursing, is a profession. Management can be practiced without special training, by natural ability, by instinct, or by trial-and-error learning. But, as in nursing, this is not desirable in view of the considerable body of knowledge that exists about management practice. For any nurse to do a good job, mastery of management as well as nursing is a requirement.

Although management practices have received considerable attention in the nursing literature, basic concepts that underlie these practices need further emphasis for the education of nurses. The nursing literature has given much attention to specialized nursing concepts, such as team nursing, primary nursing, and unit management. These are very useful concepts, but understanding of basic managerial principles will provide a broader framework for nursing management.

Depending upon viewpoint, there are many different but not basically conflicting definitions of what constitutes management work. Many different titles—executive, vice-president, manager, administrator, director, supervisor, head nurse, team leader—are used to indicate management responsibilities. There is little real difference in the problem-solving processes utilized in these positions except in terms of the level of power and prestige.

A listing of executive functions may be helpful here. Barnard (George, 1972), a pioneer in the study of management, states "The essential executive functions are: (1) To provide the system of communication. (2) To promote the securing of essential effort. (3) To formulate defined purposes."

That these functions are important in the area of nursing service hardly needs saying, since nursing is involved in complex, cooperative action requiring the services of a great many people, professional, semi-professional, and others. The nursing-service director may be responsible for at least half of a health-care agency's employees. Given these conditions, leadership and management functions in this area must have a major role. Without leadership, not everyone will see the whole picture or be aware of what others are doing, nor will everyone communicate essential information appropriately. It is doubtful that most of the leadership can come from any source outside the nursing department or from anyone but a professional nurse, particularly with respect to communication.

Managerial Requirements

A manager is commonly perceived as an individual who is responsible for getting work done through others. Some of the requirements for effective management are: to view the organization as a part of a larger system, to perceive the organization as client oriented, to establish goals and objectives, to facilitate interpersonal relationships and planning, to utilize manpower resources, communication and group techniques, and to act as the agent of change.

Supervising: A Necessary Evil

The most efficient effort is the one-person effort. When nursing was a one-to-one nurse-client relationship, the nurse did the planning, supervision, and evaluation of the care given. When nurses moved into institutional settings, the work was divided among more individuals and supervision of these workers became a necessity. Supervision, to be effective, must take place in the area where the work is done. The more workers know about the whole operation, the better they can mesh their own work with the total effort.

Supervision is more than an action taken in response to a complaint. It should be planned as a continuous process of spot checking, which can improve operation of the department by preventing mistakes and omissions that would later harm the patient or embarrass the worker. This kind of supervision is analogous to what educators call "formative evaluation"—that is, the evaluation of the effectiveness of learning during the learning process. **Formative supervision** allows a continuous process of adaptation to the requirements of nursing care. For example, an effective manager will make it part of the daily plan to spend time observing the staff in action, paying particular attention to patients with unusual or critical conditions, new employees, and new medications and treatments. Additionally, the employment of temporary staff from outside staffing services or the use of "float" personnel from other units creates a need for close supervision.

Even when employees are all well acquainted with the unit and nothing unusual is occurring, it is still necessary to continue with planned regular periods of spot checking at unpredictable times. Otherwise, even the best of staff, being human, will have a tendency to let down occasionally. This kind of checking is not "snooping," but is what must be done when the responsibilities of management are accepted. Without good supervision employees are ineffective, uncoordinated and unhappy. With good supervision, employees can be helped to work effectively in a coordinated effort and, above all, be happy in their work.

Managers fill multiple roles. It is their function to make an organization run, to make it satisfy all the demands placed upon it, and perhaps even to help it become healthy. While they are doing all of this, these same managers have to satisfy a multiplicity of personal needs, their own and others. At all times they have to maintain their equilibrium. They are also supposed to be kind and understanding under all circumstances. A leader with a headache or a problem at home is still the leader.

Management: A Learned Behavior

The major objective of nursing service is to provide quality patient care. Effective management is the key to such care. However, the management role is difficult for many nurses. A commonly held viewpoint among contemporary critics of nursing is that nurses are neither interested in nor comfortable with being leaders. This misconception arises in part, perhaps because at times a fallacy operates when promotion to nurse manager positions is considered. The fallacy is that a good clinician will automatically have the skills to be a good manager. Such is not always the case. There is a body of knowledge, a set of skills to be learned, and a set of personal attitudes required of an effective nurse manager. In the same way that learning to be a manager does not qualify one for nursing, learning to be a nurse does not qualify one for administration. Almost all nurse managers can benefit from instruction in management skills.

Of the skills required of the nurse manager, it is difficult to say which is more important—decision making or communication. But no matter how well one communicates, if one is not a good decision maker, the process of management is lost. Therefore, decision making will be dealt with first.

Decision Making

Decision making is learned through educational experiences. It represents a psychological process whereby an individual selects the best of the different alternatives available for action. But not everyone learns *good* decision making through life experiences. Many managers live a trial-and-error kind of existence, without a logical framework as a guideline for decision making. Nursing has its share of these managers.

The best decision makers share specific characteristics. First, they have the ability to quickly reduce complex situations to their essentials, to distill the problems or opportunities out of them, and then to go straight to what seems the best course of action. Second, good decision makers are generally positive thinkers. Negative thinkers often perceive new ideas in terms of the problems and risks involved, whereas positive thinkers perceive new ideas in terms of potential profit or opportunity. Third, the best decision makers, as studies have shown, are people who display confidence in their decisions and also make the best personality scores. They are self-reliant, intelligent, and balanced emotionally.

There are three commonly identified approaches to decision making or problem solving in management literature. The first is the **historical approach**. This describes the processes and techniques that have been handed down from the past. Managers using this approach are not innovative. They "force fit" the new problems into the old solution. For example, consider Mr. V., a stroke patient who was admitted two days ago. A current concept in patient care is that planning for his discharge should begin soon after admission. What decisions will the nurse manager make to facilitate the attainment of this objective? If the historical approach is used, the manager will simply make a notation in the nursing-care plan and consider the job done, without questioning whether the real need of the patient will actually be met by this action.

The second managerial approach is known as **parasitic**. This approach is learned from observing the actions of other managers. It can best be defined as "copy behavior." It has the same weakness as the historical approach—trying to fit an old solution to a new problem. It, too, is a "force fit" situation. Our aforementioned nurse manager could deal with Mr. V.'s need for discharge planning by using the solution the previous head nurse had used.

The last approach is the **professional** one, in which use is made of a theoretical system for problem solving. One such system has been developed by Odiorne (1969), a well-known management consultant.

Odiorne says "The first step in solving a problem or making a decision is to clarify your objectives. We navigate by a star or by the sun. When we manage by objectives, we mean simply that we will fix our ultimate purpose in mind before we start our journey. This objective then becomes a target, a goal, a desired outcome and a criterion for measuring progress." The decision-making system he recommends is as follows: First, have an objective in mind before starting the decision-making process. Second, collect and organize the facts. Third, identify the problem. Fourth, list possible solutions. Fifth, screen these alternatives through some decision criteria, and sixth, take corrective action as needed.

If this approach sounds familiar, it's probably because it is similar to the concept of the scientific method developed by Dewey in 1910 (1933). Dewey's system identified five factors in problem solving. First, a difficulty is felt. Second, location and definition of the difficulty is established. Third, suggested solutions of the problems (hypotheses) are formulated. Fourth, deductive reasoning of the hypothesis by action is performed.

There is also much resemblance here to the **nursing process** familiar to all clinical nurses. Nursing process is dynamic and involves constant assessment and reassessment of decisions and of the decision-making process itself. Nursing process involves problem solving for the care of patients. The steps are assessment, planning and intervention, and evaluation. The purpose of decision making in an organizational setting is to achieve coordination of goals, whereas the purpose of the nursing process is to help the client to achieve an improved health status.

Thus, the nurse responsible for Mr. V.'s discharge planning, if using the problem-solving approach called the nursing process, could take the following actions:

1. While making nursing rounds, determine that Mr. V.'s condition appears stable and that now is the time to begin thinking of activities of daily living he will need to be able to perform at home. It is noted that he has a complete left hemiplegia at this time. His wife seems worried already about how she will be able to manage at home.
2. Make the following written plan:
    a. Begin active range of motion (ROM) in the uninvolved side and passive ROM on the involved side every two hours through the day. If he wakes at night, ROM could be repeated then. In addition, Mrs. V. can be shown ROM procedure and asked to demonstrate her understanding of this procedure by doing it under supervision. Mrs. V. can then practice when she visits.
    b. Find out the physician's plans for physical therapy and for ambulation, so that nursing care can be coordinated with the therapeutic regimen and can reinforce it.
    c. Explain to Mr. V. that it is time to begin thinking of when he will be at home and how ROM, physical therapy and ambulation will prepare him for this. Repeat frequently until he appears to understand.
3. Implement the plan, making sure that nurses on the other shifts are fully informed and have input into total plan of care.
4. Evaluate the results of the plan by observing the client and communicating with him, his family, and other members of the staff.

Another example of management in nursing can be seen in the following situation. Upon returning from lunch, an assistant head nurse was informed that the following matters needed attention:

1. A visitor had fainted.
2. Mr. Smith's I.V. had infiltrated, and he was far behind on his fluids.
3. Four patients had not received their lunch trays. It was now 1:00 p.m.
4. The operating room supervisor had just called and said to "Give Mrs. Jones her pre-op Demerol now."
5. The toilet was overflowing in a patient's restroom. Water and feces were pouring out rapidly.

The following personnel were available. Who should have done what and in what order of priority?

> Assistant Head Nurse
> Ward Clerk
> LPN (Medication Certified)

The assistant head nurse had good problem-solving abilities and began by identifying her objectives and prioritizing them (reality demanded that she do this in her head). What should be done first? The true state of affairs for the visitor who had "fainted" was unknown, so the first priority was to determine the current situation there. At the same time she sent the LPN to turn off the infiltrated I.V. and then to give the preoperative medication. That left the ward clerk to call maintenance about the plumbing crisis and then to order the needed lunch trays. The nurse was then able to restart the I.V. By this time the rest of the staff had returned from lunch also. The unit was quiet for the rest of the afternoon.

There are many methods of problem solving. Another one can be seen in Box 4–1.

Box 4–1 *STEPS IN PROBLEM SOLVING*

ASSESS

1. *What* is the problem?
   What is disturbing us? What form does the problem take? What is the evidence that it exists?
2. *How* is it a problem?
   What are we trying to accomplish? What are the overall purposes, goals, or objectives to which the problem is related? How is the problem an obstacle to achieving purposes?
3. *Why* do anything about it?
   Why is it important to us? How does achieving purposes affect reaching our individual goals?
   Probable results if unsolved: harm/benefit; if solved: loss/gain.
4. What are the *facts*?
   What kind of facts do we need? Where can we get them? Survey? How can we organize, evaluate, and interpret them? Facts, opinions, or prejudices? Relevant? Causes, effects, or coincidences? All sides represented?
5. What do the facts *mean*?
   What are the causes of the problem? Specific obstacles? Should problem be restated? Are there several problems? In what order should they be attacked? What limits or boundaries should be recognized?

PLAN

6. What *kind of solution* should we look for?
   1) To remove causes or obstacles or to satisfy needs.
   2) Considering pertinent factors and overall purpose.
7. What are *possible solutions*?
   Brainstorming. No critical judgment. Quantity, not quality.
8. What is *best solution*?
   What should be done? What quantity? What quality? When should it be done? By whom? Where?
9. Will it *work*?
   What are implications and consequences? Faults, merits; effect on individuals, policies, practice, overall purpose, etc. What is the record? Where did it succeed or fail?
10. Is it *worth doing*?
    Cost/value; risk/opportunity

IMPLEMENT

EVALUATE

Should a pilot test be considered? What measurements can be set up to test results? What is the alternative, if solutions are unsuccessful? Who will be responsible? What is the report system?

Many nurses operate as if previous decisions will last forever. They fail to recognize that the work they do takes place in a dynamic environment, and that needs change from day to day. Conditions of risk and uncertainty are the norm.

Decisions must be made within the confines of the nurse's knowledge and the information level available at the time. There is no perfect decision. There is no one answer for all time. Planning is a continuous process requiring constant revision and reevaluation. Plans and decisions go together.

People vary in their decision-making styles. At one extreme are those who procrastinate for a long period in the hope that the problem will solve itself (sometimes it does, but not very often). At the other extreme are those who make hasty decisions with inadequate data. Most of us fall somewhere between these two.

Practice in decision making can improve the quality of decisions that are made. As we do more of it, we begin to see where we can decide quickly, because we have made a similar decision before and it worked well. We can also see where we need to think about the problem and increase our information base before deciding.

A formal method of decision making uses the "decision tree," which allows the visualization of the possible alternatives and their probable consequences. The first step is to construct a primary design having at least two alternatives (See Figure 4–1). The possible outcomes that could result from each of these decisions is diagrammed, and any further decisions needed are identified and made. Then the outcomes of these are diagrammed, and the process continues until a logical end is reached.

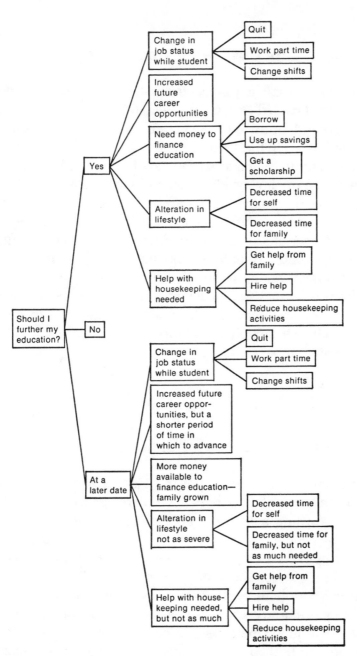

Figure 4–1   Decision Tree

Quality Circles in Nursing Service

Quality circles utilize a management technique based upon the writings of Dr. Edward Deming and Dr. Joseph Juran. This concept was invented and found to be successful in Japan and was imported to the United States in the 1970s. The idea was originally used here by business and industry leaders who saw the method as an effective way to enhance quality, productivity and job satisfaction.

In health care, quality circles are a longterm participatory management tool which employs staff creativity to improve hospital operations. This technique has been utilized to resolve problems associated with staff retention, quality of patient care and interdepartmental cooperation. The method encourages nurses to involve themselves in the clinical and administrative decision-making process. This involvement, in turn, leads to an increase in staff skills, morale and job satisfaction (see Figure 4–2). Two examples of quality circles in action appear below.

Quality Circle in a Visiting Nurse Association

The first Quality Circle formed at the Visiting Nurse Association in 1981 was made up of staff nurses who were all registered nurses. After brainstorming a list of problems the circle concentrated its efforts on the problem of the service record, primarily the amount of time required to do the opening paperwork. The service record had increased in size over the years and contained much information which was redundant and not pertinent to efficient health care delivery. Due to a time crunch the visiting nurse association had been allowing overtime for the nurses to complete paperwork. Staff were reimbursed one hour per new opening. The staff was insisting that the opening paperwork took longer than an hour. Administration was willing to consider increasing the time allotted but there was no evidence supporting the increased need.

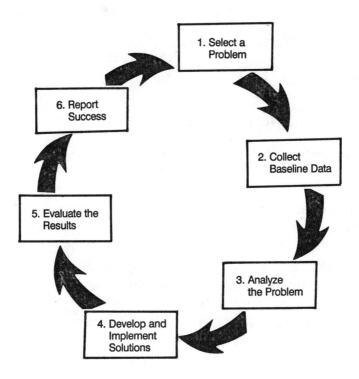

Figure 4–2   The Quality Circle Process (From Melanie Adair, Mary Ellen Fitzgerald, Kortner Nygerd, and Franklin J. Shaffer. *Quality Circles in Nursing Services: A Step-by-Step Implementation Process*. National League for Nursing. New York: 1982.)

Using the quality circle techniques of brainstorming and cause and effect diagramming the group was able to define the problem and collect data. From their investigation of the problem the team first determined that the average time to complete the paperwork on a new service record was 1.485 hours (see Figure 4–3). In addition the group identified the redundant areas in the record, i.e., the client's name in thirteen different places on the record.

Over the next couple of weeks the group met weekly to work on streamlining the record, eliminating the redundant areas as well as some of the "nice to know" but not vital information. The new record was four pages shorter and had eliminated much of the redundancy. Administration agreed to allow the quality circle members to pilot the

TEAM	A	B	C	MISC.
Number of Records	7	21	15	5
Time in Minutes	760	2200	1695	660
Average Time per Team in Hours	1.49	1.45	1.53	1.47
Average for Total Teams	1.485 hr.			

Figure 4–3 Problem of the Service Record

revised record on one of the teams for a two month period to assure that the changes were workable.

At the end of the two month period the quality circle team was ready to make the management presentation with the recommendation on the record changes. All team members were participants in the presentation which was held at the monthly staff meeting. All nursing staff were present when administration accepted the recommendations of the Quality Circle.

Quality Circle in a Nursing Home

Many of the clients at the nursing home though physically disabled were mentally alert. A concern had been voiced by the nursing staff that inadequate socialization opportunities were available for this group, especially at meal time.

The first Quality Circle formed at the nursing home was made up of nurses and nursing aides. In the first session using brainstorming the group identified the following problems:

1. lack of enough linen on the weekends
2. lack of communication between the nursing aides and the registered nurse staff
3. no scheduled patient care conferences
4. limited environment for socialization of the mentally alert residents.

Through consensus the group agreed they would concentrate on the problem of the limited environment for socialization, especially at mealtime.

The nursing home had a census of 100 patients housed on four wings. The large day room also served as a dining room. Patients were brought to the day room after morning care and were kept there until after lunch. Many of the patients required assistance with feeding and a number of them had problems associated with feeding such as drooling and regurgitation. The dining room was furnished with long tables and it was difficult to avoid seeing and hearing the feeding problems. The result was that alert patients chose to eat in their own rooms. This practice greatly diminished socialization associated with meals.

Using a cause and effect diagram to identify the problems, the quality circle members began to brainstorm causes of the problems. Input from the social worker assisted in the collection of data.

The decision was made to concentrate on the problem of the environment of the dining room. Hiring additional staff for feeding the patients was not feasible and changing the feeding habits of some of the patients was not realistic.

The group brainstormed the following available options:

1. divide the dining room having one section for the alert residents
2. small individual tables
3. feed the mentally disabled residents in their rooms.

Feeding the mentally disabled resident in their own rooms was not acceptable as this group needed the benefit of socialization also. Also in the dining room the staff could feed more than one resident at a time. The quality circle felt that the use of small tables arranged in such a way that both groups of residents could be served would be the solution of choice. The facilitator found that administration would consider the proposal depending on the cost. A circle member checked with supply houses for prices as well as with a local carpenter on the cost of cutting down the large tables.

The circle prepared for the management presentation with recommendations for changing the environment of the dining room. Costs were provided from both the supply house for new tables and from the local carpenter for remodeling the long tables. The nursing home administration accepted the recommendation and agreed to purchase some small tables and in addition have the long tables cut down. A local volunteer group heard of the plans and volunteered their time and some funds to arrange the tables and provide plants and some new pictures to add to the refurbishing.

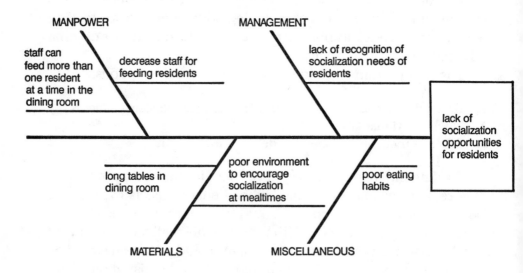

Figure 4–4 Cause and Effect Diagram

The Art of Delegation

Each person has a preferred style for solving problems. Knowing what it is and fitting it to the job can be important to career success. Whether one is planning, organizing, motivating, directing, or controlling, the first decision is to choose among alternatives in planning. For example, nurse leaders must decide who is to do what, when, where and how. When leaders have made decisions they have really only made a beginning in the process of leadership. They must next be able and willing to delegate the results of those decisions to subordinates. The process of delegation is quite elementary and is one of the most important keys in the organizational structure. Nurses may choose to retain much authority and have a strong centralized organization or they may prefer one that is more decentralized and delegate an increasing amount of authority to staff.

A common failing among new and experienced supervisors alike is that they try not only to do all the things they did before they became managers, but in addition, to find the time for supervising. To do an effective job, nurses must be willing to delegate certain functions, but one of the touchiest problems in delegating just what decisions can be delegated. Effective nurse managers never fail to make it clear from the beginning which decisions staff can make and which ones only they can make. When a person has been authorized to make certain decisions or has been given a special assignment, it is necessary that the nurse manager inform the staff. Otherwise, the individual will meet resentment and may be accused of "throwing his weight around."

Another problem that the new nurse leader often faces is that, in delegation, the person assigned the job may not do it exactly the same way that the leader would have. The leader must remember that the desired results may often be obtained in a variety of methods.

In order to delegate effectively, the nurse leader must first recognize the need to do so. Second, the talents of subordinates must be developed by providing adequate training. Third, the tasks to be delegated and the person to do the job must be chosen with equal care. Fourth, it must be clear to the staff just which decisions are theirs to make. Fifth, all concerned must be told about the assignment. Sixth, concentration should be on the results, not the methods. Seventh, there is a need for thorough follow-up. Any supervisor who wants to have maximum efficiency in operations must be willing to delegate many of the routine jobs or noncritical decisions to competent employees.

An important component of delegation is the sharing of planning. The astute nurse manager recognizes that one cannot delegate without giving appropriate authority and that with authority also goes responsibility and accountability. With delegation one must give credit for results and must show confidence in the subordinate. If this is not done, the subordinate may bypass the immediate supervisor and take feelings of frustration to the next higher level of management. One can't just delegate and forget. Even though the job has been given to someone else, it is still the manager's responsibility to follow up in a systematic way to see what is being done about the work that has been delegated.

Besides including the employees in writing goals and objectives for the nursing unit and discussing forthcoming plans and changes to be made, another way of obtaining worker input is by the use of a suggestion box. This is not a substitute for any other management system. It is not to take the place of policies or procedures, rules or regulations, nor does it take the place of a good personnel program. A well-planned suggestion program will help bring about improvement and equanimity in the operation and will also help build good morale and harmonious working relationships among employees. This suggestion program does not need to be institution wide. Any nurse manager may see its value and utilize one on an individual nursing unit.

A Game Plan

Neophyte managers frequently express the need for a cookbook method for the art of management. Blanchard and Johnson ably provide one approach in a book titled *The One Minute Manager*. The basic idea here is to set goals, praise and reprimand behaviors promptly, and as needed, encourage people, speak the truth, laugh, work, enjoy (see Figure 4–5).

The game plan incorporates a number of theoretical approaches to management and human resources management. This technique is easily remembered and applicable to many common situations encountered in daily practice.

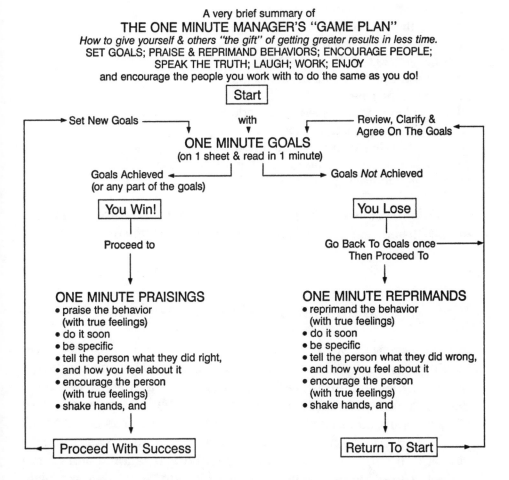

A very brief summary of
THE ONE MINUTE MANAGER'S "GAME PLAN"
How to give yourself & others "the gift" of getting greater results in less time.
SET GOALS; PRAISE & REPRIMAND BEHAVIORS; ENCOURAGE PEOPLE;
SPEAK THE TRUTH; LAUGH; WORK; ENJOY
and encourage the people you work with to do the same as you do!

Start

Set New Goals ———————→ with ——————— Review, Clarify & Agree On The Goals
ONE MINUTE GOALS
(on 1 sheet & read in 1 minute)

Goals Achieved ←——————— ———————→ Goals *Not* Achieved
(or any part of the goals)

You Win!   You Lose

Proceed to   Go Back To Goals once———→ Then Proceed To

ONE MINUTE PRAISINGS
• praise the behavior
  (with true feelings)
• do it soon
• be specific
• tell the person what they did right,
• and how you feel about it
• encourage the person
  (with true feelings)
• shake hands, and

ONE MINUTE REPRIMANDS
• reprimand the behavior
  (with true feelings)
• do it soon
• be specific
• tell the person what they did wrong,
• and how you feel about it
• encourage the person
  (with true feelings)
• shake hands, and

Proceed With Success   Return To Start

Figure 4–5   (From Kenneth Blanchard and Spencer Johnson. *The One Minute Manager*. Morrow Publishers, Inc.: New York, 1982.)

A Game Plan for Nurse Managers

There are certain behaviors that once identified assist practicing nurse managers in the strategy of becoming successful nurse managers. Many of these practical behaviors are described by Sullivan and Decker (1985) in the following listing:

1. Know who you are
2. Learn the tools of your trade
3. See the big picture
4. Have a red flag sensitivity
5. Be alert to trends or changes
6. Know time and motion methods
7. Learn the rules
8. Develop a nondefensive stand and be nonemotional
9. Avoid interpersonal putdowns
10. Learn to live with a certain amount of discomfort
11. View what you are doing as a career not a job
12. Stretch toward excellence

Pragmatically speaking, other points emphasized are: think continually, listen, learn to trust, don't give away your power, and develop a support group.

Communication in Organizations

In nearly every survey of problems in nursing service, someone will identify communication as critical. What is it about organizations that seems to make communication so difficult? Much study has been devoted to this question. An organization may be considered a system of overlapping and interdependent groups. Other things being equal, people will communicate most frequently to those geographically closest to them, even in a relatively small organization. Each one of the subgroups (departments, nursing units, etc.) within an organization demands allegiance from its members. It has its own immediate goals and means for achieving them. The groups in any organization often represent different subcultures, particularly in a health-care institutional setting in which there are many occupational and professional groups. Each of these tends to have its own value system, idealized image, and tradition. We tend to communicate differently with those who are on a different level from our own in the institutional hierarchy. What intensifies all of these factors and can create communication problems is the fact that relationships among people in an organization are in a continual state of flux. People leave, are transferred, promoted, or replaced in a situation, and the relationships change.

It is sometimes said that in any organization communication flows well only in a downward direction. The problem of the nurse is to get communication in an upward direction from below. The forces that direct communication in an organization are mainly motivational. People communicate or fail to communicate in order to achieve some goal, to satisfy some personal need, or to improve their immediate situation. Often, what we call communication problems are symptomatic of other difficulties that exist within the organization or between people and groups.

Many barriers to communication have been described in management literature. One is the problem of trust or the lack of it. We must have trust before we will take the risk of communication. Another is the problem of creating interdependence among persons, so that they have common goals and agreement about means for achieving them. Still another is the problem of withholding information. Sometimes managers will fail to communicate needed facts to persons they dislike. There is also the exceedingly important problem of failure to communicate among different groups of employees. A classic example is the lost laboratory requisition. Imagine the telephone conversation that results when the ordered lab work is not on the chart.

Another barrier to communication occurs when nurse leaders allow their own opinions to interfere with obtaining input from staff. Head nurses who call meetings and ask for suggestions on a problem, and then ignore those they have been given in favor of their own ideas, are guilty of this kind of behavior.

The essentials of effective communication begin with the individual. Nurse leaders must be role models for the types of communication they wish to encourage. There are several guidelines that are helpful in thinking about promoting good communication. The leader should:

1. withhold judgment of other people until an attempt to understand them has been made
2. be sure the person's undivided attention is obtained before giving information
3. express thoughts in clear, concise words or language that the other person can understand
4. take time to listen carefully and try to hear what the other person is really saying.

We all have a built-in filter that allows us to hear what we want to hear. We have a tendency to read our opinions into the words and actions of other people. We also have a tendency to be negative and thereby reject something new before we understand it. The leader must concentrate on building trust and acceptance. Fear causes people to communicate what they think the other person wants to hear. Only mutual trust can build the type of atmosphere in which people will communicate the truth. We must select the best types and channels of communication and feedback to meet the situation.

Nurses are becoming more and more involved in community aspects of health-care delivery. In some cases this requires them to make speeches. Many times, they are in the position of trying to market an idea as a salesperson would. There are certain tips that can help make a speech more successful:

1. Think before you talk or write
2. Spark the listener's interests by your choice of words and approach
3. Memorize ideas, not words
4. Practice what you are going to say
5. Smile and make eye contact when you speak
6. Control body language as much as you can
7. Watch the clock and end on time
8. End on an optimistic note
9. Leave your audience ready to act upon the information that you have given

Common methods of communication include use of memos, face-to-face conferences with individuals or groups, telephone communication, and statements of policies and procedures. For each of these, one must consider the cost in time and money. Memos, if clear, are inexpensive and easy, but they are best used to convey factual information or praise. They are impersonal and thus a poor way to criticize, since hard feelings may result from their use. Guidelines for writing memos include:

1. Keep sentences and paragraphs short
2. Avoid wordiness
3. Discuss one subject only
4. Be concise, but conversational
5. Adapt the wording to the reader's level
6. Use the proper form

Policy and procedural statements are also inexpensive but impersonal. If the problem is a new one, or if criticism of personnel is involved, face-to-face conferences are preferable even though they are more expensive. Of course, if criticism of an individual is necessary a private conference is most desirable.

Silence is not always golden. People want information. If it is not given to them, they supply their own ideas and interpretations: hence the proverbial grapevine. What they think may not be right, but it is true to them. Therefore, dissemination of accurate information is a never-ending process.

Communication is like a continuous chain. It is as simple as the Golden Rule and as complex as life. It is only as strong as its weakest link, it cannot be pushed, and it's up to the leader to see that it works.

Finally, a good communication program must be ongoing. It requires constant effort in order to be effective and keep up with changing situations.

Another point to be considered is that, in reality, there are two levels of communications—factual and affective (concerned with the feel and tone of the interaction). The nurse manager must be aware of how communications are being received and interpreted on an emotional level. It must be understood that feelings and purposes are communicated along with facts.

In order to make sure that communication has taken place, there must be some kind of feedback. The nurse manager, knowing the personnel, will selectively observe or check on those who may not understand the communication or value it sufficiently to comply. If the material to be communicated is critical, it can be distributed in written form prior to a staff meeting in which it will be discussed with the entire group. That old cliche, "Actions speak louder than words," is still true. Every expression, gesture, and tone of voice communicates something to somebody. Others need to understand the true meaning and not what they interpret from the body language that accompanies the communications.

In the day-to-day business of working together, sometimes arguments seem to appear out of nowhere, leaving all staff furious and frustrated. There are some pointers on how to avoid these useless battles. Refighting old arguments is a waste of time, and the leader should refuse to become involved in it. There is often a history of frequent differences over trifles among staff members. Trifles become a way to air but not resolve buried anger. In some instances the bickering is pointless and accidental. In others, it's an indicator of a deeper conflict. The leader's job is to determine which of these two cases is operating so that corrective action may be taken.

Double-message battles should also be avoided. In a double-message dilemma, it appears that there are two very different choices of behavior, but really there is no satisfactory choice. Whatever behavior is chosen, it will be wrong. For example, a head nurse determines that much of her time is spent in clerical duties. Therefore she approaches administration for a budgeted ward-clerk position. But, when the properly trained ward-clerk appears, the head nurse begins to complain that she no longer knows what is going on on the unit. She is sending a double message to administration.

Other battles result from mind reading. Mind reading is a good example of a communication mistake that lead to a variety of unnecessary problems. People who depend on mind reading manufacture trouble for themselves in a number of ways. For example, a head nurse assigns a member of the staff who is clinically very proficient to the procedure committee. The staff nurse, who was not consulted about the appointment, does not enjoy writing and would much prefer another committee that puts the emphasis on doing. Thus, her performance as a committee member is likely to be poor.

Interaction overload can also be a source of conflict. An inter-action-overload fight might start when a staff nurse who has finished assigned work requests to leave early just as the head nurse, who is having a stressful day, is about to ask for help checking charts. The busy nurse is not likely to respond favorably to the request because both nurses are experiencing different levels of stress at this time. As is not surprising, conflict results.

Other Forms of Communication

Reports and Rounds

Nurses in management positions are often asked to prepare depart-mental reports. Reports help in decision making by providing facts and ideas the receiver does not have. Reports are needed to overcome the problem of distance, to save time, to communicate information, to provide permanent records, to develop new ideas, and to facilitate evaluation by supervisors. Top management can more readily eval-uate the activities of a department by the reports that are prepared.

To make report writing simpler, a system is necessary. It is helpful to review applicable minutes and to collect any needed client statistics on an ongoing basis. Data can be obtained from the per-sonnel department, or, if there is none, the business office may have the necessary information.

Another form of communication used in nursing service is the change-of-shift report. By this means the department of nursing service can enhance quantity and continuity of care. The change-of-shift report may be defined as an oral communication of pertinent information about clients on a particular unit. It emphasizes events of the tour of duty just ending. In general it should include information identifying the client, nursing directives, and special problems. Like other common repetitive, ritualistic actions, change-of-shift reports are given daily in all health-care institutions. Some turn into personal conversations. Some give so little information that they are almost laughable. Some institutions have developed the use of the taped report in order to save time and give better information. Most nurses agree that some sort of report from shift to shift is necessary. However, the value of the report varies with the person presenting the information.

Making rounds with purpose is another means of communication. Supervisory rounds should be used for evaluation of nursing care given and for feedback to the personnel on that nursing unit. Rounds make it possible for nurse leaders to see relationships and values not obtainable in any other way. Observations can be made regarding the quality of client care, the competency of the staff, the difficulties they are encountering. Group relationships and interpersonal skills can also be observed. The supervisor can make decisions about what has been observed during rounds and can communicate back to the staff the information needed to maintain a viable nursing service.

Group Process

Nurse leaders are responsible for coordination, supervision, and administration within their areas of responsibility. This includes carrying out the plans of superiors, keeping personnel well informed, containing costs, maintaining sound organizational relationships, and providing high-quality nursing care. Nurse leaders also should take any other actions necessary for the efficient operation of their group or department as approved by their immediate supervisors. In order to do this they must be expert in the use of **group process**. Nurse leaders need to know how to construct effective groups for work projects and to be able to conduct the meetings of those groups. Although committee structures are preferable to individual effort where multiple input will provide a broader informational base for decision making, nurse leaders must also be aware of the limitations of committees; many projects are better assigned to a single individual. The individual can work more quickly and at convenient times. Committees are not designed to handle most day-to-day decisions nor to supplant the authority and responsibility of the unit manager. They are better able to handle the larger issues.

Many nurses are members of different kinds of committees in both their personal and professional lives. Some of these committees are effective, some are not. Although time and effort are sometimes wasted in accomplishing designated goals, committee work can be a good learning experience for all of those involved. Committees are especially valuable in assuring that diverse ideas and points of view are considered.

A group can take advantage of the special skills possessed by some of its members. Individual members often volunteer to do the tasks they do best in order to achieve the goals of the group. Committees are established for specific purposes. Most of these purposes are problem solving or task oriented. They are divided into several types: advisory, **ad hoc**, task force, and so on. The cynic may say that the ideal size of any committee is three, with two of its members out of town, but size really depends on the committee's function. In general it should be large enough to facilitate free discussion. There are varying ideas about the ideal number of members, but seven will usually make a functional committee. An effective chairperson facilitates the work of the committee by controlling the meeting, generating interest, coordinating group efforts, and stimulating the group to action. The chairperson must be willing to spend time in preparation for meetings so that they will proceed in an orderly way to accomplish the task at hand.

Among the witty remarks about committees is the one that suggests that "perhaps committees keep minutes because of the hours they waste." If the meeting is important enough to be held, then it is important enough to be recorded. Minutes are useful in documenting decisions and in noting progress. Effective meetings often result when each member of the committee comes to the meetings well prepared and accepts a personal responsibility for attending to the business at hand. An agenda distributed several days before the meeting facilitates this process. Committees are established in a belief in the soundness of group thought and decision making. This is participatory management in action.

Computers in Nursing

Computerized information systems have a potential for use hospital-wide in the provision, documentation, review and the development of high quality care. Computer-assisted nursing care is a description of nursing in the future. In addition to the data bank of patient information, there are various computer uses for the nurse: patient care plans, quality assurance audits and data collection, scheduling for the operating room and outpatient departments, discharge planning, and streamlining documentation.

Nursing administration can manage unit human resources by utilizing a computer to allocate staff, deliver planned care (using patient acuity) and deal with the budget with hard data. Instructional applications are many: tutorial, problem solving, simulation, classroom/instructional management as well as administrative applications. The use of the computer in retrieving patient data might be the catalyst nurses in health care services need to perform nursing research.

Representation to Other Departments

The nurse leader must represent the nursing department to workers in other departments, to medical staff, to health-care administration, and to the community. Educating others to the needs of nursing service is a major function of nurse managers. Every opportunity for interaction with these people should present a picture of professional nursing and the viability of the nursing leadership in the organization. Most people do not learn by listening to whatever is said one time. Therefore the nurse leader must take personal responsibility for education of as many people as possible to the needs of the nursing service.

Dual Role of the Director of Nursing

Ever since the advent of the professional manager in health-care operations, there has been a growing debate over who should head the key clinical areas of the hospital. Should it be a clinical professional or a management professional? For various reasons this debate frequently has focused on the nursing service. First, the nursing service is the most significant department in the hospital, if for no other reason than by virtue of the number of employees and access to the client. Second, for many years insufficient funding to support research in nursing has frequently forced nurses to rely on empirical judgment as the basis for determining methods of operation. It has been difficult for nurses to demonstrate the validity of certain practices, especially from a management standpoint. Finally, for many years following World War II, the emphasis in the nursing profession was on education rather than administration, causing a significant number of outstanding nurses to choose the former as the area where the action is. Only a nurse who is both clinician and manager can minimize the conflict in values inherent in the bureaucratic structure that is the health-care organization. A knowledge of both management and clinical skills is required.

As a key person, the administrator of the department of nursing service must be a registered nurse. This nurse needs a unique background in order to relate directly with the nursing staff, to represent and interpret nursing to other members of administration, and to work with the medical and professional staffs to develop and recommend policies and procedures relative to client care. The administrator of the department of nursing must be a member of the top management echelon and should have sound educational and professional qualifications in administration as well as in nursing.

Certain general characteristics of all professionals and professionalism apply to nurses. Nurses believe that, as a result of their education and experience, they are in the best position to determine the needs of clients. This belief tends to define an independent role for nurses. As members of an emerging profession, nurses have moved away from the total dependence on authority formerly found in the hierarchy. The independent role of nurses as professionals may conflict with the role required of them by the hospital, with its emphasis on the team approach. Similarly, the goal of nurses is to deliver the best nursing care to each of the clients for whom they are responsible, considering individual needs. Administratively, there are times when the institution's need is to consider the best interests of its entire community of clients. These needs may supercede the needs of an individual client. Many articles in recent nursing literature address the question of the crisis in nursing leadership. Certainly, the chief nurse should have a good clinical background and professional management skills, knowledge, and experience in order to be the kind of leader who insures quality care. Equally important is the ability of the leader to provide a role model for professional practice by other nurses in the department.

Nursing Directors In Longterm Care Facilities

Too often, longterm care facilities have been considered the "stepchild" in the health care delivery system. Law-makers, doctors, nurses and other heath care professionals have wanted to pattern nursing homes after hospitals. Sometimes the unfair view is expressed that nursing homes look like bad hospitals (Stryker, 1975).

There are several basic differences between hospitals and nursing homes which influence the way nurses manage. There is a difference in the way in which nursing care is provided: acute versus longterm. The major charge of the director of nursing in longterm care is to manage the environment in such a way that persons living there maintain as much dignity and independence as possible. Hospitals are geared toward providing care for a short term disruption of normal living.

The nurse manager in a longterm care facility must:

1. create an environment where psychosocial programs are emphasized
2. promote an atmosphere whereby individualism can flourish
3. provide inservice programs to fill the gaps in basic education related to gerontology and rehabilitation.

The ANA Research Foundation and the American Association of Nursing Home Administrators is piloting a self-assessment and learning package which is a home study course. It is entitled "Nursing Administration in Longterm Care" and is being offered by several universities/colleges through their continuing education program over the country.

The nurse who chooses to be a manger in this rapidly developing field has opportunities for stimulating and providing creative nursing care. Also, there is opportunity to help staff develop knowledge and skills to carry out longterm care programming.

Summary

Management is

> a group enterprise that demands the best efforts of all its members working in unison
>
> the ability to delegate so as to prevent bottlenecks and to improve employee morale by sharing responsibilities
>
> the ability to make sound decisions generally, and to relinquish decisions that have been proven ineffective
>
> the ability to provide a climate that allows for failures as well as successes

Exercise

Mr. P. Z. is the supervisor for five medical nursing units. He has been concerned about the turnover in the medical intensive care unit for which he is responsible. A personnel report, received this morning, informs him that the turnover rate on the MIC Unit for the past year has been 60 percent. He can recall two occasions in the recent past when it was necessary to schedule the RNs on 12-hour shifts in order to cover the unit. Using the problem-solving steps listed below (from Chapter 2), decide how he can make best use of available resources to solve this problem.

1. State the problem.
2. Gather the needed facts and organize them into a logical sequence.
3. Consider the alternatives.
4. Be flexible, and let new ideas hatch.
5. Make the decision.

An answer to this exercise may be found on p. 271.

Bibliography

Adair, Melanie, Fitzgerald, Mary Ellen, Nygard, Kortner, and Shaffer, Franklin. *Quality Circles in Nursing Service.* National League for Nursing. New York (1982).

Albrecht, Carole, and Lieske, Anna Marie. Automated Patient Care Planning, *Nursing Management* (July, 1985): 21–29.

Blanchard, Kenneth, and Johnson, Spencer. *The One Minute Manager.* New York: Morrow, 1982.

Carpenter, C. R. Computer Use In Nursing Management. *The Journal of Nursing Administration* 28 (1983): 17–21.

Dewey, John. *How We Think.* Boston: D. C. Heath, 1933.

Diekelmann, Nancy L., and Broadwell, Martin. *The New Hospital Supervisor.* Reading: Addison-Wesley, 1977.

Edmunds, L. Computer-assisted Nursing Care. *American Journal of Nursing* 22 (1982): 1076–1079.

Ford, Jo Ann Garafalo, Trygstand-Durland, Louise N., Nelms, Bobbie Crew. *Applied Decision Making for Nurses.* St. Louis: C. V. Mosby, 1979.

George, Claude S. *The History of Management Thought.* Englewood Cliffs: Prentice-Hall, 1972: 140, 153–154.

Johnson, Mae M., and Davis, Mary Lou C. *Problem Solving in Nursing Practice* (2nd Ed.). Dubuque: William C. Brown, 1975.

Lamps, Suans. Focus Charting: Streamlined Documentation. *Nursing Management* (July, 1985): 43–47.

Longest, Beaufort B. *Management Practice for the Health Professional.* Reston: Reston Publishing, 1976.

McCarthy, Laura. Taking Charge of Computerization. *Nursing Management* (July, 1985): 35–42.

Odiorne, George S. *Management Decisions by Objectives.* Englewood Cliffs: Prentice-Hall, 1969: 252.

Poteet, Gaye. Delegation Strategies. *Journal of Nursing Administration* (September, 1984): 18–21.

Stryker, Ruth. How Does Nursing Home Administration Differ From Hospital Administration? *Journal of Nursing Administration* (May, 1975): 16–17.

Sullivan, Eleanor, and Decker, Phillip. *Effective Management in Nursing.* Menlo Park: Addison-Wesley, 1985.

Zielstorff, R. D. *Computers in Nursing.* Rockville: Aspen Publication, 1982.

5

The
Professional Nurse
Role

IT IS A MARK of status and prestige in contemporary society to be termed **professional**. Definitions of professionalism vary. For our purposes in this text, a professional is one who:

> practices a full-time vocation that is the individual's choice
> has had advanced education
> has made a commitment to a particular calling
> is identified by membership in a formalized organization
> has a service orientation to humanity
> has expertise that permits an autonomy circumscribed only by an associated responsibility and code of ethics

Regardless of which profession is under discussion, members all appear to have the following characteristics: authority or control over their activities, a body of knowledge or theory, a code of ethics, and certain powers and privileges. Medicine has been the prototype of professionalism that the allied health occupations have emulated. Some of nursing's difficulties have arisen from this choice of model. The quest for recognition as a professional continues in modern-day nursing. One could say that nursing is an emerging profession, still in the process of becoming. Nurses have been "standing on the threshold" for a number of years (a young nurse recently commented that to her it seemed we were camped there). Nurses are moving to utilize their skills to become more responsible and more accountable (and thus more professional) in the care-cure of clients.

Professionalism in nursing is exemplified by the ANA Code for Nurses:

1. The nurse provides services with respect for human dignity and the uniqueness of the client unrestricted by considerations of social or economic status, personal attributes, or the nature of health problems.
2. The nurse safeguards the client's right to privacy by judiciously protecting information of a confidential nature.

3. The nurse acts to safeguard the client and the public when health care and safety are affected by the incompetent, unethical, or illegal practice of any person.
4. The nurse assumes responsibility and accountability for individual nursing judgments and actions.
5. The nurse maintains competence in nursing.
6. The nurse exercises informed judgment and uses individual competence and qualifications as criteria in seeking consultation, accepting responsibilities, and delegating nursing activities to others.
7. The nurse participates in activities that contribute to the ongoing development of the profession's body of knowledge.
8. The nurse participates in the profession's efforts to implement and improve standards of nursing.
9. The nurse participates in the profession's efforts to establish and maintain conditions of employment conducive to high quality nursing care.
10. The nurse participates in the profession's effort to protect the public from misinformation and misrepresentation and to maintain the integrity of nursing.
11. The nurse collaborates with members of the health professions and other citizens in promoting community and national efforts to meet the health needs of the public.*

There are those who believe that nurses hold the key to change in the health-care delivery system in this country. The reasons for this belief are several. Nursing is the largest health profession, including over 100,000 graduates with baccalaureate and higher degrees—a foundation upon which to build an extended structure closer to professionalism than now exists. Nursing has already successfully demonstrated an expanded role in community-health nursing. For example, public-health nurses have long performed more independently than other nurses and carried heavy responsibility for assessment of client needs and planning of client care. In addition, individual nurses in certain settings, such as neighborhood health centers and industry have successfully performed delegated duties beyond the scope of current nursing practice. Nurses work wherever there is a need for them. And the preparation of practitioners able to

*(American Nurse's Association, Kansas City, Mo. Copyright 1976. Reprinted with permission.)

meet some of the common health needs of a majority of people adequately would take less time, less effort, and less money if candidates for the role were recruited from the nursing pool rather than other health-care providers. Clinical privileging for nurses in advanced practice within hospital is an issue that in all probability will eventually be settled in the courts.

In order to be ready for an expanded role, our own perceptions of what nursing is must change. We have tended to see ourselves as many clients see us: the ministering angel in the white uniform. Society's expectation has been and is that a nurse's major function is to give physical care. Although many nurses still accept this view and reinforce it by their behavior, this circular pattern of limited expectations can be interrupted by demonstrating to other health-care workers and to society that nursing, although it does and should include physical care, can make a much greater contribution to health if its major force is **holism**. Holism is popularly used to describe an approach that considers the whole person and the world in which that person lives. It provides a view of humanity that allows nurses to contribute to health promotion and disease prevention as well as to acute care in illness.

The satisfaction that most nurses receive from their jobs depends in large measure on their perception that they do a good job of giving care. This feeling will be enhanced when nurses view the patient holistically and give increased emphasis to a view of nursing beyond physical care alone.

Professionalism and Job Satisfaction

Although interest in noninstitutional nursing is growing daily, most nurses are still employed by hospitals. Within this bureaucratic setting it is difficult to practice as a professional. Rules and regulations can limit autonomy and creativity. Job satisfaction thus may also be limited, and this limitation is important, because it has been shown that high morale is crucial to effective functioning.

In addition to the organizational restraints imposed on the professional nurse, there are other factors in institutional nursing that create major dissatisfaction. These include low pay, undesirable hours, and inadequate recognition by physicians and administrators. Work rules that apply to the job, though they may be necessary, are restrictive. For example, nurses may be required to punch a time clock or to take exactly 30 minutes for lunch, whereas most other professionals function with a commitment to getting the job done, not to putting in a certain number of hours or minutes in a day. "Assembly-line" nursing, geared to the nurse who defines the job in terms of the clock, does not often produce professional nursing care.

The importance of job satisfaction is hard to overemphasize. Various industrial studies have shown that there is a direct relation between job satisfaction and turnover or absenteeism on the job. Studies of white-collar workers have found that satisfaction seems to be an important factor in determining whether or not employees remain in an organization.

Various methods are used in dealing with job satisfaction. One approach is to examine the extent to which an employee's needs are met—the more need fulfillment experienced by a person in his work, the greater the job satisfaction. This seems to be an especially appropriate study for nurses employed in institutions. Need fulfillment may be appraised by means of attitude surveys or by interviewing employees during performance-evaluation conferences.

Administrative support may make the difference between the satisfied nurse and the dissatisfied nurse in the bureaucratic setting. A study by Shaefer (1973) described the relationship between perceived administrative support and satisfaction on the job. The questions focused on two aspects of administrative support: the kind and amount of support received from supervisors, and salary. Clinicians who perceived themselves as having available a nursing administration staff willing to give them help felt that they had an adequate amount of support and importance within their roles. This study has some generalized implications for nursing administration and for professional nurses as employees in institutional settings.

Professionalism and Theory in Nursing

A professional performance is dependent on more than job satisfaction. Theory in nursing is the core of the educational program students bring with them to the practice of nursing. Theory may be viewed as a network of concepts linked together by laws.

In nursing, the purpose of theory is its ultimate application to clinical practice. Integration of theories from many other disciplines is not always an easy task, but it is one that is necessary if we are to use a holistic approach to nursing.

At present, there is no generally accepted science of the whole human being, but some nurse theorists have constructed theoretical frameworks that could serve the purpose of allowing generation of such a science. In the meantime, nurses function without a well-defined theoretical base. For example, caring, as a nursing concept, is a major focus in the field, but it has not been made explicit. We do not know exactly how to define **caring** and, therefore, are unable to predict its outcome completely or use it to full advantage. The same may be said regarding other basics in nursing, especially in the area of holistic care.

Theory may originate within the classroom, library, laboratory, or work setting. It can begin with clinical observations combined with mental fragments, speculation, hunches, impressions, or even intuition. The linkage of these fragments with other accepted concepts transforms them into theories that have relevance to patient care. Otherwise the fragments may remain uncodified information. If nurses are to practice intelligently, they may alter thinking patterns from passive acceptance of facts to logical reasoning and problem solving.

Professionalism and Planning of Care

Most people would agree that caring is at the core of nursing. It is caring that most differentiates nurses from the other health professionals, who have as their major focus diagnosis and cure. The concept of caring is wider now than it used to be, including clients in community settings as well as those admitted to the hospital itself. Professional nurses need to plan for caring if they are to give quality performance.

Volumes have been written about client-care planning. Today it has evolved into one part of the overall framework we know as **the nursing process**.

Only recently has the nursing process become an integral part of most nursing-education curricula. Thus, many graduate nurses educated before 1960 may not be knowledgeable about it. A growing number of articles has appeared in the nursing literature describing the process and its component parts. Basically, the nursing process is a method for problem solving.

The simplest definition for the nursing process is that it is "the sum of the activities jointly performed by the patient and the nurse" (Carlson, 1972). The process is divided into four parts:

1. Assessment of the patient by the nurse, using the nursing history as a tool, and leading to the establishment of one or more nursing diagnoses.
2. Planning, using nursing orders and/or the nursing-care plan as tools. The planning is done wherever possible with the patient, so that he or she can have preferences honored.
3. Implementation.
4. Evaluation.

The **nursing history** is a tool that allows the nurse a means of providing individualized care. Data concerning the client's perceptions of the illness and hospitalization and preferences regarding care are collected and recorded. With this information, nursing orders or plans may be personalized, and preparation for the patient's departure from the hospital will be more effective. This type of information is secured through a nurse-patient interview. The interview is often guided by means of a questionnaire and is usually carried out at the time of admission. Below is an example of a part of a nursing history used by an operating-room nurse (Mayers, 1972).

What is your understanding of the surgery you are to have to tomorrow? Do you know why it is being done?
What don't you understand or are not sure about?
What do you expect will happen between now and the time you go to surgery?
How do you feel about having this particular surgery?
Was it a difficult decision to make?
How does your husband (or wife, or family, or closest friend) feel about it?
Will someone be with you tomorrow? Who?

Nursing diagnosis is not new to the profession. Nursing leaders have been using this term since the early 1950s. Its great strength is that it can help the nurse anticipate interventions that will be needed in the future. The ANA defined nursing diagnosis as "judgments about the health status of patients which are distinct from diagnosis of other health professionals" (ANA, 1973). There has been considerable resistance to the use of the term, since the act of diagnosing has been seen as a function solely of medical practitioners.

A number of important factors are making nursing diagnosis a more acceptable tool. The most important is the use of the nursing process as a framework for nursing practice. The goals for patient care derive from the nursing diagnosis and are fundamental to planning and implementation. Evaluation is directed toward assessing how well the goals have been met, and, thus, nursing diagnosis is crucial to implementation of the entire nursing process. Goal setting, care planning, and evaluation cannot proceed in a rational way without such diagnosis.

To arrive at a nursing diagnosis there are four interrelated, interdependent steps, all based on the collection of adequate data (Shoemaker, 1979):

1. *Data collection*: The place to start is with the collection of both subjective and objective information.
2. *Cognitive processing*: Analyzing these data is not different from the thought processes we use every day. Nurses compare their observations against a base of knowledge gained in the physical, psychological, and social sciences to identify patient needs.
3. *Recognition of a pattern*: Having identified the patient's needs and responses, nurses then analyze them to determine whether they fall into a pattern that will lead to a tentative diagnosis. It helps to make a list of problems to see whether they will group themselves naturally.
4. *Validation*: This is the step that is most often forgotten, and also the step that differentiates a nursing diagnosis from intuitive assessment. Validation consists of reviewing each of the preceding steps to be certain that adequate and accurate information has been obtained. It should lead logically to the tentative diagnosis.

Many times nurses are reluctant to commit their nursing judgments to paper, since there is always the possibility of error. But professionals must take responsibility for their actions. The professional nurse will gather all information that is reasonably obtainable, knowing that information can never be perfectly complete but that the best choice can usually be made in this manner.

A **nursing-care plan** and/or **nursing orders** are written by the nurse after the nursing diagnosis has been made. The plan may or may not be a part of the legal chart and will provide an ongoing record of the nursing process. Other names used for the plan are **nursing therapy** or **nursing prescription**. Probably it will be transcribed to the card index in pencil, so that it can be readily modified.

Nursing orders derive from the plan and are sometimes used in place of it after an initial plan has been made. They list the planned interventions, without describing the problems, approach, or rationale, in the same manner as physician's orders. Sometimes a separate sheet is provided for the nursing orders on the legal chart. The orders can then provide an ongoing record of care, just as does a nursing-care plan when it is a part of the chart.

Responsibility for making the care plan and/or writing the nursing orders may vary. Usually the nurse who has admitted the client and taken the nursing history makes the plan. Many other people then contribute to it. In primary nursing, however, the primary nurse alone is held accountable for making and revising the plan of care.

The last component of the nursing process, evaluation, is an ongoing one, continued throughout the client's stay in the hospital. The first step is to establish the **nursing prognosis** — the expected outcome of care. Then, as time passes, the client's progress is systematically evaluated against the expected outcome, and the results recorded on the nurse's notes or progress notes. These notes consider whether the plans and orders have been successful in that the goals of care are being met. If not, the nurse must consider how they can be revised. The evaluation then becomes a process of reevaluation and revision as needed.

The responsibilities of the various members of the teams toward nursing-care planning is shown in Box 5–1.

Studies show that most of the information included in nursing-care plans has to do with nursing functions directly related to the physician's therapeutic regimen. But, for comprehensive care that has continuity, more is needed. In many nursing units, the problems of comprehensiveness and continuity are dealt with by making standardized care plans available for common disease conditions. Individualization of these standard plans is provided by modifying or adding to them using data about the client obtained by nursing history and assessment. The standard plans may be preprinted on a card-index form that allows individualization to be added. This system has the advantage of not requiring the nurse to copy the standard plan over and over. In other nursing units, the standard care plans are collected together in a book. The book makes a nice appearance, but in our experience it tends not to be used as much as it should be. An example of a standard care plan may be seen in Table 5–1 (Petsel, 1980).

Mason (1984) has produced a guide to assist nurses in writing valid, meaningful standards for nursing care. The approach described in this text introduces the idea of a unit of nursing care: the cluster of process, outcome, and content standards that define the nursing care for a given nursing diagnosis, health problem or need; a definable point on the health-illness-health continuum; or a specific developmental stage. The unit of nursing care is vital to developing individualized nursing care plans, evaluating the specific care administered to clients, staffing a nursing unit, and establishing the true cost of nursing care. This text is designed as a workbook providing a step-by-step approach to writing meaningful standards; it has potential as a teaching tool for staff education programs as well as the nurse managers who are responsible for writing standards for their units.

A newer method of charting is the **problem-oriented approach** to medical records. In this system, all the client's problems are identified and charted individually. Often the same progress notes are used by all members of the health team. Thus it is possible to follow the client's progress with respect to each problem over a period of time. Care plans in this system are included on the client's chart.

Not all nurses use care plans. Some feel they are "busy work." The Joint Commission on Accreditation of Hospitals (JCAH) disagrees. It requires nursing-care plans as one of its standards of nursing practice. The Commission states that the plan "should indicate what nursing care is needed, how it can best be accomplished, what methods and approaches are believed to be the most successful and what modifications are necessary to insure the best results" (JCAH, 1981).

Table 5-1. Standard Care Plan

Preeclampsia

Unusual Problem	Expected Outcome	Deadline	Nursing Action
1. Preeclampsia	1. a. reduction of sx b. prenatal record provides RN with stats re: when sx became apparent and how pt. has progressed	On admission	1. Admission assessment a. become familiar with prenatal record b. B/P, reflexes, TPR, FHR c. urine protein d. Hx of visual disturbances, headaches, or epigastric pain e. edema
2. Elevated B/P. B/P 140/90 or 30 mm Hg above normal systolic, 15 mm Hg above normal diastolic	B/P in normal range for patient	ASAP (≈2 days)	2. a. if not in labor: B/P q. 4 hr. except at night unless midnight B/P elevated b. if in labor: B/P q. 1 hr. if in early labor and preeclampsia is mild to moderate. In active labor, B/P q. ½ hr. If preeclampsia is severe, B/P q. ½ hr. in early labor, and q. 15 min. in active c. ↓ stimulation d. complete bed rest e. explain ↓ Na diet (if ordered) to pt.
3. Fluid retention	Normal excretion	1–2 days	3. a. STRICT I&O if foley anchored, I&O q. 1 hr. If output in 4 hrs. ↓ 100 cc (25 cc/hr.), notify dr. b. daily body wt. (same scale, same am't clothing, same time of day) c. daily urinalysis as ordered d. check for edema q. shift. (may be pitting or nonpitting) e. left lateral position to promote diuresis (Wilson's obstetrics)
4. Albuminuria	Negative albumin	1–2 days	4. a. urinalysis as ordered b. explain tests to pt. c. urine dipstick for protein q. shift. If protein +1 or ↑, check each void

Continued on next page

129

Table 5-1 (continued)

Unusual Problem	Expected Outcome	Deadline	Nursing Action
5. Possibility of seizures	No seizures	Immediately	5. a. complete bedrest b. explain need for rest to pt. c. private room if possible, dim lights, close door d. B/P, reflexes, as outlined in #2, a&b e. ask pt. to report headache, dizziness, visual problems, thoracic pressure, or epigastric pain f. pad side rails g. bed in low position h. padded tongue blade at bedside or taped to the HOB i. oral airway in reach j. crash cart in pt's. room k. O₂ by mask on hand
6. Fetal hypoxia	Healthy baby	Immediately	6. a. fetal heart and uterine monitor. If no monitor, FHR q. ½ hr. and prn depending on severity of preeclampsia and stage of labor b. O₂ on hand for fetal distress c. left lateral position (this ↑ uterine blood flow due to lack of pressure on vena cava. However, the nurse should utilize varied positions during labor and always evaluate FHR and V/S while pt. is not on left side)

7. MgSO₄ toxicity	No toxicity	Immediately	7. a. monitor V/S frequently. If MgSO₄ i.v., q. 15 min. If MgSO₄ i.m., q. ½ hr.
			b. always give i.m. injections Z-track
			c. before each dose of MgSO₄:
			  1. check patellar reflex
			  2. make sure respirations are 14 or ↑
			  3. make sure urine output ↑ 100 ml/4 hrs
			  4. if any of the above are ↓ or absent, call dr. immediately
			d. have calcium gluconate on hand

130

(Petsel, Sharon. "Standard Care Plan Pre-eclampsia." Purdue University, Copyright Fall 1980. Used with permission.)

Box 5–1 *RESPONSIBILITY FOR NURSING-CARE PLANS*

RESPONSIBILITIES OF SUPERVISOR

1. Review nursing-care plans for completeness, legibility, and clarity of meaning.
2. Review responsibilities for nursing-care plans with head nurse.
3. Observe the use of nursing-care plans during conference.
4. Review nursing-care plans periodically with head nurse and team leader for completeness.
5. Use nursing-care plan as a guide when on rounds, giving reports, and orienting new staff members.
6. See that a certain place has been designated for the nursing-care plans and that they are in view for everyone to use.

RESPONSIBILITIES OF HEAD NURSE

1. Stimulate the use of nursing-care plans.
2. Assist with the development of nursing-care plans.
3. Review nursing-care plans for completeness, legibility, accuracy of meaning.
4. Explain the usefulness of nursing-care plans to all employees. (Be sure to include the unit secretary's duties toward the nursing-care plans.)
5. Use nursing-care plans as a guide when making rounds, giving reports, and orienting new staff members.

RESPONSIBILITIES OF TEAM LEADER

1. Work with the nursing-care plans and instruct your team members on how to use them.
2. Revise the nursing-care plan as needed.
3. Enter suggestions as soon as possible after the patient's admission.
4. Note needs and/or problems on the nursing-care plans as they are brought up in conference.
5. Note approaches toward solving the previously stated problem and/or need on care plan.
6. Instruct and encourage your team members to use the nursing-care plans. Always use simple and concise terminology. Write in pencil so that changes may be made to keep the plan useful. *Revise daily.*
7. Always see that the nursing goals are written on the nursing-care plan for each client.
8. Encourage team members to refer to the nursing-care plans when questions arise concerning clients and their care.
9. Utilize care plans when giving report.

RESPONSIBILITIES OF TEAM MEMBERS

1. Use and adapt suggested approaches to the care of the client.
2. Discuss effectiveness of the plan with the team leader.
3. Suggest revisions for the plan, either to the team leader or at the time of a follow-up conference.
4. Enter comments as often as necessary.

Nurses who support the idea that nursing-care plans are unrealistic and not necessary are operating under the false premise that they have everything they need to know about the client in their heads. Even if this were true (and with the information explosion of today, it cannot be), how will they communicate this information to others if they do not recognize the need to share it? How can they talk about coordination and continuity of care? How can they provide for the care of the client when they take their knowledge home with them at night or are not there at all on their day off? We have all had experience with nurses who, for a variety of reasons, withhold pertinent information that would improve the client's care if it were known by all.

In many situations the utilization of nursing-care plans may be less ideal. Simpler, more useful forms may help. Nurse managers should be evaluating the process with an eye toward improved tools and approaches. In the meantime, the care plan is what the nursing professional has available to insure that the patient receives the kind of nursing care required. Refer back to Box 5–1, "Responsibility for Nursing Care Plans," for a delineation of the responsibilities of supervisors, head nurses, and staff nurses toward the nursing-care plan.

In the past, nursing was carried out by each institution, not by use of a systematic method. The nursing process today attempts to use logical assessment to personalize care. Personalized nursing care is increasingly difficult to achieve on a busy unit, despite the fact that it does remain a constant goal of practicing nurses and that nurse educators teach that personalized care is the ideal approach. Nursing is held hostage by technology. Nurses spend increasing amounts of time dealing with the technical aspects of medical care. To that is added an increase in the amount of paper work. We need to consider ways to control these factors so that nurses can return to the individual care of the client. One attempt to deal with these problems is the use of automated nurse's notes and forms.

Professionalism and Patient Teaching

Teaching, a form of nursing intervention, is a most important role that nurses play in preparing patients and their families for self-care. Nurses should be acutely aware of their role as teachers. By knowing the principles of teaching, the professional nurse becomes more effective in communicating the ideas that are important for the better health of the client.

Because of its importance, much has been written in recent years about the need to teach the client and family, especially in chronic illness and when the client is very young. Since learning is the means by which man adapts, the staff nurse must have some basic grounding in principles of teaching, lesson planning, and basics of client instruction. The supervisor also is guiding, influencing, and teaching every day. Thus, the question is not whether to be or not to be a teacher. The supervisor and the nurse are, in fact, teachers.

Client education means more than giving information. It means learning about the specific needs of each patient and finding a way to help him meet those needs. Narrow (1979) has suggested the use of Maslow's basic human needs as a theoretical framework for teaching. Using it, the nurse can systematically consider each possible client need and provide appropriate teaching. Client teaching is usually conducted on a one-to-one basis and individualized to the client's learning ability, lifestyle, and knowledge of the disease.

Lesson plans and total programs can be prepared for diabetic teaching, pre- and post-operative teaching, parent education, and other common conditions of teaching need. Client-education programs, as a part of an inservice educational department, reflect the nursing service's commitment to quality care.

If nurses are to teach clients successfully, they must be committed to a teaching philosophy and act on the principles upon which it rests. If they believe in self-actualization and self-care, then they value client teaching highly, and much of their time will be spent on it. The nurse who maintains a traditional attitude that devalues teaching is likely to miss opportunities to provide needed information.

Many nurses are still wrestling with the question of whether the doctor or the nurse should teach the client. Most health professionals now accept the value of teaching by the nurse as a means of modifying inadequate human behavior and health practices. The challenge for nursing becomes how to teach effectively.

Effective teaching is goal directed; therefore, it is necessary to identify those goals appropriate to the situation and most attainable by the learner. The nurse teacher must understand what clients already know, want to know, need to know, want to be taught, need to be taught, and can be taught.

In addition to the traditional one-on-one teaching situation at the client's bedside, some other educational methods may be used. These include group instruction for clients having similar diagnoses, group discussion of common problems in chronic disease, and family-client participation. Instruction may begin on the client's first day in the hospital or may not occur until preparation for discharge is begun. Through health teaching the nurse may capitalize on all four modes of nursing intervention: to prevent, promote, maintain, and modify a wide variety of behavior.

If a planned, organized client-education program is carried out, it may cut hospital readmissions, provide for better-informed, more cooperative clients, relieve the over-worked physician of some of the burden of giving client information, and allow the nurse to use time in an extremely constructive way.

Courses in teaching-learning process have not been included in all basic nursing-education programs. A patient-teaching workshop could be one of the special offerings given on an ongoing basis by staff development two or three times a year.

Experienced nursing instructors know that there are a number of principles that make teaching more effective. Some of these are listed in Box 5–2.

Professionalism and the Doctor-Nurse Relationship

Another of nursing's dilemmas is the conflict, sometimes hidden and sometimes open, between physicians and nurses. Kalisch and Kalisch (1977) have described the differing perceptions that cause each group to look at the other with suspicion. Nurses need to stop approaching the problem indirectly and to start taking the lead in improving relationships between the two professions. Kalisch and Kalisch have several suggestions:

1. Work toward improving salaries. It is a fact that increased monetary reward and increased respect from others go hand in hand.
2. Work toward getting nurses back to the bedside so that the beneficial effects of good nursing care can be seen by physicians.
3. Work toward educating physicians about nursing today and what it has to offer — not that we want to become "junior doctors" but that we want an opportunity to make a real contribution to health care, especially in the areas of disease prevention and health maintenance.
4. Work toward improved communications with physicians. Typically, we complain about them only to each other. Direct confrontation is painful and does not often occur. But nurses spend a good deal of time learning communications skills. We should be able to use our skills in our relations with other professionals. We need to become more assertive and to use the power we have in numbers to promote and foster improvement of care. We need to unite under the auspices of our professional organization to accomplish nationally what needs to be done, so that needed change can filter down to the local level where nurses are already in daily practice.

Professional and Quality Nursing Practice

Quality care, one goal all nurses share, requires that we walk a fine line between caring and competence, the essential components of practice. We cannot turn back to the traditional image of the ministering angel if this means being less competent technically, but, on the other hand, we need to keep concern for the person who is our client always in mind.

The components of quality care have been debated and studied for a number of years. In general, there is agreement that nurses are responsible for observation of clients, for preparing and supporting clients during diagnostic tests, for administration of medications, for carrying out treatments as ordered by the physician, for maintenance of the physical state, for health teaching, for prevention of accidents, and for comfort needs. In all these activities, the nurse needs to consider the limitations of the client, the priorities of client care, and the need to provide continuity of care while constantly evaluating and trying to improve it. These efforts to evaluate and improve nursing care may be called efforts toward **quality assurance**.

Quality assurance has two components (Brooks, 1980):

1. Setting standards for the optimum achievable degree of excellence in care
2. Systematically comparing care with the standard and taking action to make improvements that will result in a higher quality of care in the future

These functions may be carried out by evaluating any combination of three objects: structure, process, and outcomes of care. Evaluation of structure is directed toward assessment of such things as physical facilities, educational preparation of staff, staffing patterns, organizational structure, and philosophy. Standards for these are often set by licensing and accrediting bodies. This approach assumes a positive relationship between good care and good structure.

Evaluation of process means evaluation of nurses as they deliver care. There are two methods of evaluation of process:

1. Evaluate the competency of the nurse through the use of instruments such as the Slater scale. The assumption is that if the nurse is good the care is good.
2. Evaluate the care received by the client, using instruments such as the Phaneuf audit. The assumption is that if the care is good the nurse is good.

Evaluation of outcome means looking at the results of care. For example, how has the client responded in terms of symptoms or ability to perform the activities of daily living? What are the mortality rates for the condition? The assumption is that the final state of the client's health is the result of the care provided.

None of these types of evaluation is perfect: each has weaknesses. One of the major difficulties in examining the effects of nursing intervention is that outcomes may be affected by factors other than nursing care, such as the extent of illness or the physiologic and psychologic resources of the client. Probably the most accurate evaluation is obtained by utilizing a combination of all three types of evaluation.

Quality assurance is a management process, one of the tools of nursing administration. The need for ongoing, systematic, comprehensive evaluation of services rendered and the impact on consumers has shifted from a luxury to a necessity—an expectation of professionals in all areas of practice.

The Joint Commission on Accreditation of Hospitals (JCAH) have been obliged to "demonstrate a consistent endeavor to deliver patient care that is optimal within available resources and consistent with achievable goals." A quality assurance program must have two major components:

1. securing measurements and ascertaining the degree to which standards are met
2. introducing changes based on information supplied by the measurements, with the view of improving that effect and product of the unit or agency

According to the JCAH (1981), the basic components of a quality-assurance program are the following:

Identification of important or potential problems in patient care
Objective assessment of the cause and scope of problems, including the determination of priorities for investigating and resolving problems. Priorities are determined by the extent of the impact of the problem on patient care
Implementation of decisions or actions that are designed to eliminate identified problems
Monitoring activities designed or actions that indicate result has been achieved and sustained

Documentation that reasonably substantiates the effectiveness of the overall program to improve patient care

The intent is clear: Nursing must be accountable for the care rendered by its practitioners. A quality assurance program must be developed to efficiently and effectively provide evidence that nursing is accountable to those receiving services for evaluation of standards to determine compliance. Also, a mechanism must be provided to identify, measure, and resolve those problems within the delivery of those services. Lastly, a mechanism must be developed to evaluate quality indicators to determine trends, propose solutions, and assess outcomes.

Box 5–2 *EDUCATIONAL PRINCIPLES RELATED TO THE TEACHING PROCESS*

1. Identify what the client knows.
2. Identify what the client *needs* to know.
3. Identify what the client *wants* to know.
4. Relate new learning situations to the client's past experiences, staying away from medical jargon as much as possible.
5. Progress in accord with the client's growing interest and capacities, so that new experiences are of greater difficulty than previous similar experiences.
6. Provide for repetition of vital facts, starting with the most important, since that takes best advantage of the attention span.
7. Provide for development of initiative and self-direction and an inquiring attitude of mind on the part of the client.
8. Ask the client to repeat the information to you, so that you can be sure it has been understood.
9. Correct any misunderstandings or lack of knowledge tactfully. Say "Many people think that is true, but . . . "
10. Provide for desirable balance and variety of experience using institutional and community resources. If you think it will be difficult for the client to remember, write it out.
11. If you are asked a question you cannot answer, admit it and then get the needed information. Don't fail to follow through if you want to keep your credibility with the client.
12. Plan for a follow-up discussion at a later date.
13. Summarize what you have said at the end of the teaching period.

Box 5–3 *STANDARDS OF CARE COMMITTEE*

POLICY

The Nursing Service Standards of Care Committee will be concerned with the accepted patient care outcome and nursing practice. This committee will coordinate the writing, distribution, review, assessment, evaluation and utilization of patient care standards. This committee will oversee the implementation and interpretation of standards of nursing practice. The Guidelines for Patient Care are the Iowa City Veterans Administration Medical Center's statements of patient care outcome based on nursing actions/practices. Activities of this committee will not be limited to Guidelines for Care but will encompass other areas related to nursing practice.

RESPONSIBILITY

This committee will:

a) Develop appropriate Guidelines for Patient Care
b) Review/revise guidelines on an annual basis or more frequently as needed
c) Develop methods to assist staff in the utilization of the Guidelines
d) Determine if accepted standards are in compliance with policy of the Veterans Administration
e) Make recommendations to the Chief, Nursing Service

PROCEDURE

1. The committee membership will be appointed by the Chief, Nursing Service.
2. The meetings will be regularly scheduled no less frequently than at a monthly interval.
3. The minutes of the meetings will be kept. A copy will be filed in the nursing office. Each member will be furnished a copy.
4. The committee will develop criteria for writing Guidelines for Care.
5. The committee will develop a systematic method of assigning the development, distribution, and review, and evaluation of Guidelines of Patient Care.
6. The committee will assist in informing the staff of nationally accepted standards of practice as applied at this VAMC.

Example of Quality Assurance Activity

Date: From:

To: Subject: Quality Assurance Activity

I. *Problem Studied*: Follow-up review on Change of Tour Report that was done in December, 1983.

II. *Identified By*: Previous audit findings.

III. *Objective*: To determine if action taken has corrected deficiencies found on previous review.

IV. *Planning And Programming*:

    A. Random sample of recording (giving) and receiving Change of Tour Report on all units on 2 different occasions. Exclude units 10E, 8E and Primary Care. Exclude change of tour report between evening and night personnel unless taped.

    B. Review to include only those criteria that were 85% or less in compliance on previous review.

    C. Review period, June 11 through June 25, 1984.

V. *Criteria And Standards*:

    A. Nursing Service Memorandum #83-51, dated September 27, 1983.

VI. *Findings*:

    A. Criteria #1 —— 65% Compliance. 33% improvement.
    B. Criteria #2 —— 95% Compliance. 37% improvement.
    C. Criteria #3 — 100% Compliance. 48% improvement.
    D. Criteria #4 —— 83% Compliance. 12% improvement.
    E. Criteria #5 — 100% Compliance. 29% improvement.
    F. Criteria #6 —— 90% Compliance. 18% improvement.
    G. Criteria #7 — 100% Compliance. 38% improvement.
    H. Criteria #8 —— 95% Compliance. 12% improvement.

VII. *Summation of Findings*:

A. All nursing units are now taping "Change of Tour Report" on all three tours except the Intensive Care Units.

Taping of reports has seemed to be an influencing factor in decreasing length of report and eliminating irrelevant information that should not be included in this type report.

B. MICU/CCU oral reporting was somewhat confusing to reviewer as two (2) reports were being given simultaneously at the same table as well as medical students entering room several times to "chat".

VIII. *Recommendations*:

A. Head Nurses disseminate findings of the review to their respective staff.

B. Head Nurses continue to urge staff to adhere to Nursing Service Memorandum #83-51, "Guidelines For Change Of Tour Reporting," dated September 27, 1983.

C. Review not be repeated.

IX. *Problem Studied*: Change of tour report. Suspected noncompliance to policy on content and length of Change of Tour Report.

X. *Identified By*: Previous audit study done in December, 1983.

XI. *Objective*: To determine if action taken has corrected deficiencies found on previous review.

XII. *Methodology*:

A. Random sample of recording (giving) and receiving change of tour report on all units on 2 different occasions. Exclude units 10E, 8E, and Primary Care. Exclude change of tour report between evening and night personnel unless taped.

B. Review to include only those criteria that were 85% or less in compliance on previous review.

C. Review period, June 11 through June 25, 1984.

Criteria	Yes	No	NA	Comments
1. Date, tour of duty and name of reporting nurse is given at the beginning of the taped report.				
2. Information is concise and clearly stated.				
3. Report is within 15 minute limit.				
4. Unit census is included in report. (Admission, discharges, lodgers, deaths, patients on pass, and seriously ill list are included.)				
5. Nursing Care Plan Kardex is utilized for report.				
6. Patient's diagnosis is included in the report.				
7. "Hear-say" information or verbal personal feelings that are not relevant or appropriate are not included in the report.				
8. Safety measures are reported.				

Longterm Care Standards

The Joint Commission on Accreditation of Hospitals (Long Term Care Standards Manual, 1985) has identified eight standards that apply to Nursing Services in longterm care facilities. Standard V speaks to one of the major focus differences between nursing home and hospital provided nursing care. It is as follows:

Standard V Required characteristics

Standard V

A rehabilitative/restorative nursing program is an integral part of nursing services and the multidisciplinary plan of care.

Required Characteristics

A. Rehabilitative/restorative nursing services are directed toward achieving and maintaining optimum levels of functioning and independence in patients/residents.
B. Rehabilitative/restorative nursing services are performed daily and are documented.
C. Rehabilitative/restorative nursing services include, but need not be limited to, the following:
    1. Proper body position and body alignment;
    2. Assistance to patients/residents in being up and out of their beds for reasonable periods of time, except when contraindicated by physicians' orders;
    3. Preventive skin care;
    4. Bowel and bladder training;
    5. Techniques of ambulation;
    6. Assistance and instruction in the activities of daily living, such as feeding, dressing, grooming, oral hygiene, and toilet activities;
    7. Remotivation therapy and/or reality orientation, when appropriate;

8. Active and passive range-of-motion exercises; and
9. Assistance to patients/residents in adjusting to their disabilities and redirecting their interests.

D. The nursing personnel responsible for providing rehabilitative/restorative nursing services attend educational programs in rehabilitative nursing and receive special instruction—including demonstration, supervision, and evaluation—in rehabilitation techniques.
   1. Attendance at such programs is documented.
E. The performance of nursing personnel in rehabilitative/restorative techniques is supervised.
   1. The director of nursing and/or charge nurse evaluate the performance periodically.

The Quality Assurance program in a longterm care facility has the same charge as in a hospital, but the application process is different. Major differences are explained in Chapter Four, page 116.

Professionalism and Client Advocacy

Nurses have been in the advocacy role for many years. There is no doubt many of the clients that nurses serve need this kind of assistance. But there are two dangers in advocacy of which nurses must be aware. One is that it is possible to assume so much of this role that the nurse takes over what the client should be doing. The concept of self-care and responsibility for one's own health is lost. The other is that often nurses are not assertive enough to give advocacy more than lip service. The client advocate must be honest. Probably we are most effective as we work to help clients deal with their problems themselves, doing for them only what they cannot do.

The average person in society today knows more about health, disease, and health care than the average nurse did at the turn of the century. Consumers are beginning to define their rights to health care. They are developing their own definitions of health, their own priorities, and their own options. Out of this process is coming the self-care movement. The essence of this movement is a declaration of the need for more responsibility and decision making by clients. Expanded options and an improved quality of life and health for consumers are goals of this movement. Nurses in client-care planning, in teaching, and in care must support and incorporate the self-care concept into their personal orientation. Nurses who do everything for clients do not show awareness of the current societal trend toward self-actualization. Nurses are ideally suited for placing the responsibility for health care where it belongs—making sure that the needed tools and supports that will allow for the individual's self-care are available.

Consumer participation is currently a widely discussed topic. Self-care and intelligent decision making are concepts basic to consumer participation. Consumers are becoming involved in community organizations by sitting on boards and/or participating as members of health-related associations. Here consumers and providers meet on common ground in order to discuss improvements in health care.

Nurses wanting to understand this trend would benefit from a client's-eye view of his situation as he lies in bed. Many barriers between clients and staff need to be broken. We need to recognize that clients, like all other people, have different needs, perceptions, and personalities and that one can't treat everyone in the same manner. Nurses need to recognize that all clients are dependent on them for comfort, reassurance, and understanding—even the "problem client" (anyone can nurse the simple no-problem client). The true professional uses all available skills in order to solve problems with the difficult client.

Atmosphere for Professional Growth

In order for staff to keep up with new practice ideas as well as new ideas in the management field, nurse managers in service departments must lead the way. Practicing nurse managers are role models for both leadership and quality patient care. They look for clinical problems to study and appropriate ways to use health professionals. They explore ways of harnessing the potential of the professional staff. They concentrate on building a blend of the old and the new in attempting to eliminate the generation gap in nursing. They assume the obligation of getting maximum performance from all for whose work they are ultimately responsible—the full potential from human resources.

This thought has been expressed in poetry by Nona Bice-Stephens in *The Art of Nursing*.

> Never
>> say never,
>>> for never
>>>> does not
>>> allow you
>> a place
> to go.
> Always
>> can give you
>>> the sky to
>>>> reach for
>>> and plenty
>> of room
> to grow . . .

Summary

Professional nursing is

demonstrated quality nursing care.
based on a theoretical framework.
recognizable when the nurse plans care using the nursing process, values client teaching, and acts as a client advocate.
fostered in an atmosphere that allows for autonomy.

Exercise

Miss B. C., a head nurse on a 32-bed medical unit, has decided to approach administration with a request to convert her floor from team to primary nursing. Compare and contrast the strengths and weaknesses characteristic of primary and team nursing.

An answer to this exercise may be found on p. 272.

Bibliography

American Nurses Association. *Generic Standards of Practice*. Kansas City: American Hospital Association, 1973: 2.

Annas, George. The Rights of the Hospital Patients. *The American Civil Liberties Union*. New York: Hearst Corp., 1975.

Anonymous, A Consumer Speaks Out about Hospital Care. *American Journal of Nursing* 76 9 (September, 1976): 1443–1444.

Bice-Stephens, Nona. *The Art of Nursing*. Bryn Mawr: Dorrance & Company, 1983: 49.

Brooks, JoAnne. *Quality Assurance*. Unpublished presentation. Purdue University (November 10, 1980).

Carson, Sylvia. A Practical Approach to the Nursing Process. *American Journal of Nursing* 72. (September, 1972): 1589–1591.

Joint Commission on the Accreditation of Hospitals. *Accreditation Manual for Hospitals*. Chicago: JCAH (1981).

Joint Commission on the Accreditation of Hospitals. *Longterm Care Standards Manual*. Chicago: JCAH (1985): 118, 152.

Kalisch, Beatrice, and Kalisch, Phillip. Analysis of the Source of Physician-Nurse Conflict. *Journal of Nursing Administration* 7 (January, 1977): 51–57.

Maciorowski, Linda, Laron, Elaine, and Keane, Anne. Quality Assurance Evaluate Thyself. *Journal of Nursing Administration* (June, 1975): 38–42.

Mason, Elizabeth J. *How To Write Meaningful Nursing Standards*. New York: John Wiley, 1984.

Mayers, Marlene. *A Systematic Approach to the Nursing Care Plan*. New York: Appleton-Century-Crofts, 1972: 236.

Narrow, Sylvia. *Patient Teaching in Nursing Practice*. New York: John Wiley, 1979: 26.

Petsel, Sharon. *Obstetrical Nursing Care Plans*. Unpublished presentation. Purdue University (October 28, 1980): 1–4.

Redman, Barbara. *The Process of Patient Teaching in Nursing*. St. Louis: C. V. Mosby, 1980.

Rose, Michall. Laying Siege to Hospital Privileges, *American Journal of Nursing* (May, 1984): 613–615.

Shaefer, Jeanne A. The Satisfied Clinician: Administrative Support Makes the Difference. *Journal of Nursing Administration* (July–August, 1973).

Shoemaker, Joyce. How Nursing Diagnosis Helps Focus Your Care. *RN 42* 8 (August, 1979): 56–61.

Wooldridge, P. J., Leonard, R. C., and Shipper, J. K. *Methods of Clinical Experimentation to Improve Patient Care*. St. Louis: C. V. Mosby, 1978.

The
Staff Developer
Role

IT HAS BEEN ESTIMATED that the half-life of science and technology affecting professional nursing practice is three to five years. The newly graduated nurse will soon find that school is never out. Further, more than the updating of technical and theoretical skills learned in the basic program will be required. Leadership techniques, many of which will be utilized daily in the work setting, can be applied in the area of staff development as well. The professional nurse, therefore, will be accountable not only for personal and professional growth, but also will function as a role model for other health-care personnel.

Moreover, public demand for competence in many fields, from real-estate sales to health care, has prompted some state lawmakers to require continuing education as a condition for relicensing. This development, together with an increasing emphasis on adult education, has led to the idea of education as an ongoing activity and to educational institutions as colleges of lifelong learning.

If life is a continuing educational process, and learning must be geared to meet each phase, it follows that education must be tailored to meet professional nurses' needs as they progress through each step of their careers. Society, employers, educators, and practitioners accept that professional nurses will maintain expertise in their fields of competence.

Responsibility for this competency maintenance is shared by the individual, the employing institution, professional educators, and the nursing profession. The degree of responsibility depends upon whether the primary purpose of such education is to enhance the quality of client care, to help the institution meet its corporate responsibilities in the community, to fulfill requirements of law or standard, or to be useful to the individual as a person.

The cost of recruiting, hiring, and training new staff members is sizable and considered one of the hidden costs in a nursing service. The staff education department plays a key role in orienting new staff members in a reasonable time period to the point where they are making their full contribution to caring for patients.

Once an individual has been hired, sufficient orientation must be provided to assure that the new employee is familiar with institutional policies and procedures, special patient needs, and sophisticated equipment operation. If the nursing service has a re-entry program for retraining nurses who have been out of nursing for some time, an orientation program must be especially designed for meeting the returning R.N.'s individual learning needs. Some hospitals who recruit many new graduates each year have developed special orientation programs based on the work of Marlene Kramer (1974) in reality shock.

An institution performing a service to clients and charging them for services rendered can justify the cost of education that has a direct relationship to the quality of the client care given. The nursing-service administrator of a health-care facility no longer questions whether programs are needed: the need for programs is assumed. But the kind of programs, their depth, their agents, and the method of their financing have become important administrative issues.

Definitions of Terms

Several terms need to be clarified at this point, so that they can be differentiated from one another. First, **inservice education** occurs within the agency. **Staff development**, a more inclusive term, refers to educational programs sponsored by the agency, which may or may not take place within its walls. Formerly, agency educational efforts were carried out only within the institution. However, the ever-increasing rate at which new ideas and technologies accumulate has mandated a broadening of this approach. Greater effort involving more sources of information must be made if personnel are to remain current. Thus the older concept of inservice is viewed as an aspect of the newer and broader concept of staff development. **Continuing education**, another term needing clarification, has been defined in many ways. The field is an evolving one, and it must be kept in mind that definitions and terminology change with usage. A broad definition is again most useful: continuing education in nursing includes all those educational activities beyond the basic nursing program. It includes all goal-directed educational activities: professional reading, library search, programed learning, and conferences with colleagues, as well as the planned professional educational offering. Inservice education is thus a part of continuing education, as it is of staff development, in many cases, since it is usually seen as a planned instructional or training program provided by an employing agency in the employment setting. The relationship of the three terms is illustrated in Figure 6–1.

Need for Staff Development

Staff development is both old and new. It is as old as the recognition that a better piece of work would result from increased knowledge of one's job, and it is as new as the training of personnel to care for the patient undergoing hemodialysis. Historically, staff development in the form of inservice education has long been a part of hospital

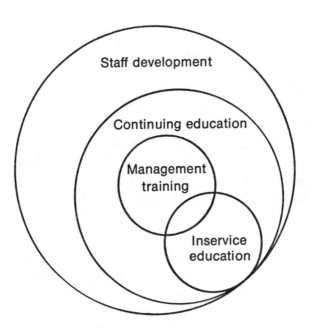

Figure 6–1   Relationship of Terms

nursing services. It has served to identify and meet learning needs of personnel. In recent years the value of inservice education has received greater recognition than in the past.

As the demand for accountability to the public for quality care has increased, evaluating performance on the job has become more important to employers. Poor client care is costly, and administrators know it. Higher costs of health care have encouraged administrators to look closely at performance in order to justify maintaining persons in their present positions, advancing them to other positions, or terminating their employment. And last, because of the vast amount of medical knowledge constantly accumulating, health-care agencies now give a high priority to providing continued learning opportunities to personnel.

The aims of a good staff-development program are to provide:

1. Self-direction and growth of the individual
2. Improved and effective performance
3. Safer working conditions
4. Reduced waste, greater efficiency, lower costs
5. Greater job satisfaction
6. A means of keeping pace with change
7. A means of maintaining continuity of qualified service

Components of Staff Development

The following usually are recognized as divisions of a staff-development program:

1. General orientation—the introduction of the new employee to position, responsibilities, and job environment
2. Job and skill training—training in the manual and behavioral skills as specified by the job description
3. Follow-up supervision of newly learned skills
4. Continuing education

In health-care institutions that do not have formally established inservice or staff-development departments, the nursing service administrator is usually the responsible person.

Establishment of a Staff Development Program

The astute and up-to-date nursing administrator is aware that continuing training programs and educational opportunities for staff development must be continuously provided. Initiation of an on-going staff-development program and the success of this venture will depend on the personnel chosen to assist in program planning.

The first step in establishing such a program is to form a staff-development committee. Committee members may be appointed by the director or the inservice director, or they may be elected by their peers. They should have interest, general knowledge, the respect of their coworkers, and a willingness to learn new things. All shifts should be represented. Ability to teach is also a consideration. There should also be a committee chairperson.

If funds and authorization are available, a department will be formed and a staff-development director 'chosen. Together, the administrator and the staff-development director define function and roles, survey the needs of the nursing staff, and assess and plan further personal-educational goals. The director of staff development makes content decisions designed to lead to improved staff competency. Choices are made between what staff members *need* to know and what might be nice for them to know. Inservice programs without a plan for separating the needed from the superfluous inevitably lead to wasted time, money, and manpower. Small agencies or individual practitioners such as school nurses or industrial nurses may be able to meet their continuing-education needs by forming a liaison with a larger local institution.

Guidelines for the operation of the staff-development department must be formulated. Is inservice paid or unpaid time? Is it to be voluntary or involuntary? Is participation or lack of it recorded in the employee's evaluation?

Even if an administrator's private view is that inservice education is not necessary, is too costly, and has not proven useful, it will occur anyway. Like sex education, if no one else provides it, the peer group most certainly will. In the case of the new employee, fellow workers give the newcomer advice on such matters as how the job should be done and how the system can be beaten. No one can deny that this is a poor way to learn the job or that it is not likely to lead to increased competency. In no way can one anticipate quality care with this sort of introduction to a new position.

Departmental Structure: Centralized versus Decentralized

An education department may be centralized, decentralized, or a combination of the two. In the centralized organization, all personnel report to a single individual or department head. The theoretical advantages of centralization are efficient utilization of personnel and consistency in the content and methodology of teaching. But the primary advantage of centralization is control. Critics of centralization argue that such control discourages creativity and encourages conformity and dependency.

In the decentralized inservice organization, instructors are assigned to clinical units and report to the nursing manager of their unit. Theoretical advantages of decentralization are immediate awareness of specific needs and deficiencies in clinical practice, a closer relationship with clinical staff, a greater opportunity to develop a specialized expertise, and encouragement of innovation. Critics of decentralization believe that the absence of control causes fragmentation and polarization.

There is no right choice. The needs of the agency and its ability to provide the necessary staff-development programs, within the limitations it has to work with must be the deciding factor.

Whatever the decision, it must be recognized that the need for inservice education in health-care agencies emerges from the phenomenon of change—change in what is known about people and how they function in heath and illness; change in the way people meet the challenges of patterns of care and what the public expects in health care; change in health legislation and in scientific knowledge and discoveries.

Planning for Staff Development

Effective staff-development programs depend upon planning. Planning involves five separate phases. The first phase involves assessing needs, stating the problems, and determining both general and specific objectives. The second focuses on gathering information on the needs, problems, and objectives and identifying the resources relevant to each. The third consists of developing a program of action. The fourth is the implementing of the program. The fifth requires evaluating the results of the program as it takes place and modifying it as necessary to meet changing needs.

Assessment of learning needs is particularly important to the development of a good learning program. It is well known that adults learn best when they have had input into what they will learn. A staff developer can use any of several techniques for obtaining information about what learners need and want to know. Below are described four methods, any of which may be appropriate in varying circumstances:

1. **The checklist.** This is easy to construct and distribute, quick, easily tabulated, and inexpensive. For these reasons it is used very commonly. But it does have some disadvantages: ideas get left out, and it may not require much thought or involvement. It should be constructed by people who are representative of the target population. Thus, a checklist of possible needs for medical nurses should be constructed by medical nurses, not nurses in maternity. A category called "Other" should allow room for respondents to add their ideas to the list.

2. **Delphi technique.** This is a more complicated technique that both assesses and ranks felt needs. It is more time consuming and more expensive than a check-list, but it gives more information. It is done by mail, so that there is no face-to-face pressure on the respondents to conform. First, each respondent is asked to list the most important skills and information needed (in this case, the needs are related to staff development for medical nurses). Then, answers are grouped and resubmitted to the respondents, who are asked to rank them in order of importance.

3. **Asking.** This can be done in a group and is very easy, but the disadvantages are that the group may be swayed by one or two people

or may represent only surface needs because there has been insufficient time to consider the issues. Questions should be open ended. Everyone's opinion can be included by going around the room to each person, soliciting ideas.

4. **Matrix assessment.** This is a group activity. It produces precise information and considers minority opinions. Its disadvantage is that it cannot be used by groups larger than 20 people (although larger groups can be subdivided). There are four steps:
   a. Each person makes a list of individual learning needs for about five minutes.
   b. The group leader makes a blank matrix (see Figure 6–2), putting the names of the participants down the side.
   c. The first respondent reads a personal list of needs, and as the needs are read they are written by the leader at the top of each column. An X is placed in the space under that column by the person's name. The next respondent's name gets an X under those needs that person agrees with, and any new needs are added at the top of the next empty column. This procedure continues until everyone's needs are incorporated into the matrix.
   d. Then the X's are tallied, and the areas of greatest felt need are seen to be those with the greatest number of check marks.

	Physical Assessment of Chest	Cardiac Arrhythmias	Cirrhosis of Liver	Fluids and Electrolytes
Mary	X			X
Ron		X		X
Lois	X	X		X
Lou		X	X	X
Total	2	3	1	4

Figure 6–2 Matrix Approach To Identification Of Learning Needs.

The staff developer must keep in mind the fact that needs assessment should be used only if there can be a serious attempt to meet those needs. If it will not be possible to meet an identified need, this should be discussed immediately with the group.

In summary, to be an effective program planner, inservice educator, or coordinator, one must ask the right questions and be a problem solver.

Types of Staff Development Programs

New employees need, and are entitled to, **orientation** and **indoctrination**. Both the employee and the organization suffer when either kind of program is omitted, has been ill conceived, or is poorly planned and executed. Kramer (1974) has identified the mechanism of "reality shock" discussed in Chapter 2, in which the new graduate has difficulty in reconciling the principles learned in school with the demands of the job. A good orientation program can help to alleviate this problem. Orientation training may be defined as "a procedure designed to enable the new employee to quickly relate to new surroundings." Simple as this sounds, the orientation of a new employee cannot be accomplished effectively unless the process is properly planned.

New workers need someone to guide them along the right path in the job for which they have been hired. Methods for doing this vary from the use of sophisticated staff-development departments with a chief and several clinical instructors, to nursing-service administrators who work alone or firms that use the buddy system where an older employee takes charge of a new employee. Whatever the method, certain information is provided to the employees in an orientation program.

The indoctrination phase includes such information as the history of the organization, its founder, purpose, growth, services, and distinctions. An introduction to the employee handbook follows, describing equal employment opportunities and temporary, part-time, and permanent appointments. Also covered are position classification, performance reviews, promotion procedures, discipline, regulations concerning uniforms, grievance procedures, working hours, wages and salaries, holidays and sick time, insurance, employee services, recognition awards, parking, safety, security, and where there is unionization, labor-management relations.

In addition, in order to assess the skills and learning needs of the new employee, a management tool such as a preorientation survey is often used. Such a survey asks a series of questions regarding the basic nursing program from which the employee graduated, previous work experience, and any specifics that are felt necessary. In most cases employees are asked to complete a skill inventory or a procedural checklist. Then the basic individualized orientation can be planned.

The recent associate-degree graduate usually arrives at a first position with a knowledge of scientific principles but without much practical experience in certain procedures. The inactive nurse returning to professional employment may also have the same difficulty. In some areas of the country, refresher courses are available to teach inactive nurses principles of care, but even the most extensive course does not provide adequate time to gain much skill. Nor is the refresher course a substitute for orientation to the specific job. However, the staff-development instructor who plans and implements a detailed orientation program for graduates both new and returning will be rewarded with a competent, self-confident staff in a relatively short period.

The program should be structured and last anywhere from four to eight weeks. The initial phase should allow for an opportunity to individualize the plan for each graduate on the basis of the preorientation information already obtained. A sample orientation plan may be seen in Figure 6-3. However, the probability of producing a more proficient, productive, and better qualified staff as a result of such a program would seem to justify the time and the effort, particularly if it can be demonstrated that quality care is the result.

Many hospitals are now using the concept of the orientation unit. In this semi-protected setting the new graduate or returning nurse gains confidence as a professional and perfects skills, within the framework of the hospital's policies and routines. Orientation takes place on a regular hospital floor with sufficient staff to allow the orientee freedom to learn.

Figure 6-3 Sample Orientation Plan The following schedule has been created to assist you in becoming familiar with the clinical area in the hospital. The inservice coordinator will be adjusting your orientation according to your nursing education and experience. Please feel free to contact her at any time.

Monday	Tuesday	Wednesday	Thursday	Friday
Date 8 AM–1 PM General orientation	Date 7–10:30 PM Primary care 1 client	Date 7 AM–3:30 PM 3 clients Admission of client Discharge procedure	Date 7 AM–3:30 PM 4 clients Team conference Care plans	Date 7 AM–3:30 PM 4 Clients Care plans Review medical system 2 PM Conference with inservice coordinator
1–4:30 PM Introduction to orientation unit	10:30 AM Central orientation 12:30–3:30 PM Admission, if possible			Primary care 7 AM–2 PM Review medical system 2 PM Conference with inservice coordinator
7 AM–3:30 PM 4 clients Doctors' rounds client-care conference	Primary care 7 AM–12:30 PM 4 clients Team conference 1–3:30 PM Central orientation 1–1:30 PM Philosophy with assistant	Primary care 7–11:30 AM 4 clients Team conference Doctors' rounds Central orientation 12–1 PM Incident reports	Primary care 7–11:30 AM ½ day with client Unit Clerk Central orientation 12–1 PM Aux. Clerical duties	

Monday	Tuesday	Wednesday	Thursday	Friday
	Director 1:30–2:30 PM Cardiopulmonary resuscitation 2:30–3:30 PM Max cart	1–2 PM Fire safety 2–3:30 PM Tour of hospital	1–2 PM A-V shunt 2–3:30 PM I.V. therapy	
	Primary care 7 AM–1 PM Meds for floor	Primary care 7 AM–1 PM 2 clients Transcription orders	Primary care 7 AM–12 PM 3 clients Transcription orders	Primary care 7 AM–12:30 PM 1–2 PM Cardiac cath 2 PM Conference with inservice coordinator
Medications system	Central orientation 1:30–2:30 PM Inhalation Rx 2:30–3:30 PM Respiratory care	Central orientation 1:30–2:30 PM Monitor and care 2:30–3:30 PM Peri-dialysis	12:30–1:30 PM Isolation policies 1:30–2:30 PM Pharmacy 2:30–3:30 PM X ray	
7 AM–3:30 PM Function with another leader	7 AM–3:30 PM Primary care	7 AM–3:30 PM Primary care	7 AM–3:30 PM With head nurse to observe duties	7 AM–3:30 PM Primary care 2 PM Conference with inservice coordinator
To permanently assigned unit				

Another useful concept for orientation is the **contingency contract**, which arises out of the principles of adult education. The dictionary defines a contingency contract as a binding agreement between two or more parties, the outcome of which is dependent on something else. That is, there is a pact in which reward is promised for desired behavior and punishment threatened for failing to meet the standard. Through the establishment of a contract the inservice instructor and the orientee know exactly what is expected, and the learner can proceed at an individual pace toward a self-selected objective. Orientees direct their own orientation and schedule their own experiences.

For example, the new nurse may have a contract with the inservice instructor to become proficient in intravenous therapy. The instructor may provide one or more of several types of instructional materials, such as programed instruction, videotapes or actual demonstration. The nurse will work through these materials and, when they have been completed, will take responsibility for securing the necessary supervised practice, as required by institutional policy. In some staff-development departments the agreement may be fortified by a monetary bonus awarded when the new nurse agrees to stay a certain period of time as an employee of the institution.

Ongoing educational programs are those presented on a regular schedule, often annually, in order to be sure that all appropriate personnel remain competent in certain important areas. For example, it is important that personnel use good body mechanics when caring for patients in order to avoid back injuries. Thus some institutions present an annual program designed to refresh skills in this area. Other programs might be concerned with infection control, review of seldom-used equipment, disaster plans, or CPR. These programs must be just as carefully planned and directed as orientation or skills-training programs. They may be designed for a particular patient-care unit or for the entire staff.

If a program does not meet the needs of employees, one may expect low interest and poor attendance. It is vital that selection and planning of the general inservice program topics be done carefully. Assessment of needs is again a prior step. The topic, the speaker, the time the program is given, the space allowed, the policy regarding who should attend, and a system for evaluation must be established with each and every educational program.

The JCAH *Manual for Accreditation of Hospitals* (1981) states "Nursing department/service personnel shall be prepared through appropriate education and training programs for their responsibilities in the provision of nursing care." Underlying this requirement is the premise that these programs will produce desired outcomes for patient care. There are, however, some things that staff development cannot do. It cannot solve problems that are not training problems. For example, complaints of poor nursing care due to a lack of sufficient staff will not usually be solved by training activities, no matter how well done. Also, staff development is not automatically the answer when the crisis syndrome appears. For example, if many wound infections are occurring, reteaching of wound care by the inservice department may not reduce the incidence rate at all if nurses are not the source of the break in technique.

Management Training

Management training is another segment of ongoing or continuing education. A new way to consider the role of management in modern societies has emerged from the humanistic movement of the 1950s. In this view, effective management must be goal oriented. To achieve goals it makes use of relationships between people. The growing concern for management education reflects an awareness that the managerial capability is essential for national economic success and that both business and government must be equipped to meet change. This idea applies also to the health-care industry. Managers in hospitals, nursing homes, and other health-care institutions must be equipped to meet the challenge of the future as well as to work with solving the day-to-day ongoing problems.

Since nursing managers are often made overnight without prior training, inservice can find in them a challenge and a fertile field for management training. Program designers need certain basic information to plan management-development programs for nurses. The designers must assess the learning needs of beginning and experienced managers. Management concepts should build upon those concepts already learned in the nurses' basic educational program, but they should be pertinent to the managerial level for which the nurse is employed—team leader, first-level manager, supervisor, or whatever job titles are used in the facility.

Nurse managers and educators should share responsibility for developing managerial skills in nursing personnel. A joint approach would be practical and theoretical with experimental teaching strategies a critical part of the program. Depending on the background of the individual managers and educators involved, not only could a viable theoretical approach be utilized but experiences could be planned using a prepared mentor.

Within the overall program or course design, nurse managers should be allowed to formulate their own definitions of the role of the nurse in professional management. Distinguishing between the provision of client care and the management of staff who directly provide it often is a source of conflict for nurse managers. They may have difficulty changing their priorities so that they are able to let others perform the client care they have previously done themselves. Basic questions should be discussed. What is a manager? Am I a manager? Do I really want to be a manager? The course plan should include information on techniques of goal setting, communication, motivation, coordination, evaluation, counseling, and teaching. Classes on basic management principles and approaches, the utilization of modern tools of management, and understanding of the employing institution's philosophy, financial position, and incentive systems are also critical in a management-development course.

The most economical approach to management development would be to have one topical outline flexible enough so that it could be adapted to the needs of the participating nurses. The core content would be the same. Basic, intermediate, and advanced segments could be presented by altering the approach and complexity of materials. Files of materials to be taught could be determined and structured during the content planning by the instructor. The problem-solving approach should be related to actual work situations whenever possible. Simulated case studies may be used as an alternate method to teach the problem-solving approach. A sample program for leadership development follows.

LEADERSHIP DEVELOPMENT PROGRAM
HNs/Supervisors

WHEN: Head Nurses —

Supervisors —

WHERE: 3W19C
3W07

FACULTY:

GOAL: To provide Head Nurses and Supervisors with the principles of management.

OBJECTIVES: At the conclusion of this instruction the participant will be able to:

1.   Demonstrate increased knowledge/understanding of the concepts related to the nurse-manager's leadership role in facilitating nursing care.
2.   Identify individual leadership potential and "unique" leadership style.
3.   Identify individual strengths and weaknesses in the leadership role of a first-line manager.
4.   Recognize the attributes which nurse leaders and followers have in common.
5.   Assess individual attitudes about least preferred co-workers.
6.   Assess the leadership approaches of those who manage supervisors and head nurses.

This program offers CEU .3 (3 contact hours).

— Head Nurses

— Supervisors

9:00 – 9:10 a.m. Introduction

9:10 – 10:00 a.m. Theoretical Approach to Nursing Leadership

10:00 – 10:10 a.m. Break

10:10 – 10:30 a.m. Assessment of Leadership Style

10:30 – 11:00 a.m. Guide for Self-Appraisal

11:00 – 11:10 a.m. Break

11:10 – 11:50 a.m. Followership: the Corollary of Leadership

11:50 – 12:00 p.m. Evaluation

DAY & TIME	OBJECTIVES	CONTENT	TEACHING STRATEGIES
I. Role of the Nurse Leader 1 hour	1. To increase know-ledge/understandings of concepts related to the nurse-manager's leader-ship role in facilitating nursing care.	Theoretical approach to Nursing Leadership: Great-Man approach Trait approach Behavioral approach Situational approach Distinctions between leadership and man-agement	Lecture and discussion Slide/tape presentation of common nursing leadership styles. Short quiz to identify difference between lead-ership and management. Utilization of Gutenberg's Leadership Questionnaire and Her-sey and Blanchard's LEAD.
30 minutes	2. To identify your lead-ership potential and "unique" leadership style.	Gutenberg's Theory Hersey and Blanchard's approach	
30 minutes	3. To identify your strengths and weaknesses in the lead-ership role of a first-line manager.	Ambiguity of leadership Organizational behavior	Review of professional assets and liabilities us-ing "A Guide for Self-Appraisal".
II. Followership: the cor-ollary of leadership 30 min.	1. To recognize the at-tributes which nurse leaders and followers have in common.	Define followership and the complementary role to leadership.	Lecture and discussion *continued on next page*

DAY & TIME	OBJECTIVES	CONTENT	TEACHING STRATEGIES
15 min.	2. To assess your feelings about your least preferred co-workers.	Fiedler and Chemess Theory.The Leader Match Concept (A Contingency Model)	Utilization of the LPC Scale
15 min.	3. To assess your boss's leadership approaches.	Bosses easy to follow. Winners	Rate your boss as a leader

Resources:
Holle & Blatchley, *An Introduction to Leadership in Nursing*, Ch. I
Hein & Nicholson, *Contemporary Leadership Behavior & Selected Readings*, Part II
Maloney, *Leadership in Nursing*, Part I and II
Fiedler, Chemess & Mahar, *Improving Leadership Effectiveness*, 219 pp.
Hein & Nicholson, *Contemporary Leadership: Selected Readings*, Part II
Townsend, *Up the Organization*

As has been discussed previously in this chapter, special orientation units have effectively helped new staff in nursing-service departments. They have been found to lower turnover rates. A similar approach may be a means of helping new nurse managers get started. Many hospital leaders have recognized that it is both time consuming and costly to allow nursing managers to acquire the skills they need through trial and error. Assigning an inexperienced manager to a good role model on a well-run nursing unit will provide the advantage of positive reinforcement for continued learning after the new manager has left the classroom.

Somewhere the potential nurse manager needs to learn how to manage—in an undergraduate course, in on-the-job training, or as part of a graduate-nurse seminar. Nursing-service administration and inservice education together can provide manager education and create the organizational climate in which a nurse can grow into a sophisticated manager.

In the present search for a solution to the supervisory problems confronting nursing-service administrators, various attempts have been made to meet the challenges involved. Nevertheless, there is increasing evidence that the number of such challenges is increasing. Although the demand for nurses varies over time, the list of openings in nursing administrative positions remains as long as ever. Though nurses in general are gradually becoming aware of the benefits resulting from the development of supervisory programs similar to those promoted by business and industry, such awareness does not necessarily convert into operative plans and programs. The professional background of nurses often does not include the pertinent knowledge to prepare new graduates for first-line supervisory positions. Thus, for various reasons depending on each individual's employment situation, management skills may not be learned on the job, and education is critical. Some criteria for selection of participants to attend management-training programs might be:

1. A desire to manage, combined with solid career objectives
2. Demonstrated ability to work well with others
3. An excellent proven record of quality performance
4. Potential for advancement and personal growth
5. A stable, responsible approach to work assignments

Descriptions of leadership programs most frequently emphasize leadership development of supervisory personnel. Equally pertinent but often given little or no attention is a leadership-development program for registered nurses assigned to client-care units. If nursing administration believes that all nurses are in some sense leaders, then leadership-development programs should be given and designed for the clinical-unit level as well as for middle and upper levels of nursing management.

Orientation of Ancillary Personnel

Many of the same concepts applied in orientation of new nurses may be applied to orientation of ancillary personnel. A preorientation skills inventory is a useful tool in assessing the present knowledge level of the nursing assistant. A basic indoctrination to the hospital and its policies plus a skills-training program can be designed flexibly enough to meet the needs of the experienced as well as the brand-new aide. Similar programs should be designed for ward clerks or ward secretaries.

Continuing Education

An active continuing-education program is a recognized need in the nursing profession for combating professional obsolescence. This need may be more difficult to meet in a small nursing service than in a larger one having greater resources.

One solution to this problem may be the sharing of education and training by several institutions. By pooling their resources (money, manpower, facilities, existing programs), several institutions in the same geographical area can combine in a formal or informal way to provide educational services. Each can receive maximum benefits at minimum cost. This approach can also be effective in large institutions. Management development, interpersonal-skills training, or patient-education programs may be shared by several cooperating agencies.

ORIENTATION FOR NEW NURSE MANAGERS

PURPOSE:

To provide newly assigned managers with a five consecutive day guided experience with their clinical supervisor.

OBJECTIVE:

At the conclusion of this experience the newly assigned nurse manager will be able to:

1. Complete a month's time schedule
2. Approve vacation and sick leave in appropriate circumstances
3. Maintain record keeping related to time schedules and use of leave
4. Make personnel assignments to patient care following Nursing Service Policy
5. Monitor for compliance with documentation guidelines
6. Demonstrate the ability to communicate Nursing Service goals and objectives, patient care needs and personnel needs to staff members, peers, and supervisors
7. Identify appropriate resources to solve patient care and ward administration problems

ORIENTATION CHECKLIST
To be completed during guided supervision by clinical supervisor.

	Discussed	Completed

I. TIME SCHEDULE
1. Prepare one month schedule according to negotiated contract.
2. Certify time
3. Document all forms of leave, excused time on certified time.
4. Develop and maintain record keeping system of leave usage.
   a. Annual leave (AL) — Requests and year scheduling
   b. Extended annual leave (EAL)
   c. Sick leave (SL)
   d. Excused time
   e. Weekends requested
   f. Holidays
   g. Off-tour relief
5. Staff member memoranda for requested time and tours
6. Request book
7. Time card responsibilities

II. SIMULATED SITUATIONS DEVELOPED AND COMPLETED IN FOLLOWING AREAS:
1. Counseling for SL abuse.
2. Complaints of hours/tour assignment
3. Evaluation — yearly routine
4. Performance improvement plan presentation.

Continuing education can be viewed as one means of ensuring the competence of health-care professionals. Although at the time of this writing no one can show a direct relationship between attendance at continuing-education programs and improved practice, it seems highly likely that there are benefits for interested practitioners. But there is debate over whether such training ought to be required for relicensing.

The pros and cons of mandatory continuing education for relicensing are many. The issue is not really whether continuing education should be mandatory, but how best to assure that nurses practice in a competent, responsible way.

"A nurse is a nurse is a nurse" is still heard in nursing circles as well as in other health-care professional groups. Will further education really benefit the nurse who has this viewpoint? Can such a nurse manager have impact on the thinking of the current generation of nurses? These are questions that have not yet been resolved, but it seems likely that managers will get the best results when they openly value education.

Nurses who indicate interest by seeking further formal education, taking specialized courses, attending workshops, or participating in inservice programs offered in the employing institution should be encouraged in their efforts. The tangible rewards of money and promotion are relatively easily accomplished. The intangible rewards are also important and must be part of the nursing department's philosophy and method of operation. How should a department head give encouragement to the nurse who has participated in many continuing-education activities?

One answer may lie in the fact that many experts in the field of behavioral psychology have identified self-esteem and recognition as being basic human needs. It costs no money to recognize a person's growth and the role it plays in providing quality nursing care. Nurse administrators are the key persons in the organization to provide this recognition. They must set out to create a climate that will generate staff growth. If they believe that the quality of nursing care is directly related to the continuing growth and development of their staff, their programs for nursing service will be designed on this premise. Their philosophy statements will identify the nurse as a lifelong learner.

Other statements will reflect a view emphasizing the relationship between continuing education for nursing personnel and quality care for clients.

The nurse administrator may decide to recognize the nurse who has just attended a workshop by asking that person to become the teacher for other personnel. New knowledge may be demonstrated in clinical practice or new information presented in a formal staff-development program. Perhaps a mini-program on an audiotape that can be played any time during the shift could be developed for every nursing unit. A written report is another possibility; copies might be distributed to appropriate members of the nursing staff. The nurse manager can develop an appropriate policy for dissemination of knowledge by considering the nature of the material and the characteristics of the presenter. The guidelines presented in Box 6–1 may be helpful to a nurse reporting on a continuing-education program.

In too many institutions, in-service education has been on again, off again, with programs that were little more than busy work for those employees who could be spared from the care of clients. This approach is of little value. It may meet the educational needs of JCAH's standard for staff education, but it will not meet the educational needs of personnel. Staff development deserves the serious consideration it is beginning to receive.

A special advantage of a planned inservice education program is that the gap between nursing service and nursing education can be bridged in the service setting by making use of knowledge gained from and shared by nursing educators. Many practicing nurses recognize that formal education stands on the shoulders of those who have gone before, and these modern practitioners value such input. Educators also need input from those in the front line of actual practice. Thus, if nursing services and nursing education are to remain viable, their leaders must maintain a dialogue with each other to keep abreast of current, practical concepts that can be shared with staff. Dialogue is also necessary to give input to educators regarding the problems new graduates face in the work setting. If the nursing profession is truly to provide quality care, then service and education must work together.

Box 6–1 *GUIDELINES FOR PREPARING REPORT OF INSTITUTE/WORKSHOP*

Name of program
Dates attended
Place

I.   VALUES OF THE PROGRAM
  A. To you in your job.
    1. What new ideas came out of the program?
    2. What direct applications to your work do you see?
    3. What long-term benefits do there seem to be for you as an individual?
  B. To your institution.
    1. What new approaches to existing problems did you learn?
    2. Did people from other institutions appear to have similar problems?
    3. How valuable was the exchange for experiences between persons attending, insofar as helping with your plans and problems?

II. THE GROUP ATTENDING
  A. What was the general makeup of the group? How large was the group?
  B. What kinds of organizations were represented?
  C. What positions and levels of organization were represented?
  D. How did the group as a whole respond to the content of the program?

III. LEADERSHIP
  A. Who were the program leaders?
  B. Was their experience and background appropriate to the program?
  C. How effective were they in conducting the program?

IV. FACILITIES
  A. Did the facilities help to achieve the objectives of the program?
  B. How well were the physical arrangements for the program managed?

V.   RECOMMENDATIONS
  A. Should others from our institution attend this or similar programs?
  B. What persons should attend, and what specific programs should they attend?

Summary

Staff development is

> necessary for acculturation of new employees and maintenance of competence of experienced employees.
>
> a crucial component of an overall nursing service program valuing life-long learning.
>
> presented in various formats to retard obsolescence.
>
> responsible for a planned management training program for all levels of nursing.

Exercise

Mr. B. D. is a new nurse in charge of staff education. He is designing a logo for the cover of a booklet describing the functions of this department. On the cover he would like to emphasize four different activities for which the staff-education department is responsible. Design such a logo, using a circle with a four-inch diameter as an outline.

Bibliography

Arnold, Phyllis. What Is an Inservice Instructor? *Supervisor Nurse* 7 (February, 1975): 56–59.

Connor, Richard, and Davidson, Jeffrey. *Marketing Your Consulting and Professional Services.* New York: John Wiley, 1985.

del Bueno, Dorothy J. What Can Nursing Service Expect from the Inservice Department? *Journal of Nursing Administration* 6 (1976): 14–15.

Holle, Mary Louise. Staff Education Programs on a Shoestring. *Supervisor Nurse* 6 (February, 1975): 17–19.

Joint Commission on the Accreditation of Hospitals. *Accreditation Manual for Hospitals.* Chicago: JCAH (1981): 119.

Knopke, Harry, and Diekelmann, Nancy. *Approaches to Teaching in the Health Sciences.* Reading: Addison-Wesley, 1978.

Kramer, Marlene. *Reality Shock.* St. Louis: C. V. Mosby, 1974: 2–22.

Tobin, Helen M., Yoder, Pat D., Hull, Peggy K., Scott, Barbara Clark. *The Process of Staff Development.* St. Louis: C. V. Mosby, 1974.

7

The
Personnel Manager
Role

THE HUMAN-RELATIONS aspect of the employee-employer relationship in health-care agencies has only recently begun to be developed into sound personnel practices. The development of personnel management that operates through a personnel department has been slow. There are a variety of reasons for this delay. One is the small size of many hospitals (50 percent in the United States have fewer than 100 beds). Another is the reluctance of boards of trustees and executive directors to expend funds for good personnel management when faced with seemingly more pressing demands for money for direct client-care activities. Still another is the hesitancy of hospital department heads to relinquish certain personnel responsibilities; and, finally, there is a general lack of understanding of the need for modern personnel management.

Most hospitals state in their philosophies that they are dedicated to the provision of quality client care and service to the community. There sometimes seems to be a discrepancy between the philosophy offered to the client and the community and that which is extended to the employee. A special social characteristic exists in health care: most women employees are concentrated in the lower-status and lower-paying jobs. Female employees may not be the primary family breadwinners, and their lack of militancy has perpetuated complacency in the past. Health-care administrators have not been required as often as other administrators to provide professional personnel management.

It is difficult to determine the exact point in the growth of a hospital or health-care agency when a personnel department becomes justified. A general rule of thumb might be that it is necessary to have a formal personnel department when the supervisors are spending proportionately more time with the functions of personnel management than they are with the functions of management of client care.

The major functions of personnel management, whether they are formalized in one department or scattered throughout many in a decentralized way, are the following: recruitment, placement, training and re-training, counseling, grievance procedures, retention of employees, wage and salary administration, safety practices, policy-information dissemination, awards and services, rewards, performance evaluations, mediation of disputes, separation and recall of employees, provision of insurance maintenance of records, administration of fringe benefits, classification of jobs, listing of job openings, handling of pension and insurance funds, employees' suggestion programs, public relations, employee health services, and an advisory capacity to management as it relates to personnel practices.

"People problems" in the work situation deal with such ideas as equitable wage scales, motivation, personality clashes, physical work environment, lack of communication, resistance to social change, obsolescence of skills, personal status, seniority, opportunities to develop skills and advance, lack of recognition, lack of initiative, ability to do the job, attendance, honesty, and unfair evaluations.

In each agency there is a different atmosphere. Therefore, the processes of personnel administration have to be tailored to the particular environment in which people are employed. The designing of a personnel system is a function of top management. Personnel policies constitute guideposts for action. Some processes of personnel management are usually carried out well. Others are not. Personnel policies that are adequately performed in most facilities are employment, compensatory mechanisms, training, employee appraisal, safety, and employee activities. Personnel processes that may or may not be performed adequately in most facilities are manpower planning, leadership identification and development, communications, increased personal productivity, and labor relations.

The personnel-management process is an integral part of general management. Personnel processes exist in all enterprises regardless of size, location, or type of industry. In large institutions, the major controllable personnel processes are usually specifically identified and assigned to a department. Personnel departments vary greatly in responsibility, size, and effectiveness. Many management writers in the area of personnel planning state as a rule of thumb that one person in personnel for every 125 employees is a reasonable ratio.

Recruiting

Since human resources are the most important assets in any enterprise, the personnel-management process should be geared toward producing the best system so that qualified employees can truly do their jobs to the best of their ability. Manpower planning is too important to be left to chance. Nursing services are just beginning to get involved in the fine art of recruiting.

A sound and effective recruiting program is comprehensive, ongoing, and thus able to avoid crisis recruiting efforts. Good recruiting should be preventive in nature, meaning that it should provide for future manpower requirements or vacancies. Effective recruiting requires a great deal of time and effort. It often has to deal with the politics of the internal organization. It can be very discouraging. Recruiting failures can be depressing to the person responsible; moreover, it is a never-completed process. An effective recruitment plan should be sketched out in as much detail as possible. The prospects for the positions must be identified. After screening, an effective placement, based on the position criteria and interviews with applicants, is the last part of the total recruitment process.

The ABC's of nurse recruitment have been identified by Hoffman (1974: 682–683), who describes an approach to attracting qualified applicants and creating the employment climate that satisfies, stimulates, and keeps them. One of the ways of insuring appropriate hiring and placement of nurses is the job interview. It is important to quality client care that a nurse who is selected for a specific position be interested, motivated, and qualified for that position. At times nursing services have been so desperate for staff nurses that they have hired anyone who walked through the door with a current license to practice in the state. Traditionally, these nurses were placed where they were needed, regardless of their previous experience, area of expertise, desires, or recency of graduation from a nursing program. From the employer's viewpoint, the nurse who needed a job took what was available. This is not effective recruitment.

To predict job success, a pre-employment interview should be conducted. Information obtained from the application form and letters of reference should be taken into consideration during the interview. The purpose of the interview is to obtain and provide information and to determine whether the applicant meets the requirements for the position. The interviewer judges the applicant's dependability, willingness to assume responsibility for the job, ability to work with others, interest in the job, adaptability, and consistency of personal goals with the available opportunity. The interviewer answers questions, explains policies and procedures, and helps acquaint the applicant with the position. The value of the interview is determined by the interviewer's ability to evaluate the applicant and to predict future success accurately. Careful consideration of both the applicant's and the institution's needs and strengths is likely to supply a good staff and a satisfactory work climate.

Kaiser (1978) describes steps to interviewing job applicants. These steps are summarized below:

1. Review the application.
2. Create a comfortable social environment.
3. Standardize the interview with predetermined key questions to get the information needed for job placement.
4. Describe the position accurately.
5. If the person does not meet the job requirements, say so.
6. Periodically evaluate interviewing methods.

There are also some guidelines to the interview for applicants. The interview is a very important part of the employment process. In it the applicant can present the most professional image and from it receive needed information about the job. Some suggestions for interviewees are listed below:

1. Submit a separate résumé—even if all of the information is included in the application form, it demonstrates initiative, organization, and courtesy.
2. Do some soul searching about your professional goals, special interests, expertise, strengths, and areas where growth is needed. The interviewer will probably ask some open-ended questions to get an accurate picture of you.

3. Decide what job conditions you expect or are willing to accept.
4. Appearance counts:
   a. Wear a simple understated outfit.
   b. Watch your body language.
   c. Maintain eye contact.
5. Manners count:
   a. Do not smoke.
   b. Do not interrupt the interviewer.
6. Limit any negative comments about your current or previous supervisor or place of employment.
7. Be honest—do not feel you must agree with everything the interviewer says.
8. Ask questions.
9. Ask for a tour of the units where you might be assigned.
10. Consider asking for an opportunity to talk with one or more staff members.

A format for a résumé appears in Box 7–1.

Personnel Policies

Health-care employees have aspirations similar to those of employees in any other business or industry. They seek individual recognition, opportunity for promotion, a fair wage, good working conditions, and other benefits of employment comparable to those available in other fields. There may be another motivating force in the health occupations: professionalism and its resulting benefits. For these and other reasons, personnel policies in health-care agencies are very important. They provide a basic set of rules for orderly goal achievement in the process of delivering health care.

The Policy Manual

The employee **personnel-policy manual** states the policies of the institution, in writing, for dissemination to all workers. It is an important instrument and is usually referred to on many occasions to clarify misunderstandings regarding obligations of the employer as well as of the employee. It is indispensable in regard to union activities.

Box 7–1 *RESUME FORMAT*

Name
Address
Telephone Number

EDUCATION
Registration: number, date, state
Name and location of nursing school, and date of graduation
Education beyond basic nursing: degrees held, name and location of school, date of graduation
Name and location of high school and date of graduation

EXPERIENCE
Titles and locations of positions held, dates of service in reverse chronological order
Principal duties and responsibilities of each position held

SPECIAL EXPERIENCE
Any experience related to health care that was not part of the requirements of a job or was performed on a voluntary basis

MEMBERSHIPS
Professional memberships or committees

REFERENCES
Persons who are able to account for your professional abilities and character (and have agreed to do so)

GOALS
(Optional) A statement of your professional goals in the work setting

---

The personnel manual usually includes an initial statement from the administrator welcoming new employees and outlining the philosophy and objectives of the institution. A statement regarding the importance of individual employees' contributions to the quality of client care should be included. Following the initial statement, policies outlining responsibilities of both employees and employers are described. They are usually presented in alphabetical order for ease of reference. A sample table of contents from such a manual is presented in Box 7–2.

Box 7–2 *PERSONNEL POLICIES AND PROCEDURES*

CONTENTS

1. Absence
2. Accidents
3. Blue Cross insurance
4. Breakage and loss
5. Cafeteria use
6. Cashing paychecks
7. Categories of employees
   a. full time
   b. part time
   c. permanent
   d. probationary
   e. temporary
8. Cleanliness
9. Coffee breaks
10. Conduct
11. Health and funerals
12. Demotions
13. Discipline
14. Educational benefits
15. Employee counseling
16. Employee recruitment
17. Employee terminations
   a. disability
   b. dismissal
   c. exit interviews
   d. resignation
   e. retirement
18. Garnisheeing of wages
19. Grievance processes
20. Health service
21. Holidays
22. Hours of work
23. Identification cards
24. Inspections
   a. infection control
   b. safety
25. Internal communication
26. Jury duty
27. Lost and found
28. Overtime
29. Pay periods and pay days
30. Payroll deduction
31. Performance ratings
32. Personnel records
33. Promotions
34. Relationships with clients
35. Sick leave
36. Social security
37. Tardiness
38. Telephone calls
39. Telephone courtesy
40. Transfers
41. Vacations
42. Valuables
43. Wages and raises
44. Withholding tax statements
45. Workman's compensation insurance

Naturally, other categories than these may be discussed as needed. Employee manuals or employee handbooks are put together in various ways. All prospective employees should have one to read and think about before accepting a position. The employee needs to know what to anticipate from the employer and what rights, benefits, and responsibilities accrue to a particular job. An example of a standard policy and procedure (**SPP**) is presented in Figure 7–1.

Personnel Practices

Personnel practices are often unwritten approaches to policies, procedures, and problem solving. They may have a great deal of effect on the morale, motivation, and productivity of the group. Though nurses generally have been exposed to a considerable amount of discussion of interpersonal skills in their educational programs, often it seems that nurse leaders do not use the same interpersonal skills with staff that they do with clients.

Certain observations merit the concern of a nurse leader who seeks satisfied employees.

1. People differ in their basic wants, and they expect to be treated as individuals.
2. The acceptance of new ideas and changes is more likely to take place if people are prepared for them.
3. Habit and emotion are of major importance in explaining behavior; reason is of secondary importance.
4. People want credit for work accomplished when they deserve it.
5. A sense of belonging to an acceptable group and of feeling important is a strong motivating factor to most people.
6. Fear is a strong motivating force but has a negative effect and normally is diminished with time.
7. Employees want to use their highest abilities and enjoy a sense of accomplishment in their jobs.
8. Employees prefer supervisors whom they respect and trust.
9. Giving information to employees about matters that concern them helps form an effective team.
10. A person is affected by the group of which he is a part and, in turn, affects the group's behavior.

EFFECTIVE: 10/8/87
CANCELS: #123

TITLE: Vacation

STATEMENT OF PURPOSE:

Annual vacation with pay is provided all permanent employees as a benefit based upon past service with the hospital. The purpose of this SPP is to set forth the policies and procedures that govern the eligibility and granting of vacation leave with pay.

TEXT:

A. *Employee Eligibility*

1. Permanent full-time and part-time employees are eligible to accrue vacation benefits and receive paid vacation leave as set forth in the provisions of this policy.
2. Temporary employees are not eligible to receive paid vacation benefits.
3. The number of paid vacation days and the employment waiting periods are determined in accordance with the established benefit codes set forth in the Employee Benefit Program policy.

B. *Vacation Benefits*

The following chart sets forth the paid vacation days based upon the number of completed work years of continuous employment. A "work year" is defined as 2080 hours of continuous employment for full-time employees, and 2080 paid hours for part-time employees.

Paid Vacation Days per Number of Completed Work Years					
Benefit Code	1 yr.	3 yrs.	5 yrs.	7 yrs.	10 yrs.	over 10 yrs.
A	15	15	20	20	20	20
B	15	15	20	20	20	20
C	10	15	15	20	20	20
D	10	10	15	15	20	20

Figure 7–1   Standard Policy And Procedure

11. Criticism or unfavorable comparison of an employee's work in public is resented by most employees. No one likes losing face.
12. When employees are doing their work incorrectly, they want to be told about it and to be told the correct way.
13. Reprimands and remedial actions are expected by most employees when they violate established rules.

Many motivational studies can be found in the management literature. Job satisfaction surveys lead one to think that it is good for production when the employee is happy in his job. This may or may not be true. It depends upon how the satisfied employee reacts. Satisfaction with everything that is going on may result in an attempt to maintain the status quo, which does not stimulate new ideas or allow for change and improvement. A chart showing the various phases of personnel management in nursing is presented in Figure 7–2.

Changes in Personnel Practices

Several changes in practice are occurring within health-care institutions. Some nursing services are changing patterns of staffing as a result of studying the effects of the placement of nurses, the hours worked, and the organizational system of nursing being utilized. Functional and team systems are being replaced by primary nursing to improve personnel satisfaction and client care.

It must also be recognized that no one can do everything. For example, nurses who become physically ill when forced to work the night shift should be placed promptly somewhere in the organization where they can work days or evenings and not be forced to wait until it is convenient for management to transfer them from nights to days. These persons may be lost to the institution because they become so ill that they can no longer function. Research on body rhythms and the related differences among individuals is just beginning to have an effect on personnel policies.

PERSONNEL MANAGEMENT
FUNCTIONS OF THE NURSING SERVICE

Personnel Management	Control of Physical Environment	Interpersonal Contact	Administration
1. Determine kind and number of positions needed	1. Plan for allocation and utilization of space	1. Develop plans to interpret nursing and to coordinate activities with agency groups a. Administrative b. Professional c. Intradepartmental d. Interdepartmental	1. Develop organizational structure
2. Define qualifications and provide job descriptions	2. Determine needs and provide for necessary equipment and supplies	2. Provide for association with community groups a. Educational b. Professional c. Service d. Publicity	2. Plan, organize, direct, control, and coordinate administrative activities. a. Set standards for patient care, personnel management, physical environment, working relationships, and administrative practices b. Assign responsibility and delegate authority c. Provide for directed group participation in projects, planning, and problem solving d. Establish program of individual conferences for direction of associates and assistants e. Establish systems for reporting and recording all functions f. Provide for systems of constant and periodic evaluation of all functions

g. Interpret nursing needs and problems to administrative officers and other hospital personnel
h. Provide channels for and methods of communication within the hospital and the community
i. Identify areas needing study, and plan for research
j. Prepare and administer the nursing budget

3. Evaluate effectiveness of existing physical environment

3. Appoint personnel and maintain staffing

4. Maintain a recruitment program

5. Evaluate performance of personnel

6. Provide opportunities for growth and development

7. Provide working conditions and economic considerations that provide for job satisfaction

8. Establish and maintain adequate records for nursing personnel

Institutional Redress of Past Grievances

Equal-rights issues and the discriminatory practices that have affected women also have to be considered when one is an employer, supervisor, or personnel manager. Affirmative action, which has been mandated in state and federal legislation, affects employment and placement procedures. Most employers must make an effort to hire individuals who are seen as members of a protected class. Protected-class status is given to several groups that have been discriminated against in the past—Blacks, Hispanic-Americans, Asian-Americans, Native Americans, the aged, and the handicapped, as well as women.

Pay scales affecting men and women reflect discriminatory practices. In recent years, some health-care institutions have been ruled in violation of the Equal Pay Act because of inequities occurring where men and women are doing the same job for different rates of pay.

Self-Examination and Career Ambition

Most nurses have not had to address the question: what makes individuals promotable? This is true partly because many nurses have been employed in part-time positions or have worked only to provide a second income for the family. There is a whole class of nurses who could be identified as "appliance" nurses—they are working to buy a stove, a refrigerator, or some other material need. They may be technically competent and caring with their clients but ordinarily they are not interested in advancement for nursing or for themselves. Therefore, money is their primary motivation. Although there is no substitute for being professionally and technically competent in a position, when one is considering moving from staff nursing into a head-nurse position or higher, the required competencies change in nature. Many nurses upon promotion become examples of the truth of the Peter Principle, which states "In a hierarchy, every employee tends to rise to his level of incompetence" (Peter and Hull, 1969). The head nurse is evaluated not only on nursing-care skills but on managerial and human-relations skills. The staff nurse who wishes to advance needs to seek out and plan learning experiences and to assume more responsibility in small enough increments to be easily handled.

Nurses too often operate under the premise that what they are doing is what they are going to be doing for the rest of their professional lives. It is just as important to have a professional goal as it is to have a material goal such as paying off the mortgage or buying a new car. The nurse who has no career plan and no professional goals tends to acquire institutionalized behaviors analagous to those one might observe in the institutionalized psychiatric patient: with the loss of high-level enthusiasm, expectations, and ideals comes the end of commitment to the profession and to the desire to be an agent of change.

At the opposite end of the spectrum is another phenomenon, identified by Kramer (1974) and discussed in previous chapters. This phenomenon is the turnover problem in nursing and the loss of nurses to the profession because of what Kramer has called "reality shock" — the shock that results when the new graduate discovers that the working world is not what it seemed to be in nursing school. These nurses leave because making changes designed to make the ideal real is often a slow and painful process.

Performance Evaluation

Assessing quality of nursing care is a controversial issue for many nurse managers. **Performance evaluation**, which guarantees to the client at least some measure of quality care, may be defined as measurement of an individual against a previously determined standard. It is concerned with assessing how an individual functions in a particular setting. Direct observation is the principal evaluation tool. Since people are all different and are neither all good nor all bad in their individual performances, ratings of different characteristics are likely to vary. Thus the evaluators need to agree on the objectives, qualities, and behaviors to be evaluated, and on the definition of high and low standards of performance. This information should be made available to those who are being evaluated.

Traditionally, evaluation of nurses has been a negative experience. Objectivity of evaluators and validity in the evaluation of performance have often been lacking. Objectives or job descriptions have not always been available to nurses, and ambiguity has clouded the endeavor. Another major problem is that many nurses who perform appraisals think of them as a clerical operation in which a form is filled out once a year for experienced employees, or sometimes more frequently for newer employees. On the other hand, if the nurse manager does recognize a problem and point it out to the employee, there will be the additional responsibility of either helping the employee to improve or making a decision about dismissal. Many nurses prefer to avoid these issues.

It takes time, energy, and thought to do evaluations well. Care is not improved when the supervisor hands the nurse manager an evaluation form and says, "Here, read this and sign it. I have to have it down to Personnel by three this afternoon." If we are going to improve nursing practice in the institutional setting, this kind of approach to personnel evaluation must stop.

Types of Performance Appraisal

Metzger (1978) has described several types of evaluation procedures in use today. There are **rating scales**, in which the supervisor chooses a particular number or letter indicating average, above-average, or below-average performance. This method is simple and therefore popular. There are also **checklists**, which are similar to rating scales except that the supervisor chooses the most appropriate among several statements descriptive of performance. The difficulty here is in writing a set of sentences that will adequately describe the various levels of performance. Another method is to compare one employee with other employees on several predetermined factors characteristic of the job.

Additionally, management by objectives, discussed in Chapter 3, can serve as a basis for evaluation. The supervisor gives a rating according to the extent to which the employee meets objectives previously agreed upon in advance by both.

Peer Review

A method of performance evaluation receiving a great deal of emphasis at this time is peer review. It is the method most commonly discussed among nurses. In this approach evaluation is performed by a person of the same rank or standing as the employee being evaluated, not by the supervisor. Peer ratings have been judged to be reliable and valid measures of an individual's performance in various situations. General findings indicate that peers have more opportunity to observe performance than do supervisors; further, because peers perform similar or identical functions in the same situation, they are more sensitive than their superiors to variations in performance.

In the nursing environment certain standards of practice are recognized as being the minimum acceptable nursing care for a given client in a given situation. Such standards have been promulgated by the ANA and by local, state, and national licensing and accrediting bodies. Principles of nursing care are constant regardless of the department involved. For example, they may be based on the nursing process. Thus, any nurse working with other nurses can be evaluated in performance by means of peer review because there are common standards of nursing care as criteria. Peer review is a formal expression of the perceptions and expectations of others in the nursing environment with respect to a given individual's performance.

The recent surge of interest in peer reviews is a result of the fact that in recent years government and the media, as well as other professions, have begun to hold nurses accountable for the quality of care provided to clients. Accountability requires a performance-appraisal system, which may or may not be a part of a formal program for quality assurance. There are strengths and weaknesses inherent in the peer-review approach. There may not be a peer available on evenings or nights. Peers may be reluctant to be openly critical, or they may be overly critical. The strength of peer review lies in the fact that the peer knows the job, its problems, and its objectives.

Goals and Objectives of Performance Appraisal

In theory, a performance-appraisal system accomplishes the goals of making satisfactory workers better, ridding the system of unsatisfactory workers, and forming a basis for recommendations for merit pay increases.

More specifically, the American Hospital Association (AHA) describes a sound employee-appraisal system as having the following objectives:

1. "Systematic analysis of *all* important aspects of an employee's performance, not just isolated incidents of behavior or outstanding examples of good and poor performance." Be warned of the halo effect in evaluating employees—that is, judge a workers's entire performance over a protracted period of time, and do not be unfairly affected by one or two incidents.

2. "Application of uniform standards or a common measuring stick that all supervisors can apply in a like manner to all employees." One of the problems in evaluation is the discrepancy between assessments made by an "easy going" supervisor as compared with a "tough taskmaster" supervisor. There should be general agreement as to the measuring mechanisms, and this is one area that requires particular attention.

3. "Reduction of guesswork, favoritism, and influence in the evaluation of employee performance." One of the sore spots in the supervisor-subordinate relationship is the playing of favorites. The standards used to evaluate one employee's performance should be the same as those applied to all other employees.

4. "Collection of objective evidence of the relative merits of various employees to enable management to justify promotion, transfer, salary adjustment, training, and termination on an equitable basis throughout the institution." There is a need for specific facts as to the merits or faults of employees. Wherever possible, evaluation should be based upon data accumulated over a period to time.

5. "Provision for a method of comparing personnel costs with actual employee performance on the job." This kind of comparison goes to the heart of employee performance evaluation—and measures employee efficiency related to the direct labor costs of running the department.

6. "Development of an inventory of the skills and abilities of the work force to ensure proper placement of each employee and to prevent wasted manpower." Most employees welcome the opportunity to be evaluated so that they may be placed in the right job and have full opportunity to make use of their capabilities. Performance evaluation programs can be used to develop an inventory of skills so that proper placement is indeed guaranteed and proper utilization is equally assured.

7. "Provision of a statement of individual progress of each employee, with specific indications of areas needing improvement." Employees want to know exactly how well they are doing and, equally important, how they can improve their performance against their supervisor's expectations and standards.

8. "Provision of a system for giving employees recognition and reward in proportion to their performance on the job." This objective fulfills the number one need expressed by employees—recognition of a job well done and appropriate rewards in relation to performance.

9. "Provision of practical instruction for training supervisory and management personnel in the evaluation, direction, and development of personnel." This training is necessary for proper implementation of evaluation programs. Special attention should be directed to development of interviewing skills and a system for standardizing evaluations.

10. "Organization of facts that can serve as a basis for agreement in labor-management negotiations." This objective underscores the use of performance evaluations for backing up decisions in the areas of promotion, transfers, and discipline.

Implementation of Peer Review

Because of the interest in peer review, special attention will be paid to it. Several rating scales that allow peers to rate one another have been developed. An example of such a rating scale is the **Slater Scale** (1975). This 84-item scale was designed to measure the competencies displayed by any nurse in providing care to clients. Each item is expressed as an observable nurse action, and a cue sheet is provided as a guide to matching observed behavior to the correct item.

The items are grouped into six subsections according to the primary scientific and cultural bases for the nursing-care actions to be rated.

The subsections are as follows:

1. Psycho-social: Individual
   Actions are directed toward meeting psycho-social needs of individual patients.
2. Psycho-social: Group
   Actions are directed toward meeting psycho-social needs of patients as members of groups.
3. Physical
   Actions are directed toward meeting physical needs of patients.
4. General
   Actions that may be directed toward meeting either psycho-social or physical needs of patients, or both at once.
5. Communication
   Communications on behalf of patients.
6. Professional
   Actions directed toward fulfilling responsibilities of a nurse in all facets and varieties of patient care situations.

These behaviors are the performance expectations for a first-level staff nurse. The assumption is made that all basic nursing programs in the United States prepare individuals for first-level staff nursing and that there is some agreement among educators and head nurses about what these skills are. This delineation of behaviors that constitute the practice of nursing care meets a major requirement for effective evaluation.

One important concern in implementation of performance evaluation is the way the evaluator's personality characteristics enter into the evaluation process. The Slater Scale was developed to enhance objectivity in the evaluation process. It was proposed that, by rating observed individual actions and by comparing them with a concrete frame of reference, objectivity would be strengthened. This concrete frame of reference is developed by each evaluator of the group by identifying the best, average, and poorest staff nurses in each evaluator's experience. The performance of the person evaluated is then compared with this frame of reference and rate accordingly. Evaluator subjectivity is not eliminated but is greatly diminished by this process. In addition, the fact that more than one person is doing the evaluation may give the subject a comprehensive overview of personal performance.

Points are then ascribed to the various levels of performance, and mean scores can be determined. An advantage of the subsections is that specific areas can be examined, scored, and compared to determine deficiencies or areas to be improved.

A rating scale can be used for a one-time evaluation or it may be used periodically to determine improvement in performance. Another use could be the identification of areas of needed instruction for inservice education programs or individual learning experiences.

How this method of evaluation is presented to the staff members involved will influence its effectiveness. Because evaluation experiences in the past may have been negative, careful explanations of the objectives and process must be offered. Improvement in performance should be represented as the main goal, rather than just the completion of all evaluations. If wage increases and promotions are going to be among the considerations involved in the use of the scale, this should also be explained before its use. Some resistance to change and fears about evaluating and being evaluated by those who "really don't know how I work" should be anticipated. An understanding approach that encourages verbalization can be invaluable in the preliminary discussions of peer review and in its actual use in evaluations.

In the intelligent use of peer review in nursing, several factors must be considered: the individual's self-concept and expectations for self and others, the relationships of staff members among themselves, expectations and communications among staff members, and the effects of all these factors upon group expectations.

Evaluation of the Manager

Evaluation of managers by their superiors is similar to evaluation by managers of their staffs. An example of a form appropriate for performance evaluation of a manager is shown in Figure 7–3.

In summary, performance evaluation must be based on clear, fully communicated goals and expectations. It offers opportunities for growth through counseling and planning for the future. Motivation of employees will be improved through adequate feedback regarding performance problems and through recognition when it is deserved.

Employee Health and Safety

The Occupational Safety and Health Act (OSHA), enacted in 1970, increased demands on hospitals for setting up employee health and safety programs and enlarging those already present. Many health-care agencies have appeared to show little interest in the health of their employees. They are sometimes not concerned with hazards of working in the agency, and the rate of injuries is high in comparison to that in other industrial settings. This fact seems strange, since hospitals, nursing homes, and other such agencies are in the business of providing health services to others. With respect to health education, preventive medicine, and job safety, health-care institutions should serve as an example to the public at large.

Employee Health Services

Regardless of the size of an institution, there should be provision for health services for employees. The main purposes of an organized

MANAGER EVALUATION

PERFORMANCE REVIEW

Name	Title	Date
Department	Location	Salary Base
Time in Position	Hire Date	Age

Managerial and Administrative Ability (Planning, Organizing, Delegating, Follow-up)

Self-Development

Personal Characteristics (Judgment, Decisiveness, Resourcefulness, Initiative, Sensitivity, Risk Taking, Independence) _____

ASSESSMENT OF PERFORMANCE (Check one)

☐ Outstanding   ☐ Excellent   ☐ Satisfactory Plus   ☐ Satisfactory   ☐ Unsatisfactory

Evaluation of Promotability

Development of Management Potential in Unit Personnel

Prepared By	Date

I have reviewed this document and discussed the contents with my manager. My signature means that I have been advised of my performance status and does not necessarily imply that I agree with this evaluation.

Employee Signature	Date

Employee Comments

Figure 7–3

employee health service are to encourage all employees to maintain good personal health, to assist them in obtaining medical care when necessary, and to promote the early return to work following work-related illnesses or injuries. Employees, of course, have a responsibility for their own good health. The health service should not be a substitute for the services of a private physician, but when the need arises, health care should be available until employees can be seen by their own physicians.

The health service should be a separate entity with independent facilities within the institutional setting. It should have a designated physician who is in charge and is responsible to administration. It may be a part of the personnel department or, in the smaller agency, it may be a part of an ambulatory-services setting. One or more registered nurses should be assigned to the unit to work with the physician.

Professional duties as well as health-care policies should be clearly delineated. Most policies relate to pre-employment physicals, to care of minor illnesses that develop at work, to immunizations, and to health education, especially for those who are not professional workers. Other policies of the health service concern counseling and maintenance of records, both of initial employment and of follow-up visits. Policies should be coordinated with current health-care practices.

Safety in the Work Environment

A hospital is not always a safe place to work. To make it safe the entire staff should be taught safety practices and be encouraged to think and act for safety first. The work environment of a health-care agency for many personnel is that of the client-care unit. The environment is varied, depending upon the area in which one is employed. For those working in the operating room the environment is often that of a chemical industry. In all units, there are hazards associated with incorrect lifting of clients or equipment, with falls when using unsafe procedures or reaching for stored equipment, or with misusing electrical equipment. There are also less obvious hazards — the ones peculiar to the various patient-care units. For example, one can contract the disease from the client one is caring for. Safe infection-control practices are just as important and necessary as such safety practices as wiping up wet spots on the floor, keeping siderails up when the client is elderly or confused, and providing handrails in halls.

Accidents in hospitals are a major problem. It has been estimated that chances are one in twelve that an injury will occur while a client is hospitalized. Employees are exposed to many of the same dangers as patients, and to others as well.

Unionization

The coming of unionization to health-care agencies both affects and is affected by the nurse manager. It has been said that the most important determinant of whether or not employees choose to join a union is the first-line supervisor. If this individual is seen as a good administrator who cares about the staff, employees are less likely to be interested in unionization. The reverse, of course, is also true.

Labor-relations experts tend to feel that poor employee relations on the part of administrators drive employees into unions. Lack of understanding of what the employee needs, inadequate salaries, poor working conditions, and arrogant supervisors are frequently cited as leading to unionism (Metzger, 1978). Overall, fairness and consistency by supervisors in dealing with staff will have a large effect on employees' need to find an organization that can speak for them.

If a union drive does occur, there are certain actions the supervisor can and cannot legally take. The supervisor must not threaten with consequences of joining a union nor promise any reward for staying out. Administrative staff may not ask employees whether or not they intend to join. Managers may state why the agency is opposed to the union.

There are also certain legal restrictions on employees during unionization procedures. They may wear union buttons if the agency allows other types of buttons to be worn. Usually, but not always, the courts have decided that solicitation for the union can take place on the employer's property as long as it is done after working hours, on meal breaks, or in rest periods.

If 30 percent of a unit shows union authorization cards, the union is allowed to hold an election. One point that employees should understand is that if they choose not to vote, that is the same as allowing others to make the decision for them. Thus, those who vote are those who determine the outcome.

Once an election is allowed, the National Labor Relations Board (NLRB) sets the date and time. The election may be on agency premises. A representative of the NLRB conducts the procedure, using a silent ballot. There must be a majority in favor for the union to be affirmed.

As more professional workers unionize, an increase in work stoppages can be expected among them. Over the last decade nurses have exhibited an increased willingness to strike. Registered nurses constitute the largest group of professional health workers in the United States and data on the incidence, cause, and scope of registered-nurse work stoppage are available.

The director of nursing, when a collective-bargaining situation occurs, is expected to wear two hats—one for management and the other for nursing. This untenable position develops from three factors: first, the principle underlying collective bargaining; second, the natural duality of the position of the employed professional; and third, the position of the director of nursing as a member of the management team. It is an established fact that collective bargaining in the health field is not acceptable to the overwhelming majority of health administrators, though it is a well-established process in most other American businesses. It is a new experience for the majority of both employees and employers in the health field.

Some find opposition to the collective-bargaining process difficult to comprehend or to justify, in view of the similarity to the missions of health agencies and labor organizations. Caretakers of the integrity of the human mind and body profess to give service and concern to the ill, the injured, and the infirm. Caretakers of the dignity of human labor profess to give service and concern to the laborer. The fundamental principle of collective bargaining is that all workers have the right to a voice in determining the conditions under which they will provide their service. The humanistic philosophy of nursing tends to reinforce this belief, and society recognizes it, as evidenced by authorization in society's laws for employees to organize collectively and to choose representatives who will assist them in the pursuit of those rights.

In a society in which emphasis upon rights in all facets of human endeavor is increasing, today's nursing practitioners feel more acutely than before a loyalty divided between their profession and the employing institution. They are likely to seek more and more the application of the principles of collective bargaining. These actions are neither an attack on the director's position nor an indictment of the administration, but a means of responding to bureaucratic constraints upon professional practice and to affronts to the dignity of people.

The duality of the position in which directors of nursing find themselves arises from their status, common to almost all nurses, as employed professionals. Their primary responsibility is to management—in this case, management of the nursing service. The staff nurse, also an employed professional, has a primary responsibility to client care.

By virtue of their positions, directors of nursing have authority over conditions of employment such as salaries, hours of work, fringe benefits, and other matters that may concern nursing practice. Collective-bargaining agreements often limit this authority. Such agreements are becoming more and more common as young nurses, with an expanding concept of professionalism, seek increased participation in decision-making activities that affect their practice. This trend is leading, for example, to the establishment of professional performance committees, in which staff nurses have a voice in recommending measures to improve client care. Thus, nurses have introduced new steps in the collective-bargaining dance, and the director of nursing is constantly grappling with the question: Whose partner shall I be?

The view of the director as a member of the management team is also undergoing a transition. The contemporary nurse director has more sophisticated managerial skills than past directors and serves more as a facilitator for nursing care than a practitioner. However, even though directors do not care for clients themselves, they are properly seen as experts on nursing care by other members of the management team. Nursing directors bring both nursing and managerial skills to the collective-bargaining table as the need arises.

However, instead of expending energy in worrying about the changes unionization would bring, the director should concentrate on developing adequate supervision and on working for good employee benefits and practices. These kinds of activities will help promote a satisfied staff.

Career Mobility

A thoughtfully planned, carefully implemented career-mobility program benefits almost everyone—the employee who wants to get ahead but otherwise couldn't, the department short on skilled manpower, and the institution as a whole. Ultimately, of course, it benefits the client. Career mobility raises morale so that when employees move up they do not move out. This kind of movement helps the turnover problem.

Many health-care institutions are becoming deeply involved in educational policies and practices that allow employees to be enrolled in advanced academic programs. The institutions may pay for part or all of these learning experiences and also assist those students who are working for certificates, diplomas, and degrees in nursing and other health fields. Establishing a functioning program of this nature can be a very great benefit to both the individual employee and the institution. The individual can develop new skills, and the institution can attract new personnel and improve performance of experienced personnel. Success depends on strong, enthusiastic support of supervisors. They must be willing to alter staffing patterns resulting from employee's shortened work weeks. They must also be responsible for evaluation of the results of study on staff performance.

Reduction-In-Force

Retrenchments, at least until the age of prospecive payment, have been unprecedented in nursing. Many nursing administrators may now be required to face this traumatic undertaking, of managing staff cutbacks constructively, but they tend to be lacking in previous experience. The process involves the following steps: determining the cutback need, figuring the cuts, implementing the cutback plan, managing the feelings of loss, and achieving a new stability.

Reduction-In-Force (RIFs) are difficult decisions. The nursing administrator's philosophy about people and nursing care will be evident in the way staff reduction is managed. All nursing managers should be included in the decision making criteria for layoffs. Staff cutbacks affect everybody: those who leave, those who stay, those whose assignments are changed, and those who make the decisions. An organization changes with RIFs and appropriate strategies must be developed to minimize stress.

Participative Management

Participative management is a valid alternative to traditional organizational behavior. A staff member whose ideas are valued and put into action tends to be productive. Careful planning and evaluation will usually effect successful implementation of these ideas. Through participation and decision making, leaders and staff can achieve higher self-esteem while becoming more sensitive to others' needs. Greater involvement in goal setting results in better communications, increased productivity, and increased motivation for both the leaders and the group members. These results are especially important to professional workers in a bureaucratic setting.

Summary

Personnel management is

- —a responsibility of nurse leaders as they recruit new personnel and evaluate the performance of present personnel.
- —a responsibility of nurse leaders as they communicate personnel policies and practices to their staffs.
- —a responsibility of nurse leaders as they plan for employee health and safety.
- —becoming increasingly important in the health-care agency setting.

Exercise

Miss N. is a newly employed staff nurse working on 1A, a medical-surgical unit. She is a recent graduate of a highly reputable local diploma program and is due for her three-month probationary evaluation in a week. The following are anecdotal notes that will be used during the evaluation conference. Describe the strengths and weaknesses of Miss N. identifiable in these notes.

5/2/86 — During this first week on the unit, Miss N. has asked pertinent questions regarding the routine and policies of the unit. Suggested having the aides listen to 7:00 A.M. shift report as this is what she "was used to."

5/7/86 — In making rounds today, I observed Miss N. giving bath to new cholecystectomy client. Dirty linen was on the floor. I later spoke to her about the dirty linen on the floor. She said that all the hampers were in use and that she remembered linen was not to be put into a pillowcase and thrown down chute.

5/9/86 — Today I observed Miss N. giving passive exercises to Mr. D., a CVA client who is semiconscious. She was talking to him and explaining everything she did even though he was not aware of what was being said. (She did not know I was in the room with the other client.)

5/23/86 — Mr. B., a three-day post-op pneumonectomy client in 342, requested "the same nurse he had today" (Miss N.) as she gave him "the best care he'd had since being hospitalized." He added that she really answered a lot of his questions as well.

6/7/86 — Conducted team conference today regarding two particular clients on their team. Aides really appeared interested and contributed worthwhile input.

6/14/86 — Did not remove dentures of operative client, and O.R. called reporting situation. Retrieved dentures from O.R. and secured them appropriately at bedside. Stated she was in the habit of leaving in dentures, since in her home school the anesthesiologist requested that the dentures be left in.

6/15/86—Several aides have asked to work on Miss N.'s team, as they say she is so interested in "what they do and how they do their care." Also mentioned they wished they had more time for clinical conferences conducted by Miss N., as she really knows a lot about nursing.

An answer to this exercise may be found on p. 273.

Bibliography

Adler, Jack. When a Nursing Staff Organizes: Management Rights and Collective Bargaining, Programmed Instruction. *American Journal of Nursing* 33 (April, 1978): 657–668.

American Hospital Association. *Employee's Performance Appraisal Programs: Guidelines for Their Development and Implementation.* Chicago: AHA (1972).

Darling, LuAnn, and Luciano, Kathy. Managing Staff Cutbacks. *Journal of Nursing Administration* (January, 1985): 29–34.

Godfrey, Marjorie. Job Satisfaction. *Nursing* 78 (April, 1978): 89–102.

Hepner, James O.; Boyer, John M.; and Westerhaus, Carl. *Personnel Administration and Labor Relations in Health Care Facilities.* St. Louis: C. V. Mosby, 1969.

Hoffman, Edin. ABC's of Nurse Recruitment. *American Journal of Nursing* 74 (April, 1974): 682–683.

Kaiser, Pamela. Ten Steps to Interviewing Job Applicants. *American Journal of Nursing* 78 (April, 1978); 627–630.

Kramer, Marlene. *Reality Shock.* St. Louis: C. V. Mosby, 1974: 2–22.

Metzger, Norman. *The Health Care Supervisor's Handbook.* Germantown, Md.: Aspen Systems, 1978: 96.

Peter, Laurence J., and Hull, Raymond. *The Peter Principle.* New York: Morrow, 1969: 26.

Sloane, Robert, and Sloane, Beverly. *A Guide to Health Facilities Personnel and Management.* St. Louis: C. V. Mosby, 1971.

Wandelt, Mabel A., and Stewart, Doris Slater. *Slater Nursing Competencies Rating Scale.* New York: Appleton-Century-Crofts, 1975.

The
Change Maker
Role

In an age in which the single constant is radical and rapid change, all human beings suffer in varying degrees from what Toffler (1970) has called "Future Shock." The concept of future shock refers to the shattering stress and disorientation that result when individuals are subjected to too much change in too short a time. Toffler's point is that the *rate* of change has implications quite apart from, and sometimes more important than, the *direction* of change. Physical and psychological distress arise from an overload on a person's adaptive systems and decision-making processes. Holmes and Rahe (1967) have proposed that change itself—not a specific change but the rate of change in one's life—is intimately related to physical health. They developed a life-change unit scale for measuring the amount of change an individual has experienced in a given span of time. They found a positive correlation between high life-change scores and the frequency and severity of subsequent illness.

Change is essential to the life of the individual, but there are limits on one's adaptability. Just as environmental overstimulation causes physical damage, so does it affect one's ability to think and behave rationally. The combat-fatigued soldier, the disaster victim, the culturally dislocated traveler, and the burned-out or reality-shocked nurse tend to respond to overstimulation in strikingly parallel ways. With sensory overload come confusion, disorientation, or blurring of the lines between illusion and reality.

Change is essential to the life of organizations also. In organizations one sometimes sees **decision stress**, which is a form of overstimulation. The increasing tempo and complexity of life in organizations causes an increased need for decision making. A delicate balance between too much change and a growth-stunting lack of change must be maintained. Any organization must be planned, organized, directed, and controlled. But no matter how carefully this is done, *changes* are essential for the organization to remain viable. The need for change comes primarily from two areas—the external environment or society and internal organizational desires for improvement. The introduction and implementation of change must be planned through a series of well-thought-out strategies that make use of an appropriate leadership style.

Resistance to Change

In looking at the change process we must examine the issue of **resistance**. Most people, even the well educated, find the idea of change so threatening that they attempt to deny its necessity. People cannot change all their beliefs and still retain their sanity. They frequently prefer familiar problems to unfamiliar solutions. In a society in which every area of life is subject to change, we should not be surprised to find individuals consciously or unconsciously digging in and hanging on to what is familiar.

Stability in one area of life often enables a person to feel comfortable enough to risk or even seek change in other areas. Frequently the area of stability so tenaciously clung to is the work area. A would-be change maker must recognize and take into account this possibility.

All psychiatric nurses are familiar with the phenomenon of resistance. A patient who, in the course of therapy, feels threatened by a painful awareness may balk, become silent, change the subject, fill the interview with irrelevant small talk, miss or come late for appointments, or become angry with the therapist—all in an effort to resist change and maintain the status quo. Similar resistance occurs when the target of change is a group or organization. Hostility, either overtly or covertly expressed, is a common defense against real or implied threats to an individual or group self-image.

A number of conditions promote resistance to organizational change. Since most nurses are working in some type of organization, they should know how to influence people in order to make the kinds of change that are desirable. Personal idiosyncrasies and life experiences cause people to read different meanings into a proposed change, and adequate explanation of the coming change does not always assure that there will be no resistance. Explanations can be distorted, and information is not a panacea for the problem of implied threat to one's personal status or power position. When people feel pressured to make a change, they may be expected to resist; when they have a say in the nature or direction of the change, resistance will decrease. Resistance is also likely if a change is made on personal grounds rather than because of impersonal requirements. And, last, if the change ignores existing alliances within a group, resistance by the individuals in the group is a certainty.

Resistance can be valuable. It can force leaders to clarify purposes and results to be achieved. It can point out inadequate communication processes. It can give the change maker pause to consider short- and long-range consequences, and it can disclose inadequacy in problem-solving processes.

Another complaint is the threat that comes with change. Some threats are real; some turn out to be nonexistent. There are real concerns in any organization that change may bring financial loss, loss of power, threat to a vested interest, or loss of social status.

Theoretical Framework for Change

In providing leadership for change it is better to avoid dependence upon the personal force of the change maker, using instead a conceptual and operational framework for bringing change about. Although personal charisma may help some people effect change, the use and understanding of the processes of change are more reliable. **Change theory** is derived from learning theory, communications theory, systems theory, and interpersonal theory. We have all had experience with those whose approach to change is "You should want to make this change because I ask you to." This strategy, used by nurses for many years, is often not effective.

Any organization, once established, becomes a system rather than a random collection of individuals. We need to understand the components of the system.

We need first to identify the **repetitive patterns** whereby the organization operates. Most health-care facilities state in their philosophies that their primary function is to provide quality care. Yet, in the hospital situations, is the bath given at a time conducive to relaxation for the client because it fits the client's bath patterns, or is it given at a time convenient to the nursing staff? Are meals served at a time usual for the client or convenient to the dietary department? Are clients prepared and held ready for X rays scheduled at the convenience of the client or of the doctor? Even though we say we arrange for individualized care, all of these questions are valid.

The Maker of Change

There are a number of characteristics basic to the role of change maker. The change maker is a professional who relies heavily on a body of knowledge to realize certain aims. Frequently an individual having only a marginal membership in the group, the change maker may draw suspicion and hostility from others who do not appreciate the need for the change. At the same time, to be effective, any person intimately concerned with change needs patience and tolerance both for uncertainty and for a certain amount of personal stress. The role of the change maker is both insecure and risky. Besides evoking suspicion and hostility, she or he may frequently be viewed as a most expendable person, and with the complexity of any organizational change, unanticipated consequences of actions can lead to totally undesirable outcomes. For example, proposed changes may lead to backlash from superiors as well as from peers and subordinates. At a later time, however, the change maker may find that the superior has adopted some of the proposed changes.

Probably the most singular skill of successful change makers is that of **interpersonal competence**. *Competence* implies the capacity to meet and deal with the changing world, to formulate ends, and to implement them. Interpersonally competent individuals are intelligent, empathetic, autonomous, sound in their judgments, and innovative. They can assess a situation while maintaining an awareness of the human factors involved, and they can develop a diagnostic sensitivity as well as behavioral flexibility in dealing with human problems.

Leadership is the process of developing plans and strategies for getting work done and for effectively accomplishing objectives through others. The nurse leader must look for changes through which the organization or specific group can function more effectively to get the day-to-day work done, to carry through those activities that maintain the organization, and to plan for continued growth and development. Planned change is helping people to develop appropriate behavior in a new environment so that they can continue to be effective and creative. The following are useful guidelines for the prospective change maker:

1. One's attitude toward other persons is more critical than the change itself. The change maker, therefore, should be person-centered, friendly, and supportive.
2. It must be recognized that people fear change because it undermines their security. A change of any magnitude requires that support and help for the people affected be planned.
3. The process of change is helped when the persons affected can participate in the decision-making process and in the planning for change. The greater the participation, the more assurance people have of being able to influence the direction and impact of change and consequently to identify and resolve their personal resistances.
4. A plan must be made for both emotional and informational aspects of the change. The staff needs to be allowed to express its feelings and to be fully informed about objectives and procedures.
5. The prospective change maker may at first assume that the situation needing alteration is firmly established and unchanging. But this appearance of stability covers a constantly shifting set of forces the change maker must analyze before trying to make modifications.
6. To change nursing practice, the nurse leader seeking change must serve as an example and stimulus to the staff.

Lewin (in Cartright, 1951) has described a balance of opposing forces that impact on change. **Driving forces** move the situation in the direction of anticipated change; **restraining forces**, in opposition, tend to prevent the situation from moving in the direction of anticipated change. These two sets of forces working against each other tend to create a dynamic equilibrium (see Figure 8–1). There are three possibilities inherent in this situation that could tend to cause change: the numbers or strength of driving forces might be incomplete and in need of strengthening to allow change to occur; the strength and number of restraining forces might be decreased, so that change can occur; or a combination of the first two methods may operate to initiate change. In addition, other contributing forces need to be identified. **Interference forces** take time and energy, diverting the change maker from change making. **Interdependence forces** exist when two or more individuals form a power coalition to promote or restrain change.

The change maker should identify and rank all these forces prior to developing a blueprint for change. By limiting the forces to be considered to no more than the three most important in each of the four categories (driving, restraining, interference, and interdependence), the change maker will have a manageable number of factors to deal with.

The next procedure is to rank the identified forces according to the change maker's ability to influence them constructively. Again, no more than three of the most important of these forces in each category should be isolated. Both lists should then be combined, and the best and most realistic choices should be selected. Next, at least one alternative action should be developed for each identified force. The action should be one that will move forces in the desired direction. The most promising action or actions from this list should be determined.

For each action, the change maker should list the resources available at the present time. Resources that are not available but will be needed for implementation should be listed also.

The relationships between the two lists should be reviewed with a consideration of new or less expensive ways in which the needed resources may be obtained. From this review, a comprehensive action plan can be developed.

Image of Potentiality (Desired change) ————————————					
Restraining Forces	a^1	b^1	c^1	d^1	n^1
	↓	↓	↓	↓	↓
Status Quo (Present situation)	———————————————				
	↑	↑	↑	↑	↑
Driving Forces	a	b	c	d	n
Interference/Independence Forces	←——————— ————————→				

Figure 8–1 Lewin's Force Field Analysis

As planning is carried out, the change maker should consider and list ways to evaluate the success of the proposed change. Furthermore, once implementation begins and the action plan is carried out, feedback should be obtained. As the force field shifts, the experienced change maker should expect the unexpected to occur. As the results of ongoing evaluation accumulate, the action plan can be revised and refined as necessary.

A last and most important step in change making is **internalization**. A change that has been instituted must be carefully nurtured and/or monitored. The period of time varies with the amount of distress the change produced. If this step is not taken, old methods tend to reappear even after the new method has made a promising start.

A hypothetical example of Lewin's force field analysis in action is shown in Figure 8–2. The proposed change is the institution of primary nursing on a 52-bed surgical unit in a small hospital. The figure shows the existing forces.

The interference forces identified in the situation include the demands of day-to-day operation of the unit and the heavy committee assignments carried by nursing personnel. Interdependence forces include the existence of a group of four influential head nurses who are led by a fifth highly respected head nurse. These five nurses usually respond as a group.

Ranking the three most important restraining forces from most to least important produced the following list:

1. Shortage of RNs
2. Budgetary constraints
3. Lack of maturity among RNs

Ranking the driving forces in the same manner produced the following:

1. Greater patient satisfaction
2. Decreased staff turnover
3. Greater job satisfaction for RNs

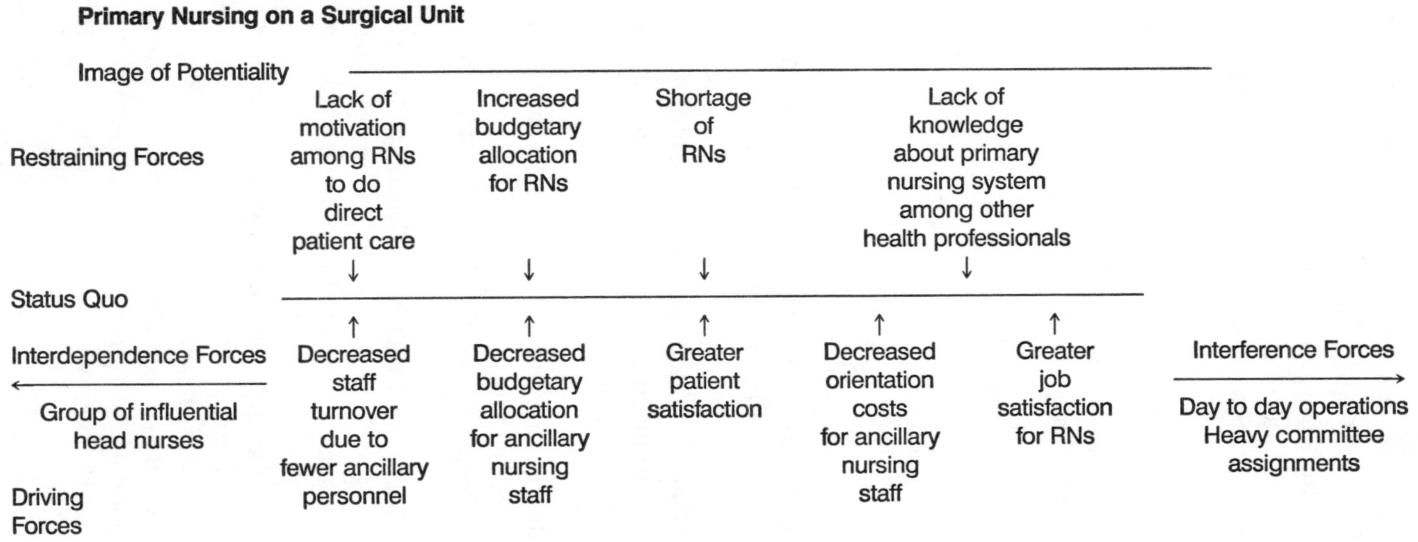

Primary Nursing on a Surgical Unit

Image of Potentiality

Interference Forces

Restraining Forces
- Lack of motivation among RNs to do direct patient care
- Increased budgetary allocation for RNs
- Shortage of RNs
- Lack of knowledge about primary nursing system among other health professionals

Status Quo

Interdependence Forces
- Decreased staff turnover due to fewer ancillary personnel
- Decreased budgetary allocation for ancillary nursing staff
- Greater patient satisfaction
- Decreased orientation costs for ancillary nursing staff
- Greater job satisfaction for RNs

Group of influential head nurses

Driving Forces

Interference Forces
- Day to day operations
- Heavy committee assignments

(Figure 47 (p. 263) in *Field Theory in Social Science*, by Kurt Lewin. Copyright 1951 by Harper & Row, Publishers, Inc. Reprinted by permission of the publisher.)

Figure 8–2   Lewin's Force Field Applied to the Process of Installing Primary Nursing on a Surgical Unit

217

Interference forces, when ranked, showed that day-to-day requirements for operation of the unit were most important.

The next step is to rank the same forces, identifying the three restraining forces that the change maker can influence most constructively. These are ranked from most to least amenable to influence:

1. Lack of motivation among RNs
2. Lack of knowledge among other health disciplines
3. Need for increased budgetary allocation for RNs

The three driving forces most amenable to influence were:

1. Greater patient satisfaction
2. Decreased orientation costs
3. Greater job satisfaction

Interference forces, when ranked, indicated that heavy committee assignments would be easier to change than the demands of day-to-day operation.

Combining and making a plan including all restraining and driving forces, with consideration given to interference and interdependence forces, resulted in the following plan:

1. Shortage of RNs: Establish active recruitment of nurses interested in primary nursing. Evaluate by keeping a record of nurses recruited.
2. Budgetary constraints: Reallocate money within the nursing-service budget for this pilot project.
3. Lack of motivation among RNs: Send the group of five influential head nurses who act together to an institution in which primary nursing is correctly and enthusiastically used. Evaluate by counting requests to participate in the project.
4. Planning for evaluation and obtaining feedback: Invite the executive committee of the medical staff, selected leaders in the medical community, a hospital department head, and the community advisory board to a breakfast where the advantages of the project can be presented. Evaluate six months later by a follow-up questionnaire to elicit satisfactions and dissatisfactions with system from their point of view.

5. Greater patient satisfaction: Search the literature for documentation of patient satisfaction in primary-nursing situations. Develop a rating scale to assess patient satisfaction.
6. Greater RN job satisfaction: Invite a staff member from the institution the head nurses visited to come and describe the satisfactions of primary nursing to the nursing staff. To evaluate, conduct a pre- and post-project attitude survey of the nursing-staff encounter.
7. Decreased staff turnovers and decreased orientation costs: Collect information from similar institutions concerning the effect of primary nursing on staff turnover and orientation costs. Evaluate by comparing these costs with project costs after one year of operation.
8. Heavy committee assignments: Reduce the committee assignments of those nursing-staff members who will be involved in the change.

At this point, the plan can be implemented and will have a good chance of succeeding, provided there is continued evaluation and support until primary nursing is clearly well established.

Some other good ideas for making changes include the following categories:

What?   The change that will occur must be defined or identified in specific and concrete terms.

Why?   There must be a valid reason for making the change and persons concerned must be aware of the reason.

Who?   The individuals who will be affected by the change must be identified by the person initiating the change.

When?   Timing is crucial; change requires time.

Where? The place involved in the change must be identified.

How?   Consider the key concepts in making change — readiness, repetition, reinforcement.

Obtain strong approval and sanction from the highest administrative person.

Inform administrative personnel up and down the chain of command of what is being planned.

Spell out the advantages to the organization and the individuals affected.

Link the change to the group's existing values, beliefs, and needs.

Provide for easy feedback to clear up any fears, doubts, or

confusions that those affected may have.

Indicate what criteria you will use to judge success or failure.

Give facts about the change without painting too rosy or too negative a picture.

Spell out the process in small steps.

Involve personnel in the planning as much as possible and practical.

Proceed one step at a time.

Build on skills already available.

Provide opportunities for individuals who are expected to implement change to learn the skills necessary to perform the new tasks.

Build peer reinforcement by circulating information about the favorable reactions of others.

At the appropriate time, announce that the experimental stage is over, that the method has proved itself, and that all who have participated in implementing it are to be congratulated on a job well done.

Common Errors Made by Nursing Managers

Today's nurses are seeing many changes in the field of patient care and nursing management. New medications, new equipment, and new methods of treatment are being introduced at a rapid rate.

The ability to introduce change with a minimum of resistance is a key managerial skill. The nurse leader will be involved in most of the changes introduced in the institution. Too often, nurses concern themselves with the technical aspect of change and fail to consider the human-relations problems that many changes generate.

Nurses helping to introduce change need to seek out the reasons for resistance to change. It is critical to determine how the change will affect the people involved and particularly how it affects their interpersonal relationships. The first step is to bring any problems out into the open, allowing for two-way communication. Objections and suggestions for modification should be carefully considered. Some suggestions may not be realistic but their airing lets the nurse know what the staff is thinking. Some objectives and modifications may be useful, and their acceptance will improve the overall quality of the proposed change.

Change Can Be a Creative Process

"Management by memo," whereby change is mandated by a single decree from above, is rarely effective except where the change is minimal. The nurse leader must use judgment in determining how much time and how many meetings will be needed to effectively implement the change, at the same time avoiding unnecessary delay.

In recent years much new light has been shed on the problem of what makes some people more creative than others. Research conducted at a number of universities suggests that creative people differ significantly from those who are less creative in a number of characteristics. Interestingly enough, most of these attributes are not directly related to intelligence, which until recently was assumed to be the key trait of creative people.

Among the most pronounced attributes of creative people are their sensitivity to their surroundings and their ability to see things to which the average individual is blind. They also are mentally flexible and have the ability to adjust quickly to new developments. They show independence of judgment and have the assertiveness to insist on evidence, while at the same time recognizing the importance of deeply felt but more vaguely defined feelings. They have a tolerance for ambiguity—a continuing confidence that contradictions, complexities, and apparent disorder, if allowed expression, may generate richer types of experience. Finally, they have the ability to break down problems into their component parts and the skill to combine several elements in a creative way to form a new whole.

Almost everyone encounters daily the many common obstacles to creativity. In bringing to each situation a unique personality and the sum of an individual's life experiences, one may be hemmed in by forces that prevent the free unfolding of creative potential. Among the most significant inhibitors are lack of self-confidence, resistance to change, perceptual rigidities that prevent one from seeing things in a new or different way, conformity, and lack of opportunity for innovation.

There are also many barriers to group creativity. It is probable that every nurse is a member of some formal group that meets periodically for a specific purpose. In any group there are some familiar problems that limit creative output, such as lack of clearly defined goals, lack of leadership, breakdowns in communication within the group, lack of decision-making skills, and uneven participation among members. There may be members of the group who have a "hidden agenda" that may limit productivity since only certain topics may be considered, or there may be a leader who pressures for an answer before the group has explored all the alternatives. There may be a lack of willingness to share needed information, or administrative pressure for immediate success, or excessive work pressures. All of these will interfere with creative group outcomes.

Creativity needs to be developed and nurtured. With the proper motivation, with the stimulation of other creative people, with the courage to take risks and innovate, much progress can be made. Although individual learning is helpful, organized educational activities can do a great deal to speed up the process whereby individuals, groups, and organizations can develop their creative potential.

Various approaches have been used to stimulate creativity. Most people will recognize the term **brainstorming**, where all are encouraged to express their ideas without worrying about whether they are sensible or not. This process often leads to new solutions. Then there are **creative growth games**, which require the participant to abandon stereotyped thinking. An example in Raudsepp and Hough (1977) is as follows:

> Stereotyped thinking is one of the major barriers to creative problem solving. The impulse to overgeneralize about human beings is one most of us never fully conquer. But it is worth struggling with, because it can grossly mislead us—as this little puzzle illustrates.
>
> A young man, badly injured in an auto accident, is brought into the emergency room of a hospital. It is determined by the attending physician that immediate brain

surgery is required. Accordingly, the brain surgeon is summoned. Upon seeing the patient, the surgeon exclaims, "I can't operate on that boy! He's my son!"

That is so, but the surgeon is not the boy's father. How do you explain the apparent contradiction?*

Creative growth games will enable people to discover new facets of their imaginations and inventive powers that will help them cope with the chronic problems that weigh them down in day-to-day living. Many people in business and industry are beginning to look at a lack of developed creative ability as a factor that tends to inhibit progress in an organization.

Sensitivity training is another form of creative effort designed to help individuals to become more effective in their interpersonal relationships. The trainees are encouraged to relate to one another as openly as possible. The interactions among them provide the primary subject matter for discussion and analysis. During the training experience, the *process* that goes on between people rather than the *content* of what they say receives great attention. The participants deal with their feelings about themselves and others. They explore the impact they have upon one another, examining feelings, expressions, gestures, and subtle behaviors often taken for granted or not seen at all in everyday life.

Another method of creativity development is a cooperative group action called **diagnostic-skill training**. The diagnostic process utilizes a specialist in group work who observes the ongoing interaction and identifies the symptoms of common "group ills," in order to understand their causes and help correct them in constructive ways. Conflict among members, power struggles, apathy, indecision, conflicting loyalties, and many other factors can reduce group efficiency. Diagnostic-skill training is designed to help people to identify, as well as eliminate, the blocks that prevent them from working together effectively.

Here are two examples of creative approaches to the procedure for bathing clients. The first requires only two minutes. Developed by Gus Totman, RN, staff member at Tucson's Veterans Administration Hospital, it is known as the towel bath. This novel procedure employs

---

*If an answer is needed, see footnote to end-of-chapter exercise.

a quick-drying solution containing a cleansing agent, a disinfectant, and a softening agent mixed with 110-degree water. The solution is poured over a seven-foot terry-cloth towel. The towel is wrung nearly dry and unrolled over the client, wrapping him in a moist sauna-like heat. Working from the feet to the head, the nurse massages the client clean using a fresh section of towel for each body area. To finish, the nurse turns the client, flipping the towel and rubbing his back clean with an unsoiled section. Nine out of ten clients find the towel bath extremely relaxing, and arthritic clients particularly praise the way it soothes their painful joints.

The second type of creative way to provide baths is the portable shower for bedridden clients. The shower is a stainless-steel box mounted on four wheels. Eight shower heads are attached near the top. The heads have inner rotating vanes that spin the water into tiny droplets. This provides a soft, dense full-coverage spray that massages the body. A shower bed on rollers is placed on a standard stretcher, which has a set of rails attached. The client is placed on the shower bed and rolled to the shower. The rails on the stretcher are locked to mating rails on the shower similar to those in a car wash. After the shower bed is pushed into the shower, the stretcher is unlocked from the shower and moved away. If the client cannot bathe himself, the shower can be turned on to wet the client. Then he can be pulled out of the shower onto the stretcher, where the nurse can wash him, return him to the shower for rinsing, and pull him out again for drying.

Lewis (1971) has described the "ostrich" nurse:

You are an "ostrich" nurse if you:
Don't read
Don't learn new techniques
Don't share ideas with others
Don't belong to your nursing organizations
Settle for the same methods of doing things you learned in nursing
   schools 10, 20, or 30 years ago
Don't use the humane methods of modern management
Don't communicate with your patients any more than you have to
Make excuses about why other duties keep you away from the bedside
Don't learn how others view you, especially if you continue to believe
   that you are seen by others as you see yourself

Don't keep an open mind, especially if you close it for fear you will hear
    something upsetting
Support the status quo with every fiber of your being.*

Change in Health-Care Institutions

The convergence of a variety of factors in our social environment
make change mandatory in our health-care institutions. All of the
problems coming about with cost-containment programs are really
only the tip of an iceberg that is just beginning to surface. As noted
earlier, nursing for many years has answered requests for more
efficiency with the excuse, "We can't do that because we work with
people, not machines." But, with the high cost of health care, nurses
must begin to look creatively and with willingness to change toward
becoming more efficient—what many call "working smarter, not
harder." Although tradition has a role to play in any profession, and
particularly in nursing, to continue to use "We have always done it
this way" as an excuse for not seeking newer or better ways of doing
things is really an archaic approach that is no longer affordable.

Nurse leaders need to look at various systems for simplification.
Essentially, there are five steps in work simplification. First, a specific
procedure must be selected for study. Then, all the relevant facts
must be collected. Next, every step of the procedure must be ana-
lyzed. An improved method is then developed and either implemented or presented to administration for consideration.

One area in serious need of such study is evaluation and promotion within nursing. Are nurses advanced for their clinical skill
and knowledge? And, if so, do they receive additional compensation
for giving good client care? Or are they promoted to a higher position
in management as a reward and thereby taken away from the
bedside? Experienced nurses know that the second case is by far the
more common and that expertise in care tends to vanish behind a
desk. Thus, the whole system of career advancement in nursing
needs to be examined. One approach that is being advocated is a

*(From Edith Lewis, "The Expanding Circle," in *Changing Patterns of Nursing Practice—
New Needs, New Roles,* © 1971, p. 73. Reprinted by permission of the American Journal of
Nursing Company, New York.)

system for clinical advancement within the nursing department, allowing the nurse to be rewarded for her nursing knowledge while remaining at bedside.

Two other innovative approaches to management have recently appeared. One is the development of organizational bylaws for nursing service, and the other is the autonomous nursing staff.

Guidelines for Nursing-Staff Bylaws

These bylaws are patterned along the lines of medical-staff bylaws. The parallel structure allows an increased collegial relationship between nursing and medicine. The Tennessee Nursing Association Board of Directors (1978) approved the following *Guidelines for Nursing Staff Bylaws in Health Care Institutions* as recommended by the Council on Practice:

> The nursing staff is responsible for the quality of nursing care provided in an agency. The Director of Nursing Service holds administration responsibility and authority. Members of the nursing staff are responsible for their actions not only to the agency, but to the patient/client. The philosophy, goals, and objectives of the nursing department should be congruent with the philosophy and goals of the institution.
>
> The nursing-staff organization shall functionally provide a mechanism for self-governance responsible to the governing body of the institution; provide freedom for nursing to develop professional relationships with other structural units within the agency; provide a vehicle for orderly change in improving patient care; and project a positive image of nursing to the public.
>
> It is recommended that nursing-staff bylaws be established to facilitate the above functions and that they be flexible and consistent with the philosophy of the nursing department. These guidelines are developed to assist nursing departments to write their own bylaws that will meet their needs relative to the size and function of the institution.

Proposed Nursing Staff Bylaws Content of nursing-staff bylaws shall include the following broad areas of content. Some examples of content are included:

— Delineate the organizational structure of the nursing staff.
— Define purposes of the organization to include such things as:

1. Provide nursing care to patients served by the institution according to professional standards.
2. Delineate responsibility, authority, and accountability of the employed nursing staff and nurses holding practice privileges.
3. Provide the structures through which nursing will participate in policy-making processes including budgeting, allocation of personnel resources, and so on.
4. Facilitate communications within the nursing department.
5. Provide for continuing education and professional development of the nursing staff.

— Define membership on the nursing staff including provisions for appointments, retention, conditions, scope, and duration of privileges. Suggested membership should include registered nurses and all other nursing-care providers within the institution.
— Specify a method of performing the credentials-review function. Establish a Credentials and Appointment Committee.
— Provide an appeal and grievance mechanism relative to nursing-staff recommendations for denial of staff appointments and reappointments, as well as for denial, curtailment, suspension, or revocation of clinical privileges. This mechanism shall provide for review of decisions, including the right to be heard at each step of the process upon request. The final appeal shall be to the governing body.
— Define expectations of clinical practice for all nursing staff. Delineate how the nursing process will be carried

out, including responsibilities for record keeping. Delineate the scope of practice of nonprofessionals.

— Require that each nurse will practice in accordance with ethical standards of the profession.

— Provide for a mechanism for staff development, including support of staff in pursuits of continuing education within or outside the institution, sufficient orientation for new appointees, criteria for extended-education leave, and provision for a nursing library.

— Develop criteria for appropriate reward mechanisms and incentives for the nursing staff.

— Provide for nursing involvement in the development of institutional policies and procedures.

— Establish a framework for communications between the nursing staff and other providers as it relates to patient care. Establish expectations for nursing referrals.

— Provide methods for selection and term of office of nursing-staff officers. Outline responsibilities of the executive committee.

— Specify composition and functions of standing committees as required by the size and complexity of the nursing staff and institution. Suggested committees might include the following: Professional Practice; Credentials and Appointment; Research; Audit and Peer Review; Evaluation; Grievance; Continuing Education; Professional Liaison; Policy; and Bylaws.

— Establish requirements regarding the frequency of and attendance at general and/or departmental meetings of the nursing staff, a quorum for same, and a record of proceedings and actions. Establish a staff newsletter to facilitate communications and preclude unnecessary use of meeting time.

— Provide for a mechanism by which the nursing staff consults with, and reports to, the governing body. Because the governing body of the institution, acting through the chief executive officer, has the overall responsibility for the conduct of the institution and the nursing staff has the overall responsibility for the provision of nursing care to clients, there must be full communication between these two bodies. Both must be informed adequately regarding institutional activities. Further, representatives of the nursing staff should participate in any institutional deliberations that affect the discharge of nursing-staff responsibilities.

— Provide for an amendment procedure for the bylaws.

(From "Guidelines for Nursing Staff Bylaws," in *Health Care Institutions,* © January 1981. Reprinted by permission of Tennessee Nurses' Association, Nashville, Tennessee.)

Autonomous Nursing Staffs and Other Innovations

The other innovative development in management, the autonomous nursing staff, is separate from the nursing-service department but carries out some of the functions described in the *Guidelines for Nursing-Staff Bylaws.* The autonomous nursing staff reports to the Board of Trustees, as do the medical staff and the hospital administrators. Thus nursing has similar direct access to top policy making for client care. Both the development of organizational bylaws for nursing service and the autonomous nursing staff are radically new ideas and are going to require some time for acceptance.

External pressures for change and increasing complexity in nursing departments are resulting in disjointed operations that are difficult for the nurse leader to coordinate. Traditional organizational patterns must be changed in line with improving communications among physician, nurse, and client. The **client-centered approach** has been developed as one answer to this problem.

A few institutions have made a determined effort to put the client ahead of the system by eliminating a central nurse's station and keeping everything the client needs, including his medications and his chart, in the client's own room. Routine procedures such as TPRs are done only when ordered by a physician or professional nurse. Meals are available whenever the client is ready. Most importantly, nursing personnel spend 75 to 80 percent of their time with clients in clients' rooms (Porter, 1973).

Other approaches for better care make use of the **clinical specialist** as a change maker or may offer an **externship** for new graduates. Externships may be a way to bridge the gap between the educational process and the first job, improving the clinical skills of new nurses.

Valuing

In organizations where membership involves paid employment, it is important to consider individual interests when assigning work. Many supervisors assign people to jobs or tasks in which they are not really interested on the assumption that "somebody has to do it." Often, there is someone else immediately available who would prefer to do the task in which the other is uninterested. But to find this out the supervisor must be open to mutual planning and must recognize that individual values differ.

For example, a staff nurse on the evening shift may have a particular interest in client teaching. Her supervisor is planning to develop a teaching unit on the stress of hospitalization and is preparing to select someone to be responsible for its implementation. If she chooses a nurse on the day shift because it will be convenient to work with her during this time, the evening nurse is likely to be disgruntled and unhappy because her values and skills have not been considered.

The foundation of effective management is in identifying and setting a favorable climate fostering mutual planning among key participants and carefully assessing individual organizational and community needs, interests, and values.

Human energy is the critical key to success. When one has only so much energy to expend, the value that one places upon what is to be done determines effective performance.

Conflict and Change

With the right amount of conflict (not too much, not too little) and an appropriate skill in handling it, a job can be exciting and challenging. If there is not enough conflict, a job becomes boring and monotonous; if there is too much, a job is overwhelming. Constructive, growth-producing conflict resolution requires both awareness of the factors likely to cause tension and the possession of skills needed to manage the tension.

Human-relations theorists see conflict as a normal result of the fact that people have different needs. Communication between them is the prime requisite for resolution of conflict. The methods used are discussion and problem solving, with the goal of including the thoughts and feelings of all parties concerned. If issues are brought out into the open there is often a rise in group performance. If issues are not discussed openly, there is a tendency for tension to build. Thus, if there is too little open conflict, issues are not resolved. It is also true that, if there are high levels of conflict, progress toward resolution may not be made. Moderate conflict is most productive.

Nurses are often handicapped in the area of conflict resolution because they have been taught from childhood to avoid open disagreement. But conflict is inevitable and can be an aid to improved performance. According to Douglass (1980), compromise, in which each side gives in a little, may be a useful technique, but usually an even better approach is that of **integrative problem solving**. When this method is used, both parties involved recognize that there is a conflict and look for a resolution satisfactory to all. Values, purposes, and goals must all be identified. There must be open communication, a sense of responsibility, and a sense of mutual trust among all who participate. Alternative ways to solve the problem can then be identified and evaluated. The function of the leader is to keep communication going, making sure that all group members have had enough time to make their ideas and feelings understood. Outside help can then be obtained if needed, and a satisfactory solution can often be found.

Nursing Leadership, Power, and Authority

If, indeed, the test of leadership is the wise use of power, how can power be meaningfully defined, and how can nurse leaders learn to use it wisely? These are questions that have plagued nursing for many years. Is the problem truly a lack of power, or is it a failure to use it? If nurses really lack power, the question for nursing becomes "How do nurses obtain power?" If nurses merely fail to use power available to them, they need to ask, "How do nurses become involved in the legislation that affects nursing practice?" and "How do nurses affect nursing goals and health care?"

The first question leads directly into a discussion of the need for more **assertiveness** by nurses, particularly female nurses, at all levels, for no one will hand over power that nurses do not claim as their own.

The women's movement, which has made great strides since the early 1970s, has made the public aware of how the special socialization processes women experienced as children shape their actions as adults, teaching them to be dependent, passive, nonaggressive, and noncompetitive. If they had been male, an entirely different and opposite set of attitudes would be expected of them. Chenevert (1978) has described in an amusing way how these socialization processes affect adult behavior in female nurses.

Dependency and unassertiveness may be appealing in teenagers but they will not serve mature women and practicing nurses well. Many times, however, when nurses recognize the need to be independent and try to behave in that manner, they run into barriers to action erected by society's expectations and their own. Many nurses are not comfortable being aggressive, even when to do so on the client's behalf will clearly improve care. This dilemma can be resolved by learning to be assertive, not aggressive. Being assertive means serving others without being subservient. Nurses are usually extroverted—sometimes so much so that they lose themselves, depending on others to tell them what they are.

Assertive nurses recognize that both they and their clients have value equivalent to anyone else's. They know what they want for themselves and what their clients need and want, and they are able to insist, and persist, politely, until those needs and wants are met. This attitude, although a little uncomfortable at first, will lead to increased self-respect and ability to function for all concerned. The hard part is to make a start, because initial success in assertiveness is needed to breed more success. Chenevert's advice is to start small and persevere with strangers whose opinion doesn't really matter, before moving on to more important needs involving closer relationships. In this way nurses can learn how to gain the attitude they can use to further their clients' best interests and their own.

Summary

A change maker is

— a manager of change.
— a creative person who is sensitive to surroundings, flexible.
— able to make use of conflict as a way to improve performance.
— able to be assertive when necessary.

Exercise*

One of the financial effects of prospective payments has been to increase the number of seriously ill patients in nursing homes, causing a need for more RNs to work in that setting. Mrs. A. C. has been charged with the responsibility for recruiting more RNs for the chain of nursing homes that employs her. She and her staff are having a brainstorming session in which all ideas, wild or not, are encouraged in the hope that some ideas usable for recruitment will develop from the free flow of the discussion. Contribute five ideas to the brainstorming session, using the form below.

In five minutes or less, write briefly and quickly. Do not judge your ideas — the wilder, the better. Shoot for at least five ideas — more if possible. Consider combining some into new approaches. Remember: work fast, defer judgment.

1.
2.
3.
4.
5.

Some possible answers to this exercise are found on p. 273.

*Answer to creative growth game: The brain surgeon is a woman.

Bibliography

Asprec, Elise. The Process of Change. *Supervisor Nurse* 75 (October, 1975): 15–25.

Brown, Barbara J. Politics and Power. *Nursing Administration Quarterly* 2:3 (Spring, 1978): 17–32.

Cartright, Dorwin, (Ed.). *Field Theory in Social Science: Selected Theoretical Papers by Kurt Lewin.* New York: Harper Brothers, 1951.

Chenevert, Melodie. *Special Techniques in Assertiveness Training for Women in the Health Professions.* St. Louis: C. V. Mosby, 1978.

Douglass, Laura Mae. *The Effective Nurse Leader and Manager.* St. Louis: C. V. Mosby, 1980: 173–189.

Holmes, Thomas, and Rahe, Richard. The Social Readjustment Rating Scale. *Journal of Psychosomatic Research* 11 (1967): 213–218.

Levinstein, Aaron. Effective Change Requires Change Agent. *Hospitals J.A.H.A.* 50(24) (December 16, 1976): 71–74.

Lewis, Edith P. *Changing Patterns of Nursing Practice.* New York: American Journal of Nursing Company, 1971: 73.

Porter, Karen. Change for Patient's Sake. *Journal of Nursing Administration* III (March–April 1973): 37–42.

Raudsepp, Eugene; and Hough, George P., Jr. *Creative Growth Games.* New York: Jove Publications, 1977: 26.

Sample, Sally. Development of Organizational By-Laws. *Nursing Clinics of North America* 13 (March, 1978): 91–102.

Tennessee Nursing Association. *Guidelines for Nursing Staff Bylaws in Health Care Institutions.* Nashville: Tennessee Nursing Association, 1978.

Toffler, Alvin. *Future Shock.* New York: Random House, 1970: 4.

The
Advocacy
Role

NURSES TODAY are very much aware of the increased emphasis being placed on consumer needs and rights in all areas of health care. It is the responsibility of the professional nurse to keep current with consumer movements concerning health-care delivery systems. In the past, the role of the nurse was confined strictly to the hospital setting, and responsibility to the client terminated with discharge. With the current trend toward the use of ambulatory-care settings, long-term care facilities, community-health nursing programs, and other nonhospital types of care, nurses must think about the continuity of total care and extend their roles into the community. Part of this continuity involves advocacy of clients' rights. Nurses have always been undeclared advocates for their clients, but now there is increased awareness of the need to risk speaking out when violations of rights occur.

An example of the need for advocacy is seen in the nursing-home industry. Complex social, economic, and medical developments in the United States since the 1930s have blessed nearly every American community with an increasing proportion of elderly citizens. These same developments have challenged communities to provide the necessary facilities and to satisfy the social and medical needs of the senior population. By and large, the American response has been a proliferation of nursing homes, where medical assistance and opportunity for the client to associate with a peer group were intended to be assured. In recent years, communities have responded to the needs of young physically handicapped and/or mentally retarded citizens in the same way.

Nursing homes have lately come under careful scrutiny by government officials and agencies as well as by private consumer groups and the media. The interest of the public and the media has been aroused primarily in response to tragedy and discontent. There has been considerable clamor for reform and much of it is justified. Continuing efforts on the part of the industry and of the government to improve the care of the nursing-home resident are vital. The nursing-home **ombudsman** (a Swedish term) is one answer intended to help meet this need.

The ombudsman is a person who acts as a speaker for people who do not have the power or ability to speak for themselves. Some ombudsmen have been nurses. Any persons acting in this role must above all be able to present the needs of nursing-home residents in an articulate and forceful manner so that client abuse, physical or psychological, becomes a rarity.

Some nursing homes now ask their residents and new staff to read and sign a copy of the Patient's Bill of Rights (Moss and Halarnandaris, 1977) (Box 9–1). The purpose is to assure that all residents and staff know what kind of care a resident can expect in each facility.

In November of 1972, the American Hospital Association (AHA) also proposed the adoption of a patient bill of rights. The hospital Patient Bill of Rights was designed in the interest of more effective client care and greater client satisfaction. The AHA proposed these rights in the expectation that they would be supported by each hospital on behalf of its clients as an integral part of the therapeutic process. The bill recognizes that the personal relationship between the physician and the client is essential for the provision of proper medical care. The traditional physician-client relationship takes on a new dimension when care is rendered within an organizational structure. Legal precedent has established that the institution itself

---

Box 9–1 *NURSING-HOME PATIENT BILL OF RIGHTS*

1. The right to be free from mental or physical abuse.
2. The right to voice grievances to staff or outside representatives of his/her choice, without fear of reprisal.
3. The right to manage his/her own finances.
4. The right to receive his/her mail unopened.
5. The right to be kept fully informed of his/her medical condition unless otherwise indicated by a physician.
6. The right to retain and use personal clothing and possessions as space permits.
7. The right to be treated with consideration, respect, and full recognition of dignity and individuality.

also has a responsibility to the client. It is in recognition of these factors that the bill was developed.

Other groups in the United States have been developing programs concerning clients' rights. In 1973 the Family Life Bureau of the United States Catholic Conference developed a program called Respect Life. This group is dedicated to the promotion of life for such groups as the unborn, the mentally retarded, youth, and the aged. The Euthanasia Council is also campaigning for the individual's right to have a "good death," not prolonged by technology if the individual does not desire it.

What Is an Advocate?

An **advocate** can serve in two different roles—as one who pleads another's cause, or as one who speaks or writes in support of some particular belief or program. Recent graduates in nursing have learned that they are first and foremost the client's advocate. Although current curricula have a heavy science component, major emphasis is still appropriately placed on the art of caring for people.

The origins of advocacy programs lie in the concept of representative government. In 1908, the Swedish parliament created the office of ombudsman in a political setting. This advocate's function was to receive complaints from citizens and protect them from injustice. In 1919, Finland adopted the Swedish model. After World War II the idea spread rapidly throughout the United States.

The condition that generated the ombudsman boom was a resurgence of the feeling that people have a right to a voice in matters that concern them. Typical citizens felt left out of the decisions affecting their lives. In the same way, typical citizens who become health-care clients may feel left out of the decisions affecting their lives.

The advocate or ombudsman for client care renders a very specific service to persons who question the way they have been treated. The ombudsman provides an independent, impartial, and professional review of complaints. Neither a jack-of-all-trades nor a trouble-shooter, the ombudsman functions as an agent for the citizen with the goal of solving specific problems of care. Ombudsmen are becoming increasingly visible, particularly in the nursing home setting through federal legislation (1978) that requires each state to set up an ombudsman program.

A different form of client advocacy is offered by programs emphasizing human-development services. These include services for health needs as well as other necessities of life. Such agencies are either being developed or are already in operation in many communities. Their aim is to direct individuals to the resources existing in the community and to prevent duplication of services already established. The same referral service is offered by the nurse in the institutional setting who operates in the advocacy role for clients.

In this age of consumerism, nurses are more interested than before in clients' feelings about their care. Most institutions routinely conduct a survey of client attitudes. Usually this survey is a questionnaire, sent as a follow-up after discharge. In some nursing-service departments there is a client representative/advocate who is responsible for attitude surveys. This person carries out a number of other functions to assist nurses (see Box 9–2). The attitude surveys may be written or may be completed by means of an interview.

Since the mid 1960s nurses have been studying clients' perceptions of care. These studies deal with issues such as the client's acceptance of authoritarianism in the nurse and the client's perception of the personal care provided. Through these investigations, nurses aim to foster self-care and the client's ability to control personal destiny.

The attitude of the nurse providing care to the client has also been studied in recent years. Investigators have asked, for example, how involved with the client the nurse should be. Most nurses have been conditioned to develop a degree of emotional distance. From the client's point of view, this distance may involve many difficulties. The nurse may be seen as uncaring, rejecting, and mechanical; these perceptions may add to the client's sense of loneliness, isolation, and helplessness. From the nurse's point of view, work may lose some of the opportunity for human interaction that was the original attraction to nursing. As a result, the nurse may become increasingly dissatisfied and even bored by the more routine tasks that permit the maintenance of emotional distance from clients.

Other aspects of the nurse's attitude have been investigated. Should nurses feel guilty when they can't respond sympathetically to

---

Box 9–2 *JOB DESCRIPTION*

TITLE: CLIENT REPRESENTATIVE

Basic Function: The client representative, under the direction of the nursing director, acts as an advocate for the client to any department or service; represents the hospital to the client, family, and visitors, interpreting policy and procedure; confers with hospital personnel seeking solutions to client problems and meeting client needs.

Details of Duties:

1. Call on all new clients, providing information about the hospital and advising them of client-representative services.
2. Listen to client's complaints and problems and seek solutions to them.
3. Confer routinely with nursing personnel on the condition of clients and any problem or complaint of client, family, or visitor.
4. Responsible for safekeeping of client's valuables; process lost and found client items; aid with insurance information; assist with transfers.
5. Assist families of critical and deceased clients in any way possible.
6. Assist in procedures concerning Medicare certification and bed utilization.
7. Initiate discharge planning and provide information about nursing homes and community services.
8. Assist in procedures related to client evaluations of hospital services.
9. Attend appropriate meetings and interdepartmental conferences.
10. Maintain a file of individual client cards with documented client information.
11. Revisit clients routinely and perform other duties as required.

Minimum Qualifications Required: Two years of college, preferably with major courses or a field of study in psychology or public relations.

---

clients? How do nurses' feelings influence the effectiveness of nursing care? How do nurses handle the anger they sometimes feel toward clients? Do nurses see more value in relieving physical pain than in comforting a client in psychological distress? The older generation of nurses seems to have more difficulty responding to psychological aspects of suffering than to physical pain. All of these questions relate to the attitude of one human being, the nurse, toward another human being, the client. As human beings, we have the ability to react to each other in an attitude of sharing, caring, honesty, and love. This is the newer or **humanistic** approach to nursing care.

The Humanistic Approach

Nurses often develop habitual modes of behavior toward clients that interfere with giving successful nursing care. Some nurses always smile. Others hum constantly. Still others always answer clients' questions about medications or treatments with the phrase. "This will make you feel better." This fixed way of behaving, sometimes called the **bedside manner**, appears to be something that the nurse puts on with the uniform. A psychologist would identify it as "character armor," a rigid interpersonal behavior that effectively hides a person's real self, both from self and from others. Character armor is acquired in situations marked by anxiety. It protects a person from recurrence of that anxiety and from guilt-provoking impulses and actions.

Early in the educational process, the nurse asks the question, How should I behave in the presence of clients? By trial and error and perhaps by emulating highly esteemed role models, neophyte nurses arrive at a formula that works for them. But what does it do to clients? Nurses generally will tell you that they are dedicated to the promotion of health and well-being in their clients and that they do all they can to promote recovery from illness. But perhaps their bedside manner blocks the highly important relationship that will elicit the optimum response to the client to treatment.

It is sometimes difficult for nurses to accept the fact that they cannot really know another person until they have taken definite and specific steps to find out who that person is, whether a student, friend, family member, or client. The alternative to the bedside manner is the **humanistic** approach, in which nurses freely disclose their real selves, are not afraid to be wrong, and work to find realistic and feasible ways to identify with their clients.

Nurses may think that they do their jobs well, but do their clients think so? They may be technically capable but may have forgotten or perhaps never known what clients value most. These nurses may totally miss the relationship that can be had with another human being. Most clients will value a nurse who is concerned enough to smile at appropriate times, to listen, and maybe even to stretch the rules or question orders if doing so is in the client's best interest.

Some nurses may not be able to employ a humanistic approach because of their own lack of self-esteem. De Filippo (1978) has expressed the view that more women with "little egos" enter nursing than enter other professions. Because nurses value themselves and their judgment too little, she says, some of them hesitate to do anything they are not specifically ordered to do by someone else in authority. This attitude has two results: the clients' individual needs often are not met (the physician is not likely to have time or interest in identifying or planning for needs other than those directly related to diagnosis and treatment), and the nurse, confirmed in the belief that she is not capable of making decisions on her own, becomes frustrated as a sense of personal inadequacy becomes a self-fulfilling prophecy. More importantly, such a nurse's attitude tends to spill over and infect other staff.

Some of these attitudinal problems derive from the commonly accepted stereotype of nurses as handmaidens to physicians. A study conducted by Lee (1979) indicates that, although most people, including doctors, see nurses as professionals, they are valued on a lesser scale than other professionals. Nurses are seen to provide compassionate care based on physicians' orders. The majority of the general public (and physicians) also feel that nurses have sufficient control over nursing care and do not see any reason for nurses to practice independently. It is interesting to note, however, that people who have recently been hospitalized, and thus are likely to have been exposed to the new and broader ideas about what nursing is, are significantly more likely than others to see nurses as colleagues of physicians rather than as physicians' assistants.

It appears that nurses cannot value clients' needs more than the needs of physicians or administrators until they can value their own needs also. Much has recently been written about the real need of many nurses for a better self-image. Nurses need to accept the fact that they have a contribution of their own to make to client care. They need to learn to be assertive—politely, but definitely. They need to work together with other nurses, and with physicians whose trust they have gained, to improve their image as contributing members of the health team. And, of course, all of this assumes that nurses either have or are working to acquire a real clinical competence that can be made visible to others.

Nursing and Image Building

As more nurses think about their relationships and their advocacy role with clients, they come to realize that, to some people, nursing has a shopworn image. The profession has changed and is in the process of changing, but the image hangs on. When nurses want to change the care provided to clients in institutions, they encounter and become victims of stereotyped ideas of what constitutes good care. For example, cleanliness is important, and at one time it was deemed necessary that a patient have a bath every day. In the routine that many nurses developed, this principle meant that the client needed a bath between 8 and 11 A.M. each morning. Nursing staff patterns still are designed toward this kind of care.

Yet, if individualized nursing care is truly a goal, the nurse in the admission assessment will ask the client when he ordinarily bathes and whether he prefers a bath or a shower. The nurse then will make use of this information in the nursing-care plan. If the client is accustomed to a bath at bedtime and finds it a relaxing activity that helps promote sleep, then, logically, he should take his bath at that time. However, we are all familiar with what usually happens: he takes his bath between 8 and 11 A.M. like everyone else. If the client routinely takes a tub bath, forcing him into the shower can be an exercise in futility. True, the body is clean, but the client experiences none of the other beneficial effects that result from carrying out his own routine. Most nurses can think of many examples to add to this simple one. Perhaps the most extreme example, and the most ridiculous from the consumer's point of view, is of the client who has worked nights for a number of years, and yet when hospitalized is expected to sleep all night. If he doesn't, he is usually given one or more sleeping pills so that he will be a good client and sleep when everyone else does.

The image of the nurse as a handmaiden was created by nurses who saw themselves in this role. The image of the professional nurse will be created by nurses who see themselves as professionals. Until nurses begin to see nursing from the point of view of the people they serve rather than according to the needs of the system, they will not be functioning in a manner that can be designated professional. We all know that for some nurses the determining principle for planning their work is their own convenience.

Robinson (1978) found that consumers still have a traditional view of the functions of the nurse. Most of them still identify provision of physical care, administration of medications, and teaching patients to care for themselves as principal activities. The more recent nursing functions, such as performing physical assessments, acting as client advocate and counselor, and acting as agent of referral, were not as well accepted as the traditional activities.

To broaden this common perception of nursing to one that includes functions designed to meet the human needs of clients, maintain their health, and prevent further illness will require a concerted effort on the part of nurses. Professional nursing, according to Ashley (1976), must begin to "exert open and public leadership in meeting consumer health needs." This will not be an easy task, but it will allow nurses to do what many of them thought they would be doing when they chose nursing: act as advocates for clients.

Much has been written, here and elsewhere, about meeting the human needs of the client. Working staff nurses, attempting to do the best job they can in the circumstances in which they find themselves, cannot be blamed for wondering what all the fuss is about. Nurses carry out orders to the best of their ability, and within the limits of the time that is left then try to keep their clients as happy as possible. And, until recent years, this approach has been adequate.

But now, many knowledgeable consumers and many health professionals agree that the health-care delivery system operating today is very inadequate in some areas. The reasons for the inadequacy are well known to reading, thinking consumers. The increasing age of the general population means that too many old people don't receive needed care. The same is true for those having chronic illnesses. And too many poor people, both in the inner city and in rural areas, find that the often excellent care available to upper- and middle-class persons is not accessible to them.

Many busy working nurses may see the truth of these ideas and still wonder why the problem should be of immediate concern to them. In the past, the policy decisions necessary to solve these problems have not been a part of nursing's domain. Bates (1972), a physician, has put forth a convincing argument in favor of involvement of nursing in such decisions. First, she points out, client care as a whole is largely composed of medical and nursing care. Any definition of nursing care should minimally include the functions of "caring, comfort, guidance and helping the patient to cope." Medicine, on the other hand, is concerned primarily with diagnosis and treatment. Unfortunately, client care today tends to have a narrower structure, in reality, than that described above. Yes, diagnosis and treatment are there, even though admittedly there are gaps in this area. But the other components, those of nursing care, are usually limited to delegated therapeutic tasks and simple physical care.

In contrast to this picture of what client care actually is, what do clients need it to be? One inner-city clinic study cited by Bates indicated that most clients, at least, have the following needs for care: a trusting relationship; skilled understanding of behavior; a patient advocate; medical technology, such as physical examination or laboratory work; and medications. These same clients needed such medical technologies as diagnosis and treatment more than 90 percent of the time on their first visit to the clinic. However, on subsequent visits they needed the medical technologies only 22 percent of the time, because their need after the first visit was primarily for a trusting relationship. Four out of five clients had needs, often unmet, that fell into the realm of nursing.

At the same time that more clients are requiring care that goes beyond diagnosis and treatment, nurses, in the wake of social change, are becoming aware that the routine technical tasks that fill most of their time use only a small part of their capabilities. Nurses could do much to meet the support, education, and understanding needs that total client care requires.

What can the nursing profession do to help put unused nursing skills together with unmet client needs? Bates (1972) suggests that "if nurses have something to offer to health care they had better learn how to compete." They must also be clinically and politically competent and able to clearly articulate the full range of client needs to others, particularly physicians and administrators. In this way both nurses and physicians can provide the kind of care that each is best prepared to give.

Sexism in Health Care

In every society there exists a set of values that permeates its major institutions. Among these values are cultural norms or behavioral expectations for men and women. Norms vary from culture to culture and reflect differences in the socialization experiences of children as seen in the work roles assigned to each sex. Most people identify the profession of nursing as "women's work," and, thus, many do not value it highly. In every society there is also an ethnocentric belief that one's own way is naturally correct and hence superior to other ways. Appropriate behavior for males and females is part of the cluster of beliefs held by a large segment of society as absolute and correct. The belief that socially prescribed differences between the sexes are inherent and biologically based and that one sex is limited or in some sense inferior has been termed **sexism**. Nurses have often been victims of sexism from other health workers, just as women in general are sometimes victims of sexism when they require medical care for women's conditions—as when some male physicians have expressed the view that most of the gynecologic complaints of women are "all in their heads."

The nursing profession in its advocacy role must deal with the sexist experiences of nurses as workers in institutions, as well as those of all women as individuals. Nursing must address the question of how to successfully make the changes that advocacy requires. Sometimes there will be failures, at least at the first attempt. Other times there will be success. Wiley (1976) has given some "Tips for the Timid" that can help make the successes outnumber the failures:

1. Find out what the grievance procedure of the institution is and use it to start the ball rolling. Bypassing the immediate supervisor usually does *not* work.

2. Choose an approach that fits the person. A personal presentation is usually most persuasive, but not if either party will be threatened. In this case, a written approach is usually best.
3. Try to fit the proposed change to the supervisor's ideas and values.
4. Use the nursing process on the problem—define it clearly, outline the alternatives, select the best plan, and outline how it can be implemented and evaluated.
5. Support the final solution, whatever it may be.

To summarize the description of the nurse who acts as an advocate for clients and for the nursing profession, Chenevert (1978) has listed both rights and responsibilities. They are described in Box 9–3.

Networking

In addition to acting as advocates for their clients, nurses have a responsibility to act as advocates for themselves and to plan their own career goals. The concept of networking is applicable here. Networks are support systems for the practitioner formed through professional organizations, alumni groups, and personal friends and co-workers. Trust and confidence between all persons involved is implied and must not be abused.

Steps in the process, according to Moses (1980), are:

1. Be assertive—approach people.
2. Keep a file of names, addresses, phone numbers.
3. Keep in touch.
4. Share useful information with others.
5. Don't ask people to give support they are unable to give.
6. Recommend new nurses only when you're sure of their reliability.
7. Be honest with contacts.
8. Don't burn bridges; they may be needed some day.

This kind of honest approach allows nurses to help themselves and others to advance when the opportunity arises.

Box 9–3 *TEN BASIC RIGHTS FOR WOMEN IN THE HEALTH PROFESSIONS**

1. You have the right to be treated with respect.
2. You have the right to a reasonable workload.
3. You have the right to an equitable wage.
4. You have the right to determine your own priorities.
5. You have the right to ask for what you want.
6. You have the right to refuse without making excuses or feeling guilty.
7. You have the right to make mistakes and be responsible for them.
8. You have the right to give and receive information as a professional.
9. You have the right to act in the best interest of the client.
10. You have the right to be human.

RIGHTS	RESPONSIBILITIES
to speak up	to listen
to take	to give
to have problems	to find solutions
to be comforted	to comfort others
to work	to do your best
to make mistakes	to correct your mistakes
to laugh	to make others happy
to have friends	to be a friend
to criticize	to praise
to have your efforts rewarded	to reward others' efforts
to be independent	to be dependable

---

*From Chenevert, Melodie: *Special Techniques in Assertiveness Training for Women in the Health Professions*, St. Louis: The C. V. Mosby Co., 1978.

Summary

An advocate is

— willing to defend the rights of the client.
— able to employ a humanistic approach that allows a view of the client as a person.
— able to internalize the rights and responsibilities of men and women in the health professions.
— able to exert leadership in changing the image of nursing to one in which a real contribution to health-care delivery is made.

Exercise

As an ombudsman who is responsible for your own development as well as that of the client, you are planning your own personal career goals. The form below will be helpful. Be as specific as possible when you fill it in.

Growth Factors	Needs	Goals	Target Date
Knowledge	Education Formal		
	Informal (work-shops, other sources)		
Skills			
Attitudes			
Personal Desires (for fun)			

Bibliography

Annas, George J. *An American Civil Liberties Union Handbook: The Rights of Hospital Patients*. New York: Avon Books, 1975.

Ashley, Jo Ann. *Hospitals, Paternalism, and the Role of the Nurse*. New York: Teachers College Press, Columbia University, 1976: 133.

Bates, Barbara. Nurse-Physician Dyad: Collegial or Competitive? In *Three Challenges to the Nursing Profession: Selected Papers from the 1972 ANA Convention*. New York: ANA (1972): 6, 10.

Chenevert, Melodie. *Special Techniques in Assertiveness Training for Women in the Health Professions*. St. Louis: C. V. Mosby, 1978: 20.

Corea, Gena. *The Hidden Malpractice: How American Medicine Mistreats Women*. New York: Jove Publications, 1977.

De Filippo, Anne Marie. Big Nurse, Little Ego. *Supervisor Nurse* 78 (August, 1978): 23–27.

Lee, Anthony. Nursing's Shopworn Image. *RN* 42 (August, 1979): 42–47.

Moses, Knooly. Networking. *Black Enterprise* 11(2) (1980): 29–34.

Moss, F., and Halarnandaris, V. *Too Old, Too Sick, Too Bad*. Germantown, Md.: Aspen Publications, 1977.

Robinson, Beverlyanne. A Study of Consumer Perceptions Relating to Nursing. *Nursing Leadership* 2 (June, 1978): 14–18.

Wiley, Loy. Tips for the Timid. *Nursing '76* 6(5) (May, 1976): Career Guide (CG)1–6.

10

The
Strategist
Role

BISMARCK, the Prussian statesman who lived in the mid-1800s, said, "Fools say that they learn by experience. I prefer to profit by others' experience." This aphorism tells us that there are two forms of practical experience, direct and indirect. Of the two, indirect practical experience may be the more valuable because it is infinitely wider (and safer). Even in the most active career, it is impossible to live long enough to have a great many direct experiences or to make all the mistakes oneself.

If one subscribes to this belief, then one must hold that successful nurse managers are in effect strategists. They have learned from their own experiences and from others' a method, or a series of strategies, for obtaining a specific goal or result. The measure of their success as leaders is their effectiveness in resolving the variety of difficulties and problems that arise hourly, daily, and monthly.

Contemporary nurse leaders who can be judged effective appear to have several characteristics in common:

1. They think in advance carefully about possible strategies in decision making.
2. They are forceful and outspoken in getting ideas across.
3. They have creative ideas and seek the help of others in developing them.
4. They like challenges.
5. They are viewed by others as courageous, visionary, and humble.

At this time there is an acute shortage of nurses with the characteristics and skills just listed. Because too few nurses have been adequately prepared as nurse leaders, nurses are wasting their resources as human beings and not contributing enough of their skills to the solution of present and future health-care problems.

Leadership needs to be viewed as a process that can be taught. Moloney (1979) has defined it as "an interpersonal process of influencing the activities of an individual or group toward goal attainment in a given situation." In the 1980s there are numerous problems that demand the best possible application of the leadership process if they are to be brought under control.

Leadership will be especially needed as nurses develop new roles, increase collaborative work with other disciplines, and become involved in a wider variety of services directed toward health maintenance and disease prevention.

The aim of this book has been to help remedy the present state of inadequate preparation for leadership among many nurses. In this chapter, the main points of each previous chapter will be summarized and some practical strategies for achievement of the objectives of each will be suggested.

Chapter 1

Chapter 1 can be neatly summarized in the words of Douglass (1980):

1. All nurses lead and manage to some degree.
2. Leadership can be an exciting experience.
3. Leadership/management is a learned process.
4. Effective nurse leaders/managers know themselves—they can identify their strengths, weaknesses, and capacities for growth and development; have knowledge of leadership and management theory; and can use self to get the right things done at the right time.

Some of Douglass's other ideas summarize further key points in the chapter:

1. Leaders must have followers.
2. The leadership process operates when others are influenced to accomplish a goal.
3. No one particular set of characteristics describes a leader. However, traits such as self-confidence, responsibility, persistence, energy, and influence are often present.
4. Most leaders don't have great talent—instead, they have worked long and hard to become effective managers.

New nurse leaders, with these ideas firmly in mind, need to have at their disposal some practical strategies to help them begin to function effectively as managers.

Strategies in Leadership Style

1. Nurse leaders who are not adequately prepared for leadership should get needed preparation as soon as possible. There are many books, workshops, and courses that can help.
2. Nurse leaders need to engage in introspection to identify their leadership styles. Does the autocratic style come most naturally? The laissez-faire? Since the multicratic style is most effective, new nurse leaders who have identified their own styles can practice using others (in which they are weaker) as needed.
3. Nurse leaders should be sure the jobs they have are those that allow them to use their natural tendencies best. If they are most comfortable with a democratic approach, they should not take jobs that preclude use of this method of working with people. The same principle applies to staff assignments.
4. To the greatest extent possible, staff should be assigned to the jobs they like most and do best. For example, a nurse who is especially interested in and knowledgeable about diabetes should be assigned to plan and carry out the diabetic-teaching program.

Ideally there should be enough challenge in assigned activities to give performers a sense of accomplishment but not too much to overwhelm them.

The leader who arranges for staff to work in their preferred areas as much as possible, within the bounds of fairness, will benefit from the "If I win, you win" effect. When the staff is happy and has self-esteem, the leader is successful.

Chapter 2

Chapter 2 is concerned with the attitudes, philosophy, and beliefs of nurse leaders. These must be individually defined if a sound basis for actions and policies is to be established. Leaders must also be aware of the different factors that motivate people. Only when leaders have identified each staff member's motivation and self-concept can they help others to develop to the maximum.

These ideas are related to job satisfaction, an area where it has been shown that immediate supervisors have a great impact on staff. High levels of satisfaction with the job can result when nurse leaders consider the needs of each member of the staff and individualize their approaches, based on those needs, as much as possible.

Self-assessment by leaders is essential. They need a positive approach to themselves and others (and, if they lack one, they need to begin to develop one immediately). Leaders must be able to deal with complaints, solve problems, and encourage innovation. They must be able to respond to the special needs of the new employee, the nurse who is returning to service after a long absence, the handicapped, male, older, or disabled employee. Discipline must be managed. Clients must be cared for in the most efficient way possible, and yet, whenever possible, the requirements of humanism must outweigh the dictates of pragmatism.

In addition to all this, the nurse leader, who is probably a woman, must meet the needs of her family and find some time for herself. A little strategy is definitely in order to help her perform needed activities effectively and enjoy doing it.

Strategies for Attitudes and Beliefs

1. Nursing should not consume all of one's life. Play and love are equally essential, but it's easier to put these off. If a nurse does so for a long enough time, opportunities for outside satisfactions will come up less and less often. This is the way to burnout. None of us can be model nurses, model wives or husbands, and model parents all at once. Compromise and help with the less enjoyable chores will be necessary, and recreation is essential.
2. Nurses should make a real effort to know themselves and those around them. What motivates others? What are their needs? What are the nurse's?
3. Nurses should recognize that stress is a necessary (and, if not overdone, beneficial) part of life. They need to be aware of the physical symptoms—headache, sleep disturbances, tight muscles, loss of appetite, fatigue, accident proneness, and many more—that can result from too much stress. To reduce these effects, a good safety valve is the

use of the large-muscle groups in physical exercise such as hard walking, jogging, swimming, or even vigorous housework. A friend to confide in, enough personal time, and routines to maintain good health will help.

4. Criticism by others should be taken objectively as feedback that can be used to improve performance. It should first be evaluated for validity: is the nurse leader the cause of someone else's wrath, or merely the nearest convenient object for it? Is the critic competent to make the criticism? Is he trying to make himself feel better by making someone else feel worse? These kinds of feedback can be ignored. However, if the criticism has been heard before and may be valid, it can point the way to change and more effective performance.

5. Managers should do everything possible to establish trust between themselves and staff and among the staff members themselves. People learn to trust others in situations where positive results occur. This implies both that another individual (or group) will do what has been promised and that, if feelings and values are communicated from one individual to another, the second individual will listen with respect and will not use the information to hurt the first individual.

Chapter 3

Chapter 3 deals with the health-care organization and the management activities associated with it. Nurse leaders need to know how to define both short-term objectives and long-term goals for themselves and for the area for which they are responsible. They need to understand how to generate and implement policies and procedures and how to formulate an appropriate budget. They must know what staff is doing on a continuing basis. Activity analysis for this purpose should be a part of the management plan to insure efficient staff functioning.

Managers must also be able to plan the staffing for their units and appreciate the growing need for cost analysis and cost containment in health-care agencies. They must make client assignments that match the needs of clients with the skills and interests of personnel. Finally, they must keep accurate records and file complete reports of work activities in their designated areas of responsibility.

The primary task of management is to use available resources effectively—whether these resources are economic, technical, or human—in order to meet organizational goals and objectives and merge them with professional goals.

Strategies for Organization

1. Encourage staff members to set personal and career objectives for themselves. Provide opportunities for growth—personal as well as career—when possible. Plan for periodic review of goal achievement.
2. Set personal goals, and review them periodically. What improvements have been the result of work efforts in the last six months? Take stock of both successes and failures.
3. Adopt the philosophy of what is known as the open-systems organization. According to Beckhard and Harris (1977), the organization, when seen as an open system, exists in an environment with permeable boundaries and therefore interacts with that environment. These interactions affect the development and performance of the organization. Nurse leaders can adopt a philosophy in which they consciously try to provide a balance between the needs of the organization and the needs of personnel, knowing that these needs will sometimes be in conflict.
4. To keep the organization viable, adopt a process such as open-systems planning for analyzing the increasing number of environmental forces that affect the organization. These include factors such as increased governmental regulation and the consumer movement. Open-systems planning resembles the scientific method. It requires the following steps:
    a. Determine the one most important goal among all the goals in the organization—"the core mission."
    b. Test reality—map the demand system. Make a visual chart listing the ten most important groups that have expectations or make demands of the organization.
    c. Describe the extent to which the organization currently responds to the demands listed.
    d. Look into the future and project the demands that will probably be made in the next three or four years if the organization makes no changes.
    e. Describe personal choices for conditions in the next three or four years.

    f. Identify the changes that would be necessary to meet the desired state.

    g. Assess the social and economic cost effectiveness of the plan.

5. Recognize that nurses work in an industry that often does not make use of what is currently known about managing today's complexity. Nurse managers now must take a larger view of the organization's function than has been taken previously, according to Allen (1978), who says the nurses need:

    a. To develop a functioning, coordinated intelligence network in order to gain enough information to make informed decisions.

    b. To consider that some desired outcomes may be too big or too different to handle with existing resources, but may require major shifts in priorities, joint ventures with others, or other innovative approaches.

    c. To build as much flexibility as possible into planning, using contingency planning—there must be a "Plan B" or even "Plan C" if "Plan A" does not work.

6. Consider the use of nontraditional approaches to planning. For example, if representatives of *all* departments are consulted when making changes in nursing practices, rather than only nurses, one can often prevent some of the disastrous ripple effects that can result from insufficient outside input.

7. Encourage employee self-management and an increase in employee voice in decision making. Could nurses decide how many hours they will work on a given day? Could two half-time nurses take one full-time job together? Could a nursing-practice committee composed of nurses initiate a policy requiring assessments of the health status of all clients, to be followed by an individualized plan for health teaching by nurses? These kinds of self-management activities will change the role of the manager from that of a benevolent dictator to a new and more participative role.

Chapter 4

Chapter 4 describes the professional managerial role. It is particularly concerned with decision making and communication as functions of the manager, and with forms of communication used by managers.

The need to develop an assistant and the dual role of the director of nursing are also discussed.

Strategies in Engineering Care

Strategies in this area are particularly important. If they are utilized appropriately, crisis management can often be prevented. Crisis management occurs when the leader is not in control of events but only reacts to actions initiated by others.

1. For important decisions, use the "decision tree." This process requires that the primary decision have at least two alternatives. The outcome for each of these is predicted, and the need for further decision is considered as each decision point is reached.
2. Separate judgment from decision making. Decision is the process of choosing a particular course of action; judgment is the process of forming an opinion or evaluation by discerning and comparing (Woolf, 1976). However, if judgment is not accurate, decisions cannot be optimal either. Judgment can be improved by gathering as many relevant facts as possible and by remembering that:
   a. We all have a great tendency to stereotype people. Our perceptions may not be true at all.
   b. Events that occur together do not necessarily have a cause-and-effect relationship.
   c. Behavior can stem from both situational factors and inborn predispositions.
   d. We tend to focus on the desirability of an event rather than on the probability that it will occur in real life.
   e. We tend to persevere in our judgments even when there is much evidence that we are wrong.
3. One can avoid "management shock" by the development of a "managerial bank account." This concept, put forth by Elbing (1978), describes the building up of employees' trust in managers to the point that, when managers must make changes quickly, employees will cooperate willingly. In the long run, participative management unleashes more creativity and commitment in staff than does an authoritarian approach. However, one can benefit from employee goodwill when rapid action is needed if a bank account of trust has been established.

4. When one has established a managerial bank account, it can serve to improve leadership skills, especially in communication. An effective approach is to use the active-listening model, in which the listener acts as a receiver of information (Muller, 1980) and then repeats it to the sender in his own words. This simple act permits ventilation of the staff's feelings and then allows the discussion of alternative solutions to the problem. It is effective in one-to-one relationships as well as in meetings, particularly when one is faced with making changes. Ventilation of feelings, combined with trust, will often act to improve acceptance of change.

5. Write complete, clear, concise memos—don't leave instructions to chance. Use the old advice given to newspaper reporters: include, the *who*, the *why*, the *what*, the *when*, and the *where*.

6. In meetings, make an agenda and think through the approach to be used. If staff is likely to be unhappy with what will be said, rehearse responses to possible comments.

7. When acting as spokesperson for a group, prepare the presentation thoroughly. Decide how far to go. Have an alternative plan. Do not be discouraged if there is rejection the first time—regroup and try again at a later date.

8. Management of time is an important administrative objective. Managers need time to think out policy. Consequently, they must arrange priorities so that they do only the important work in the available time. Routine duties should be delegated.

9. Qualified assistants must be recruited and developed so that, if the leader is not there, activities go on as usual. Assess an assistant's managerial strengths and weaknesses, and plan for experiences designed to remedy any shortcomings. Always be alert for managerial possibilities in the staff. In general, an assistant should report to his immediate superior, not to those above the superior in the administrative structure.

10. Plan for cost containment. Some suggestions in this area are those made by Faneuf (1979):

    a. Put up a suggestion box for employees. Form a committee to screen the suggestions, and reward the donors of those that prove useful. Monetary rewards and such forms of public recognition as those given at an awards banquet or in letters of recognition have been used for this purpose.

    b. Stress good health practices among employees. Staff development may be able to help. Programs and posters, for example, can keep employees aware of the dangers of smoking, obesity, alcoholism,

and hypertension.
c. Follow up on abusers of sick time.
d. Form a committee to consider the methods of conserving energy in the work situation.
e. Periodically, put the prices of materials used on display.
f. Make use of all methods for increasing job satisfaction.
g. Keep track of savings that result from the cost-containment program so that the effectiveness of the program can be evaluated and communicated to staff.

Chapter 5

Chapter 5 deals with professionalism in nursing. Planning of care, use of nursing-care plans, client teaching, and relationships between nurses and physicians are considered. The characteristics of an atmosphere for professional growth are discussed.

Strategies for Professional Practice

1. Review the characteristics of a professional and make a conscious effort to be a role model for a professional practitioner.
2. Emphasize the importance of nursing-care planning. Make updating of written nursing-care plans a part of regular daily nursing practice.
3. Make a file of printed materials that can be used for client teaching. Restock it on a regular basis.
4. Make available written client-teaching guides for common conditions.
5. Become informed about currently accepted methods of evaluating nursing care. Determine what quality care is, so that contributions can be made to decision making for nursing-care evaluation.
6. Acquire the skills necessary to perform an in-depth health assessment.
7. Make a point of participating in committee work related to professional practice. Be alert for opportunities to improve the status of nursing.

Chapter 6

Chapter 6 is concerned with staff development as a major focus of the nurse manager's effort. The need for and components of staff development are discussed, as are methods of planning for and implementing it. Various types of staff-development programs are described. Planning for continuing education is explored, and guidelines for writing and disseminating reports on workshops attended are given.

Strategy for Staff Development

1. Form a staff-development committee to plan for needed programs, including single offerings as well as those that will be repeated at regular intervals. Committee members should include both staff and administrators and should represent as many nursing divisions and shifts as possible.
2. Explore the possibilities of competency-based orientation programs for new nurses and ancillary personnel, or skills-training programs for present employees. This approach gives emphasis to expected performance outcomes. One model, developed by del Bueno, Barker, and Christmyer (1980), has the following characteristics:
    a. Uses self-directed learning activities.
    b. Is flexible in time required for achievement of outcomes.
    c. Uses instructor as a facilitator and resource person more than as a lecturer.
    d. Assesses the level of previous learning.
    e. Assesses learning styles of learners.
3. Design a leadership-management program appropriate for the new graduate who does not have background in this area.
4. Design a higher-level management program for those nurses who are being promoted into leadership positions.
5. Design a plan for continuing education that allows all nursing personnel an equal opportunity to attend.
6. Design a report mechanism that allows others in the institution to benefit from the information obtained by those who attend continuing-education conferences.

Chapter 7

In Chapter 7 the functions of the manager as a substitute parent are described. Procedures for recruiting and interviewing are delineated, together with some hints for résumé writing. Personnel policies and practices are discussed, as is employee-performance evaluation. Some ideas are presented concerning health services for employees, employee safety, unionization, and career mobility.

Strategy for Personnel Management

1. Design a viable recruiting program by collecting information concerning what nurses really want. Would a day-care center allow more nurses who are mothers to work? Is salary the main issue, or is there also a need to make real decisions about nursing practice? Would more flexible hours for nurses help?
2. Be sure that personnel policies and practices are in line with those of other institutions in your locality.
3. Administration of personnel policies and practices should be equitable for all employees across departments and job classifications.
4. Be aware of the importance of counseling when it is time for employee-performance evaluation. Evaluation interviews provide a fine opportunity to show appreciation for good past performance and/or to motivate for needed improvements. They can also be counterproductive if not handled properly. Some guidelines may be found in Chapter 2.
5. Knowing that inadequate supervision promotes unionization, be as effective a supervisor as is possible.
6. Acquire and disseminate information about career mobility to employees.

Chapter 8

Chapter 8 deals with the long-standing human problem of how best to induce needed change. A theoretical framework for change is discussed, as is the role of the nurse as a change maker. Common errors in making changes are identified, together with some creative approaches to change. Special problems of promoting change in health-care institutions are noted. The ranking of elements in conflict for purposes of resolution is discussed, along with ideas concerning leadership, power, and authority in nursing.

Strategy for Change Making

1. Approach the process of making change in a planned, systematic way.
2. Form a group that believes in the proposed change to help put the change into operation.
3. Provide the proper climate for change, calling upon the "managerial bank account" that has built up in the past.
4. Show how each person will gain from the proposed change.
5. Be a role model, showing willingness to try pertinent new ideas.
6. Encourage individual employees to be creative and to make suggestions. Point out that two heads (or more) are better than one in problem solving, and everyone's input is needed. Stress future gains that are possible.
7. Learn techniques for dealing with conflict, rather than suppressing or ignoring it.
8. Analyze the power structure in the institution, since persons who have power can support the effort for change.
9. Recognize the power of nurses as a group.

Chapter 9

Chapter 9 is concerned with the nurse as an advocate, both for self and for clients. The value of the humanistic approach to client care is reiterated, and its positive effect on nursing image is considered. Sexism as it relates to women as clients and as professionals is described.

Strategy for Advocacy

1. Follow the Golden Rule.
2. Be aware that the manager must be an advocate for staff and for the entire profession of nursing.

3. Be a role model for your staff and others in the work setting.
4. Plan to educate the boss about the needs of the various areas of responsibility and about the potential for growth in nursing.
5. Correct misinformation about what nursing is now.
6. Move to take a rightful place with respect to decision making in nursing practice and in client-care management.

Exercise

Miss J. V. has just returned from a meeting in which **networking** was discussed and recommended as a strategy for nursing managers. You learn from Miss J. V. that networking is a systematic process of making and utilizing contacts to further one's personal career objectives and those of one's protégés. Networking has always been used, but, although all of us are involved in networking whether we are aware of it or not, it functions much more efficiently when it is a planned activity.

As a member of Miss J. V.'s staff, utilize the information from Chapter 9 and plan a personal network for yourself. List the names of ten people you know professionally. They can form the nucleus of a widespread group if an active effort is made to contact others.

Bibliography

Allen, Stephan. Fourth Generation Organizations. In Elbing, A. O. (Ed.), *Behavioral Decisions in Organizations*. (2nd ed.). Glenview: Scott, Foresman, 1978: 3–8.

Beckhard, Richard; and Harris, Reuben. *Organizational Transitions: Managing Complex Change*. Reading: Addison-Wesley, 1977: 3–8.

del Bueno, D. V.; Barker, F.; and Christmyer, C. Implementing a Competency Based Orientation Program. *Nurse Educator* 5(3) (1980): 16–20.

Douglass, Laura. *The Effective Nurse*. St. Louis: C. V. Mosby, 1980: 1–2.

Elbing, Alvar (Ed.). *The Managerial Bank Account, Behavioral Decisions in Organizations* (2nd ed.). Glenview: Scott, Foresman, 1978.

Faneuf, Patricia. *Cost Containment at the Staff Level: An Approach for Nurse Management*. Unpublished paper. Purdue University (1979): 31–36.

Moloney, Margaret M. *Leadership in Nursing*. St. Louis: C. V. Mosby, 1979: 10–11.

Muller, R. A. Using an Active Listening Model. *Supervisor Nurse* 11(4) (1980): 44–46.

Woolf, H. (Ed.). *Webster's New Collegiate Dictionary*. Springfield: Merriam, 1976.

Epilogue: Formula for Success

To SUM UP, the many roles of the nurse-manager can be identified in the acronym below.

Success in the Manager's Role =
       C + O + M + P + E + T + E + N + C + E

C = Care-giver Professional: One who provides for others, on a temporary basis, what they cannot do for themselves.

O = Organizer: One who relates people and things to each other in such a way that they form a unit capable of being directed toward organizational goals.

M = Manager of Personnel: One who is responsible for producing the best system for employees to do their jobs to the best of their abilities.

P = Professional Manager of Care: One who is responsible for planning, organizing, measuring, and integrating human and material resources.

E = Employee Educator: One who provides programs of learning based on the knowledge deficits of personnel.

T = Team Strategist: One who uses a series of tactics designed to obtain a specific result.

E = Expert in Human Relations: One who establishes significant associations among people.

N = Nurse-Advocate: One who pleads the cause of another or herself, or who speaks or writes in support of some particular belief.

C = Change Agent: One who takes the initiative to transform or modify.

E = Executive and Leader: A leader possesses a set of skills—a way of behaving—that can be identified, learned, practiced, and applied. An executive is one who has administrative authority.

Answers
to
Exercises

Answer to Exercise, p. 20 (Chapter 1)

In the usual situation, Miss J. V. would probably begin by asking herself what she knows about leading a group. If her answer is "not very much," then she might either seek more information from written sources or use a leader she admires as a role model. She may approach her immediate supervisor for help or may copy the style of the previous committee chairman.

Ideally, the neophyte nurse leader should start by recognizing that, although she has not had formal leadership experience, she has had informal experience. She needs to think about that experience and determine what patterns of leadership behavior she has chosen most frequently in the past. Further, a determination must be made of the style of leadership that would be most effective in the present situation. Does she need to choose new behaviors? In most cases a group-centered approach is usually successful in securing a productive response from the committee members.

A further question to be asked is "How well do I understand the factors motivating each group member?" Time must be spent in getting better acquainted with each individual.

Next, what are the long-term objectives of the committee? Do these mesh with the identified factors motivating the members?

Finally, there is a need for the leader to evaluate her own performance. On an ongoing basis, she must ask herself "Is the task being accomplished?"

Answer to Exercise, p. 51 (Chapter 2)

Number of Action

2. Use other personnel to meet patient needs during report. Have a preplanned system for handling interruptions. Ask a day nurse to give the needed medication.

4. Nothing can be done at this time to change the situation, but make a note to talk to supervisor about problem—perhaps Admitting might agree to wait until after report before sending up new patients.

5. Report is taking too long. Can chitchat be reduced? Limit report to unusual happenings and additional pertinent information about each patient.

7. It would be better to orient and assign the student first so that medications are given on time.

8. Send clerk for needed equipment, rather than self. Make note to talk to head nurse about the inadequate supply.

9. Make note to send aides to each bedside unit during slow time to locate i.v. poles and replace them so that each bed is completely equipped.

11. If report had been shorter, K. W. would not have been delayed in meeting this patient for so long.

12. Better use can be made of K. W.'s time—send an aide to work on the bed.

Answer to Exercise, p. 85 (Chapter 3)

Key: 1 d, 2 e, 3 b, 4 a, 5 c

Answer to Exercise, p. 117 (Chapter 4)

1. State the problem: Insufficient information exists at this time. Why is there such a high rate of turnover?

2. Mr. P. Z. could:

   a. Read the exit interviews on all personnel who have left the unit within the last year.

   b. Interview the head nurse on the unit for her view of the problem. Discuss with her ways of getting needed information from the staff. Consider the use of a questionnaire to be completed anonymously and returned to Mr. P. Z.

   c. Tally all responses and make a list of factors that seem to be most important to the problem.

3,4. Alternatives will depend on factors that have been identified as part of the problem. Some possibilities are:

a. Does the head nurse need additional education for better management skills or better communication? Is there a useful continuing education course or workshop the head nurse could attend?

b. Is caring for this client population too stressful to the staff? Would they benefit from better orientation or better inservice programs? Would a rotation system, allowing staff to work two or three months on a quieter unit at regular intervals, be helpful?

c. Is physical layout of the unit stressful? Are there other environmental factors that interfere with optimal function? What can be done?

d. Can interested nurses now working in other parts of the hospital be prepared to help in the MIC unit as needed?

e. Decide which alternatives to adopt.

Answer to Exercise, p. 146 (Chapter 5)

Possible pros and cons might include:

	Pro	**Con**
Primary Nursing	Increased continuity of care	Incongruity with traditional hierarchical structure
	Better flow of information to physician	Increased staffing costs when initiating
	Better documentation of emotional and physical needs of client	Changed role of head nurse
	Greater focus on clients by nurses	Lack of appeal for some nurses
	More autonomy for nurses	Possible shortage of available nurses
	More job satisfaction for nurses	Dislike by some physicians of relating to many nurses

Greater appeal for clients and families

Greater opportunity to individualize care

Lessened orientation and training costs for aides and new graduate nurses

Less absenteeism among nurses

Elimination of nurses' aides

Team Nursing	Written care plan	Frequently incomplete implementation
	Team conference	
	Matching of client needs with individual nursing skills	Undervaluing of listed advantages by nurses, leading to fragmentation of care
	Potential to produce best care at lowest cost	

Answer to Exercise, p. 206 (Chapter 7)

Strengths: Enjoys teaching and does it well. See 5/9/81, 5/23/81, 6/7/81, 6/15/81.

Weaknesses: May be a little rigid and slow to accept change—see 5/2/81, 6/14/81. May need to consider more alternative solutions to problems—see 5/7/81.

Answer to Exercise, p. 233 (Chapter 8)

Some Possible Ideas Are:

1. Set up a day-care center.
2. Double the pay on nights and evenings.
3. Pay eight hours' salary for four hours' work on nights or evenings.
4. Allow two nurses to fill one job—one can recruit the other.
5. Increase the input of nurses into client-care decisions.

Index